IDENTITY AND ETHNIC RELATIONS IN AFRICA

To Ayanda, Michael, Luvuyo and Thembelani,
quasi-sons and genuine friends,
from whom I've learned much about
how it is possible to grow up as
decent people in an indecent,
racist society.

Identity and Ethnic Relations in Africa

LEONARD BLOOM

Ashgate

Aldershot • Brookfield USA • Singapore • Sydney

Published by
Ashgate Publishing Ltd
Gower House
Croft Road
Aldershot
Hants GU11 3HR
England

Ashgate Publishing Company
Old Post Road
Brookfield
Vermont 05036
USA

British Library Cataloguing in Publication Data
Bloom, Leonard
    Identity and ethnic relations in Africa : towards
    collective and individual psychotherapy. -
    (Interdisciplinary research series in ethnic, gender and
    class relations)
    1. Africans - Psychology 2. Africa - Ethnic relations
    I.Title
    305.8'96

Library of Congress Catalog Card Number: 98-73507

ISBN 1 84014 529 3

Printed and bound by Athenaeum Press, Ltd.,
Gateshead, Tyne & Wear.

Contents

Foreword   vii
Preface   xi
The Series Editor's Preface   xvii
Acknowledgements   xviii

Chapter 1   Toward a Relevant Psychology   1

Chapter 2   Social Science in Africa: Problems and Prospects   40

Chapter 3   Psychotherapy and Culture: A Critical View   58

Chapter 4   Cultural Fragmentation and Mental Distress   89

Chapter 5   Ethnic Identity: A Psychoanalytic Critique   103

Chapter 6   The Emotional Damage of Apartheid: A Psychoanalytic View   121

Chapter 7   Apartheid's Children: The Emotional Costs   141

Chapter 8   Quasi-family, Quasi-psychotherapy: Six Years of Living Together, Black and White, in South Africa   157

Chapter 9   After the War is Over: Truth and Reconciliation? Reflections from South Africa   186

Contents

Foreword

In 1976, when living in London, I went to Lancaster University to participate in a *Colloquium* on *Psychology and Religion*. One lecture was being given by an absurd exhibitionist and, deciding I would tolerate no more of it, I left the lecture hall and there, to my surprise and joy, found someone else who had left for the same reason. That someone answered to the name of Len Bloom. We spoke and chatted for the duration of the lecture and the next day when the conference was finished we returned on the train together. By the time we reached London a firm friendship had been cemented and, I believe, will only dissolve when the blow of death falls upon one of us. At the time I was new to Psychology, new to Psychoanalysis, an ex-public schoolboy, a failed priest and like an alien from Mars who had been suddenly cast upon a new planet. The friendship that was established on that train journey I could only attribute to my new friend's peculiar genius for relating to any human being whom he encountered on this earth. So many of us can only relate to people within our particular village whether its inhabitants be all of one race, one class, one age or one outlook. We were from different villages and Len's special gift was his ability to bridge the gap. This remarkable book validates that first impression. For six years Len has lived with three teenage African 'street-kids'.

It is notoriously difficult to bear the bitterness of a deprived person at close quarters. I have, as a psychoanalyst, occasionally managed it on the basis of a daily contact of 50 minutes but to invite three deprived youngsters into my house to share my homelife with me is heroism of a high order. But what Len has achieved is more than this because three adolescents are all Africans whose childhood years were spent under the regime of Apartheid. It is impossible to think that they would have had no hostility towards the white man. To have bridged this and become to them a

vii

surrogate father and mother is an heroic triumph of the human spirit. It is the sort of achievement that sparks the spirit of hope in a world so torn with ruthless self-interest, cynicism and generalizes despair. Len is a realist and he knows well enough the corruption and mismanagement by governments of the countries in their charge but he decries those social scientists who despair and say there is nothing to be done. Psychology has a task and he has no doubt about what it is. It is a breath of fresh air to read Len Bloom's definition of what constitutes Psychology:

> Psychology is more than skills and techniques. It must also generate insight into the human condition and stimulate sympathy for the pains of living, even though the pains may be caused by socioeconomic and political factors. (p. 7)

So here is no sentimental idealist but someone who realizes what Psychology needs to be if it is to have an impact upon our social world. Len Bloom has a scientist's passion for the problems throbbing in the hearts of people in the numerous societies of post-colonial Africa. He has worked in Nigeria, Zambia and South Africa and I doubt if there can be many with such a penetrating understanding of the currents of suffering afflicting these ancient cultures. So Len believes that the Social Sciences have a role to play in shaping the structure and ethos of post-colonial societies in Africa and says trenchantly:

> ...social scientists do both their profession and their societies a disservice if they surrender the study of social problems to politicians and administrators. (p. 39)

Psychologists have an active role to play in society. Cynicism is the emotional attitude of passive spectators. This book of Len's is a clarion call to action.

Len Bloom believes that there are certain factors that are shared by all human beings no matter to which culture they belong. He is not a cultural relativist. He believes that there are certain fundamentals that we all share and this gives him a basis for saying that we need both as psychologists and human beings to find the common ground and then from this to be tolerant of cultural differences. For instance he criticizes severely those African psychologists who deride any psychology which has been spawned in the First World. Len Bloom knows that there is much of value in the psychological traditions in the western world. He clearly favours the understanding that has come from psychoanalysis and believes that its insights into the emotional life of humans are of great value to the emerging problems in Africa. He is more sceptical of the psychometric tradition within Psychology, believing that the obsession with accurate measurement is at the cost of missing what is most essential in human life. He is clearly struggling to find a psychological outlook that is adequate to encompass the depth and richness of his diverse experience of human beings in the birth-pains of a great social crisis. I doubt if he has found a model that satisfies what he is looking for but clearly psychoanalysis both in its theory and practice approximates best to what he is looking for.

There are two snares for the anthropologist or social psychologist engaged in experiential research work within a foreign culture. He may either remain so academically detached that he fails to get any insight into the minds of those whom he is trying to understand or he submerges himself into the culture so entirely that he loses the observer's perspective. Len Bloom avoids both these traps. He never for a moment pretends he is other than English, than Jewish, than White and it is clear that his 'adopted family' respect him for maintaining his integrity. With this stance firmly in place he is able to empathize truly with his subjects. He does not pretend to understand things which may be baffling and disturbing. When Bongani and Danilé announced that they must follow the rites of circumcision by going into the jungle as *abakhwetha* (initiates) he does not hide from the reader how disturbing this was to him especially as he knew of cases where initiates had died subsequently through infections contracted through an unhygienic operation. I think it is also clear that Len was not sympathetic to the motivating religious principle that underlay such a rite. He believes that the symbolic meaning of this rite is that the boys are being punished for growing up to be rivals of the adults and that the circumcision signifies a surrender to the adults and thereby remaining in submission to their ancestors.

Len Bloom also interviewed many children to try and discover the effects that Apartheid had had upon them. With so many variables it is clearly difficult to isolate those factors which can be attributed to the Apartheid system but he clearly came to believe that to invest a government with the power to intervene directly into people's private lives was harmful because it inhibited children's spontaneous contact with attuned adults. I suspect that Len would probably generalize this further and say that any system that places a taboo on contact between one category of human being and another is harmful. Len's life has become a testament to the value of emotional contact between human beings from different cultures. One of the saddest insights that Len records is that children blamed their parents for not protecting them from Apartheid (p. 146, this text).

Hating the horrors of the Apartheid regime Len is clearly in sympathy with the humane attitude of the Truth and Reconciliation Committee which he compares with the punitive attitudes of the Nuremberg trials. The merciful attitude of Mandela who has expressed no bitterness to his former captors who imprisoned him for 27 years clearly has Len Bloom's wholehearted approval. When reading this book I was several times struck by the similarity of outlook that Len Bloom shares with Mandela. I do not think I can offer a higher recommendation to the reader than this.

Neville Symington,
88b, Warragal Road,
Turramurra,
NSW 2074   AUSTRALIA

Preface

Writers have many motives for writing their books. I have two. This book is an extended 'thank you' to the many Africans who have shared with me, a psychologist from far-away London, their life-stories and their feelings and thoughts about their lives and the world in which they have been living. My 'professional detachment' has done little to insulate me from being moved, sometimes to anger, by the stories that reveal how individuals have reacted bravely against demeaning poverty and social and political repression.

My other motive is to bring together some of my writings that may merit discussion for a little longer, since the issues and problems they dealt with are still topical. I hope that my book will be read and debated both by lay-persons and the professionally interested. It would be optimistic to expect that more than a handful of administrators and politicians might glance through the book and become aware that what they are doing may hurt rather than help individuals and communities.

I am by profession a social psychologist with a pychoanalytic orientation, whose professional writing has become more political: not by adopting a party-political programme, but by being motivated by a humanistic social and political position. That motivation is derived from my having lived and worked in Africa for some twenty years among people hurt and damaged by the 'inequality, prejudice, violence and lack of imaginative vitality' (Samuels, 1993, p. ix) that characterise authoritarian, racist and obsessively 'ethnic' societies and their rulers.

The *latent* content of the book is broadly about how 'power is held or deployed by the state, by institutions and by sectional interests to maintain [emotional] survival... [and] gain control over others...'(ibid. p. 3). The focus is therefore on how individuals respond *as individuals* to their experiences of power. The powerful, the would-be powerful and the powerless each have their own anxieties, fears and defences. Perhaps the central issue is how individuals neutralise power emotionally so that the Self is not defeated by the assaults endured from those with authority. 'Ethnic' identification is one of the many defences against assaults of the individual's sense of being an autonomous self.

My central theme, implicitly or explicitly, is about the gravest contradiction on human life. Even though we live collectively, we remain individuals. Even though we are our idiosyncratic selves, we live embedded in many collectivities. One of these collectivities is the 'ethnic group', which in Africa as elsewhere, has often been a major political and social threat to individuality. Another theme is a psychoanalytic social psychology interpretation of 'ethnicity'. In post-colonial, post-apartheid Africa, individuals and communities that have been torn apart by racism or ethnicity have yet to be put back together again.

Rationally, one cannot even begin to write such a book as this, because - as Virginia Woolf observed - 'everything has already begun before ... The lives of individuals of the human race form a constant plot' in which there is always one bit jostling unpredictably against other bits and setting yet other bits in motion. A life, yours or mine, a community's, a group's, is made up of these bits, and even the most insightful social scientist cannot with certainty spell out the 'causes' of our lives. But I have to start somewhere - not to establish boundaries between 'my' psychology and competing or complementary perspectives, but to expose my understanding of human experience to appraisal. Maybe even a critical reader can learn something from an approach with which he or she is unsympathetic.

Chapters one and two debate two fundamental, interlocking issues. Can there be a psychology relevant to the 'Third World'?, and What are the problems and prospects for social science in Africa? There *should* and *could* be a relevant psychology, but it should also be relevant to the 'First World'. The human problems of striving for emotional independence, despite living with economic and political conditions that obstruct independence exist in *all* worlds. I argue for a humanistic psychology that tries to understand what motivates people in their everyday lives, and how they dream and symbolise to make sense of the confusion in which they live.

I reject the crypto-racist views of those ('white' and 'black' alike) who deny the universality of human affective and cognitive processes, by grossly exaggerating the emotional and cultural differences between groups of individuals. I have, therefore, no sympathy for the covert racism of Howitt and Owusu-Bempah, (Howitt and Owusu-Bempah, 1994, 1995), nor for the less strident Manganyi, (Manganyi, 1991), all of whom (and others more cynical) march into the racist trap of arguing that there is more than one kind of human - and who imply that the *other* kind is non-human compared with us. Parker has also pointed out the crypto-racism of the phenomenological, Heideggerian approach of, e.g. Manganyi, which 'repeats the very essentialising of black experience that apartheid insisted upon' (Parker, 1997, p. 40). (A similar critique is that of Couve, 1986.)

Chapter three on psychotherapy and culture, elaborates critically the view that 'western' psychotherapy only applies within 'western' cultures. Psychotherapy is *not* the white man's personal *juju*! Emotional problems in Africa are similar to those experienced elsewhere, and have to be similarly understood and treated. This again challenges the view that 'ethnic identity', totally or largely, seals people off from one another.

Chapter four explores further the relationships between culture and emotional distress. I consider how cultural themes and economic and sociopolitical stresses may give rise to emotional problems. Individuals may defensively adopt behaviour that leaves them internally unstable yet socially functioning. Adopting an ethnic identity is one form of defence.

Chapter five is a psychoanalytic critique of ethnic identity as a collective defence mechanism. Ethnicity is the collective equivalence of individual narcissism: an attempt to defend the self against feelings of threat, vulnerability and inferiority. The core psychodynamics of ethnicity is the retreat into narcissism. It is essentially 'a hatred of the relational - a hatred of something that is inherent in our being...and one of the ways that narcissism operates is to destroy separateness' (Symington, 1993, p. 18) by destroying the Others' right to exist on their own terms.

Chapters six, seven and eight are focussed on the emotional consequences of apartheid's enforced and arbitrary 'Ethnicity', which was intended, *inter alia*, to destroy individuality. Children and adults were demeaned and their sense of autonomy diminished by the stringent constraints on their freedom to develop as individuals.

Chapter six examines the emotional impact of apartheid, and maintains that so intensely paranoid and narcissistic a society was pathogenic. I suggest that the emotional ethos and social institutions must be modified if a democratic South Africa is likely to last.

Chapter seven continues the theme of the previous paper: how have many African children and young adults succeeded in developing a relatively normal True self in such a violent and impoverishing society? This chapter is partly based on the life-stories of about thirty young people.

Chapter eight goes more deeply into the problems of emotional impoverishment. It is an account of the experiences of three Xhosa youngsters and myself who have shared a home since early 1992, despite the efforts of officialdom to separate us. Although partly a narrative with psychoanalytic comments, it also addresses ethical and theoretical issues about the formation of individual identity both within a culture and in opposition to it. It is also about the formation of family sentiments in a family whose members are from different ethnic and cultural backgrounds.

Chapter nine concludes the book by posing questions about freedom and anti-freedom. Ethnic myths, and relationships based on them, divert political attention and energy from the building up of an emotionally stable democratic ethos. It examines the work of South Africa's Truth and Reconciliation Commission (TRC), which I believe has failed to deal directly and decisively with the enduring myths of ethnicity and their effect on freedom and democracy. It has also failed to meet the challenge to democracy of the collective desires for reparation and revenge, which are beginning to cohere as a political force. There are analogies between the work and relationships of the TRC and those of psychoanalytic psychotherapy, in particular between the dissolution of myths and the ending of the work. Freedom begins when myths are dispelled.

References

Couve, C.(1986), 'Psychology and politics in Manganyi's Work: a materialist
   critique', *Psychology in Society*, vol. 5, pp. 90-130.
Howitt, D. and Owusu-Bempah, J.(1994), *The Racism of Psychology: time for
   change*, New York: Harvester Wheatsheaf.
Howitt, D. and Owusu-Bempah, J.(1995), 'How Eurocentric Psychology damages
   Africa', *The Psychologist*, vol. 8(10), pp. 462-465.
Manganyi, N.C.(1991), *Treachery and Innocence: Psychology and racial difference
   in South Africa*, Johannesburg: Raven Press.
Parker, I.(1997), 'Psychological Discourse in new South Africa', *Social
   Psychological Review*, vol. 1(1), pp.37-41.
Samuels, A.(1993), *The political psyche*, London: Routledge.
Symington, N.(1993), *Narcissism: A new theory*, London: Karnac Books.

The Series Editor's Preface

I am pleased to preface this collection of recent essays by Len Bloom, who taught me sociology of the family in Nigeria. He focuses on the tensions between collective identity and individual difference, with a special emphasis on the threat of ethnic identity to personal liberty. As he puts it, 'Even though we live collectively, we remain individuals. Even though we are our idiosyncratic selves, we live embedded in many collectivities.'

This is a paradox at the heart of all social theory addressing the Hobbesian question of order: how is society possible if we are all such selfish individuals? Len Bloom answers, in the liberal tradition of Locke and Rousseau rather than in the authoritarian, absolutist style of Hobbes, that we are not all that selfish since many of us remain generous in spite of all the threats and dangers that we are forced to live with. However, unlike the social contract theorists, he applies the insights of Freudian psychoanalysis to a traumatised society like post-Apartheid South Africa even though Freud developed his ideas specifically as a response to traumatised individuals.

This represents a major contribution to social thought, that could be debated and advanced by theorists and practitioners concerned with gender, class and ethnic relations. If there is no such thing as African Psychology, is there a working class, feminist, Western or bourgeois psychology, or simply a relevent one that is applicable to any person or group with modifications?

Biko Agozino, Liverpool

Acknowledgements

Every book has its co-authors who lurk in the acknowledgements and may not appear on the title page. I hope that I have remembered them all. So, my thanks to Carol Hammond and Chris Maddox who first urged me to put together these papers; to Biko who took the bold step of taking an editorial chance, and with whom I've discussed many of these issues during many years of friendship; to Abel, who has gently encouraged me; to Rosanna and Idong who pre-typed Chapter 5 and the Preface; a thousand thanks to Jean Sharrock, who did the bulk of the typing and edited all the text to Ashgate's exacting standard; and above all to Rosemary Galli, whose academic and humane standards and integrity I have long tried to meet since we met in Nigeria many years ago. Finally, thanks to the patient, helpful and professional editorial team at Ashgate, without whom these papers might have remained hidden in professional journals.

1 Toward a Relevant Psychology

Against a Defeatist Psychology

Can there be a psychology relevant to the Third World? Should there be? There both should and can be such a psychology. We must create one. The alternative is that psychology professions will continue to stagnate, remaining conservative and satisfied with merely maintaining their scientific and political respectability. A revivified psychology could emerge from comparative research and the cross-fertilisation between Western techniques and methodology with the individual and collective problems of the Third World.

Kagitcibasi (1982) pleads for an independent, socially relevant and policy-oriented social psychology, staffed by Third World psychologists and working in interdisciplinary teams of social scientists. But his position conceals rarely examined problems. Are Third World psychologists more independent than others? Are they exceptionally sensitive to local problems? I am not as optimistic as Kagitcibasi that a new and more policy-oriented breed of psychologists is maturing. A major problem in establishing a relevant psychology is developing a professional identity and confidence that supports the professional in holding at bay suspicious and authoritarian administrators, who too often lack knowledge of the social sciences and who are too interested in immediate solutions to problems that they have themselves defined. Moreover, many Third World psychologists are as firmly locked into technologically biased, antihumanist and uncommitted philosophies of science as their Western colleagues.

I have another misgiving about Kagitcibasi's optimism. Some psychologists have spent too much ingenuity in demonstrating the dangers of the exportation of the social sciences and on attacking the colonial mentality of Western psychology (Moghaddam and Taylor, 1986). It would be more useful if they began to create a critical and constructive psychology.

Yet as long ago as 1973, the Pan African Conference of the International Association of Cross-Cultural Psychology (held in Ibadan, Nigeria) was almost entirely devoted to the problems and prospects in Africa for a young but relevant profession. It is, however, encouraging to read a paper published in a South African journal, *Psychology in Society*, which advances a theory and practice of a relevant psychology, and doubts that the ideological and institutional foundations of psychology are appropriate and directed to 'do work relevant to the vast problems posed by our own needs as a Third World society' (Dawes, 1988). Dawes describes how South African psychologists (and related workers) work among the poor and the persecuted - both children and adults. They use their professional skills to strengthen those whom we chillingly call 'subjects' to protect their integrity against the assaults of a violent society. Most South African psychologists are white. Most 'subjects' and 'clients' are black. One might cynically observe that even the most uncommitted white psychologist could gain professionally by working in a huge and largely ignored population. Dawes argues for a self-questioning psychology, collectively concerned pragmatically with transforming itself from a discipline largely constrained by the concepts, values, and problems of the urban industrialised one-third of the world, into one responsive to the massive problems of the nonurban, nonindustrialised two-thirds.

Abdi (1975) flatly asserts that 'the concepts of psychology, its theories and methods as understood by Westerners are alien to the thinking of Africa', and a fortiori to the thinking of other non-Western people. This is cryptoracism. Africans and other peoples of the Third World are no more aliens to Western people than they are to other people of the Third World. Many Westerners 'think' and 'feel' African. Many Third World people think and feel both Western and Non-Western! One of my African friends crisply observed to me: 'I think like an African. I think like a Westerner. I think like Memoye!' A relevant psychology will be remodelled from both Third World and Western thinking. It will happen only if psychologists reject the racism of those who claim that there are such gross divergencies between the affective and cognitive processes of different peoples that mutual understanding is, if not impossible, then, at best, difficult.

Other Third World scholars have argued that psychology is essentially so detached from the problems of the Third World that it is pointless to discuss ways in which it might be made more relevant. A detached and alien psychology must forever remain so. In a tendentious and bitter paper, Mehryar (1984) consigns his own profession to the rubbish bin. He writes that the problems of the Third World are, by their very nature and etiology, unlikely to be solved by psychology because the problems are economic, political and sociocultural. Not only are psychologists irrelevant to the Third World (Mehryar excepted, no doubt), but they are also agents of colonialism. Mehryar writes: 'The social sciences in general, and psychology in particular, have in practice turned into another means of cultural dependence and colonialism'. Contradictorily, he rejects psychology in the Third World as insignificant in numbers and influence! He ignores the living influence of Frantz Fanon who seized Western psychiatric and psychoanalytic insights and transformed them into a potent social philosophy and psychology of resistance to colonialism. Fanon used a Western notion to create a Third World and liberating psychology.

Mehryar evades the real problems of a relevant psychology, which is not to exert social and political influence directly but, rather, indirectly to influence national ideologies and policy by demonstrating that political and social problems may be better solved by professional research and skills than by political passion. Psychology may, moreover, reduce the influence of colonial dependency by showing what can be done during the early years of childhood to encourage independence.

Ardila (1983) is as defeatist as Mehryar. Ardila, a Latin American psychologist, rejects Western psychology because it is, he claims, 'an Anglo-Saxon discipline' and 'alien to the Latin American way of thinking'. He does admit that there is psychology *in* Latin America, 'meaning the investigation and application of psychological principles in a particular context'. But all psychology refers to particular contexts. The important question is consistently to compare what we learn from one context against what we have learned in other, comparable, contexts. Ardila makes much of the complexity of Latin America, but fails to see that complexity is a challenge to the investigator. Latin America has twenty nations, three major languages, many ethnic groups, and peoples at many different levels of socioeconomic and political development - an excellent opportunity for cross-cultural research! An opportunity for a liberating psychology to evolve! The Third World, as indeed the rest of the world, offers similar and challenging opportunities for research at once relevant and possibly theoretically significant.

A non-Eurocentric psychology dates back to the early 1900s, yet these pioneering efforts have been almost totally ignored. The work from the 1920s onward of Bartlett, Nadel and Margaret Mead, for example, already indicated (on the basis of experimental or observational studies) that affective-emotional and cognitive-intellectual processes are essentially universal, although influenced by social and cultural variations. If the pioneers had been within the mainstream of the development of psychology, we might have had a relevant and culturally sensitive social psychology a generation earlier than it appeared in Otto Klineberg's highly original *Social Psychology* in 1940.

I am, I believe, following an old trail that is now largely hidden by the flourishing of a narrowly conceived scientistic psychology. I argue for a contrasting approach - for a committed psychology that neither patronizes people nor surrenders to the cryptoracism of those who reify social and cultural differences into a somewhat outmoded quasi-biological determinism. I insist (perhaps a little too obsessively), that there is no place in a relevant psychology for either Abdi's barely concealed racism, or for its Western counterpart that limits psychology to the known parameters of the Western, urban world.

Four Issues

Four issues will recur in my critique of nonrelevant psychologies, in my exposition of relevant psychological issues, and in my suggestions for a relevant psychology.

1. Should Western-trained psychologists extend their professional and political interests to Third World problems? Are there any gains for Western psychology from such extension, or would this be little more than adding an exotic but marginal element? I strongly believe that a relevant psychology is an essential and central part of all psychology, and that the comparison between mainstream Western psychology and Third World contributions may productively unsettle Western psychology.

2. Some psychologists have attempted to construct a relevant psychology, and, although I welcome their attempts as far as they go, I am sceptical about whether they add much to either our approach to Third World problems or to extending the aims and methods of mainstream psychology. Their essential deficiency is the result of their lack of involvement with their subjects in their

subjects' real world. This is not a radical notion: Kurt Lewin pleaded for such a relevant social psychology in the 1920s.

3. Western psychology is, I maintain, inadequate because of its overly behaviouristic and psychometric methodology. Many contemporary, Western-trained psychologists are timid about approaching such complex areas as motivation and socioemotional development. They also tend to reduce to psychometrical studies the complexities of the relationships between individuals and society. Whatever is difficult to shape in a statistical and testable form tends to be banished from mainstream psychology and to be regarded as unworthy of scientific psychology. So, out goes the psychodynamic perspective! But it is not essential to be a committed Freudian to adopt the psychodynamic perspective with its insights into the universal process of domesticating the antisocial (or asocial) human infant into the more-or-less socialised human adult.

4. I have been influenced by three complementary psychological perspectives: humanistic, psychoanalytic and social-gestalt. I adopt the positions that people are often motivated by goals and hopes, and that psychologists would do well never to ignore nor minimise individual strivings toward finding meaning to their lives. The psychoanalytic perspective contributes two related emphases. It is essential to understand the unconscious conflicts and anxieties that motivate much human behaviour. It is equally important to trace the emotional origins of behaviour and experience. A relevant psychology depends on these three perspectives, and is, thus, far away from most of mainstream psychology.

Sharing Psychologies

Internationally, psychology has been grossly wasted. The British Psychological Society has 22,605 members. It is most unlikely that there are even twenty thousand fully qualified and trained psychologists spread throughout the Third World, and the number and range of social and individual problems that might be better understood and alleviated by professional psychologists are immense and largely neglected. Yet, not one

major association of psychologists has made an open social and political
commitment to sharing collectively the skills and experience of its members
with the handful of psychologists in the Third World. On the one side, the
associations placidly wait for governments to ask for help. On the other
side, Third World governments are reluctant to ask for help, partly because
few governments have any idea that psychological research could help in
understanding and solving social problems, and partly because most
governments are politically sensitive to accusations that they might be
depending on outsiders for help. But a major reason is that no professional
association has declared boldly: 'We have skills and experience. We have
mutual problems. Can we get together, learn from each other and see what
can be done to understand the problems and mitigate them?'

Owing to the passive indifference of the Western professional
associations, the latent belief that Western psychology is the Westerner's
personal magic and Third World suspicions, psychology has been almost
totally isolated from the problems of the majority of the world's peoples.

This almost total apartheid within psychology is regrettable because
of the universality of some psychosocial problems such as (1) alienation and
the development of a sense of identity meaningful to individuals and not in
conflict with their societies; (2) the control of aggression and of sexuality;
(3) the most useful form of education for the development of cognitive skills
and for the development of independence; and, most broadly, (4) the
contribution of childrearing to the mitigation of tendencies toward learned
helplessness, the readiness to attribute decisionmaking to individuals and
groups over which the individuals feel that they have little or no control;
and (5) the little recognised problem of encouraging cooperative and
nonauthoritarian social and political relationships. None of the attempts to
define a relevant psychology shows much awareness of the gravity of these
problems, much less to investigate them with our sophisticated research
techniques.

Possibly this neglect is a result of the attitude that the Third World
has been little more than a theatre of operations, a convenient and interesting
venue for research. Sharing psychology has meant no more than using
Western research skills and experience to investigate specific empirical
questions in which Western-trained psychologists have been interested. The
resulting studies have usually been technically competent, but have rarely
been applied to Third World problems. Western experimental design
decorated by Third World palm trees remains Western-oriented psychology.

Connolly (1985) proposes that 'if we are to grow a psychology for the Third World...such a programme would...lead to the development of "appropriate psychological technology" '. But is this enough? Psychology is more than skills and techniques. It must also generate insight into the human condition and stimulate sympathy for the pains of living, even though the pains may be caused by socioeconomic and political factors. The essential and almost totally neglected basis of a relevant psychology is the study of the obstacle-bestrewn journey 'from metaphor to meaning' (Stein and Apprey, 1987). We live within an atmosphere of metaphor that gives meaning to the goals and relationships of individual and collective life. A relevant psychology must, therefore, share more than its skills. It must even share more than the spirit of a scientific psychology. To share skills is not difficult. To communicate how it feels to think as a mainstream psychologist is more difficult but still not impossible. It is almost unheard of to explore the implications of extending psychology beyond mere 'appropriate psychological technology' to incorporate the enthusiasms of humanism's approach to working with people rather than with subjects, for people are not subjects. A Third World psychology must become actively involved in the neglected question of the assessment and evaluation of the actual and potential psychological hurt or damage that policies may inflict. Western psychologists should lead the profession internationally to become the professional advocates for the more vulnerable members of society - the poor and the uprooted, those who are regarded as politically or socially dangerously deviant, the mentally disturbed, the ill-treated and ill-educated children.

So dramatic a shift in orientation will expose psychology to accusations that it is subversive or radical and, in both cases, politically tainted and, therefore, unscientific. But psychology is already implicitly political in being detached from the more urgent contemporary issues as well as in its hesitation and moderation when it does criticise social policies. But are not 'subversive' and 'radical' any more than synonyms for what is socially and politically disturbing? No psychology can be relevant to the Third, or any other, World unless it does unsettle those whose policies affect the happiness and welfare of the community.

From the psychoanalytic-cum-anthropological perspective, Stein (1985) suggests that there are theoretical reasons to share psychology. It is, maintains Stein:

> ...essential to understand what is now a mystery: how feelings
> come to be articulated in social institutions, symbols and rituals,
> and are enacted in social policy. The study of a society's

psychodynamic process and structure [is] a springboard for
studying unconscious influences upon cultures.

Very little is known about how emotional influences and relationships in
childhood shape adult relationships, although the broad principles are clear.
Broadly the relationships and social sentiments that we acquire during
childhood determine our adult relationships and social sentiments. We lack
specific insights into what is probably the key variable - identity. One
universal problem is learning how identity is formed in societies that are
experiencing rapid change and, consequently, dual processes of
disintegration and new forms of reintegration.

Moghaddam and Taylor (1986), in their critique of Western
psychology observe that Third World psychology must consider the 'dualism'
of Third World countries. They define dualism as 'the presence of a modern
and a traditional sector functioning alongside each other in the same society'.
Ignoring for the moment the objection that these sectors interact rather than
operate independently, identity formation is a particularly painful process in
such riven societies, and therefore, a particularly central feature of a relevant
psychology.

Questions of Methodology

The methods of psychology are as important as its content. Although
psychology was introduced to the Third World from the Western and more
urbanised-industrialised part of the world, this does not, in itself, justify the
argument that psychology is irrelevant to the Third World.

The basic scientific methods of proposing testable questions and
hypotheses, gathering data or evidence and evaluating its relevance, validity
and reliability apply to all kinds of psychological questions and societies.

But this view is not without its critics, who appear to deny that the
Third World should even consider how far these principles are applicable
and worth sharing. Asante (1987) has a persuasive, although not fully
convincing, argument for a specific research methodology for Africa, and,
by implication, for the Third World. Asante criticises the Eurocentric
perspective of both classical and radical streams of social analysis. Marx,
Freud, Habermas and Marcuse are dismissed as 'captives of a peculiar
arrogance, the arrogance of not knowing that they do not know what it is
that they do not know'. Their views of reality are limited and are, therefore,

of limited significance to the Third World.

And what is it that Europeans do not know that they do not know? It is nothing less than that 'the African perspective [is] a part of an entire human transformation'. Asante's 'search for an Afrocentric method' is succinctly expressed in a section almost at the end of his book, entitled 'Other Ways of Knowing', and has three strands. First, 'Western...objectivity has often protected social and literary theory from the scrutiny that would reveal how theory has often served the interests of the ruling classes'. Second, and 'more damaging still has been the inability of European thinkers, particularly of the neopositivist or empiricist traditions, to see that human actions cannot be understood apart from the emotions, attitudes and cultural definitions of a given context'. Third, 'the Afrocentric thinker understands that the interrelationship of knowledge with cosmology...and traditions [is a] principal means of achieving a measure of knowledge about experience'. Asante seems to forget that Marxism and psychoanalysis meet many, if not most, of his criteria for the study of human transformation. It is, however, timely to have Asante's 212 pages that add from a non-Eurocentric perspective to widely accepted caveats about the sociocultural limitations of much of contemporary psychology.

No startling novelty here! But it is startling to read Asante's ambivalence about the reality (or otherwise) of two worlds - one black and the other non-black. He writes that although 'it would be nonsense to...claim uniformity in black behaviour, the variance among blacks is less than between blacks and non-blacks' (Asante, 1987, p. 37). It would indeed be an 'entire human transformation' if the Afrocentric view taught Western thinkers that a common humanity can be found concealed by the apparent variance between blacks and non-blacks. An Afrocentric research methodology would, I believe, be based upon the postulate that universality and variance are equally significant features of humanity.

A more radical methodology than Asante's would describe and analyse the immense range of variance, within both black and non-black societies, so that we might better appreciate their essentially common humanity. We might also investigate ways in which specific economic, social and political contexts create specific stresses and frustrations - regardless of the skin colour of individuals. We should be questioning what there is in common and what is divergent among, for instance, inhabitants of a Kalahari Bushmen community, unemployed and undereducated black youths in a deteriorated inner city and professional blacks in a leafy suburb of New York. We should be asking the same questions of, for instance, members of a Greek peasant community, white youths in deteriorated Liverpool District 8 and professional whites in London's green suburbs.

Contemporary psychology underestimates the common human responses to social contexts and finds it difficult to appreciate the rich variety of psychologies among blacks and whites. An Afrocentric perspective should be destroying the stereotypes that whites have about blacks and that blacks have about whites. Any philosophy that fails to object to categorising whites *as a group* and blacks *as a group* is an antihuman foundation for psychological enquiry.

An essential question of methodology is the difficulty that individuals have in understanding other individuals. Black and non-black psychologists are unscientific if they fail to explore both the emotional and cognitive bridges and barriers between individuals and communities. The psychoanalytic discussion of positive and negative transferences bears directly on this problem.

Mainstream psychologists such as Connolly and Moghaddam and Taylor ignore the problems of transference in research. Others too readily assume that there are such strong emotional antipathies between blacks and whites that investigations of blacks by whites (and whites by blacks) predictably arouse negative transferences. But is this necessarily so? Psychologists still have to test the limits of this pessimistic notion, and my experience leads me to doubt its universal applicability. I have, for example, found it easier to evoke a transference in therapy with young Africans than with young English clients. As an outsider to my African clients I was considered safe: I was outside the authoritarian family structure and relationships. I did not belong to a threatening kinship, ethnic or national group. I was unlikely to possess supernatural powers that I might use to punish or control my client. Above all, my concern and interest was highly charged emotionally. I am a white man committed to helping an African in trouble or distress! And when I have an insight that leads to a meaningful interpretation, the cathartic release of tension is often dramatically stronger than for a white client.

It is a methodologically significant question to ask: to what extent and in what ways can people move through the intangible barriers of collective identity - the familiar and accepted contrasted with the alien and unaccepted. We are not helped by the metaphysical assumptions of 'human nature' of Dixon and Foster (1971), that Asante quotes with approval. Dixon and Foster describe what they call the 'black referent'. This includes six factors: 'humanism, communalism, the attribute of oppression/paranoia, empathetic understanding, the importance of rhythm and the principle of limited reward'. It seems (but it is uncertain), that these generalisations were drawn from the experiences of American blacks, both during slavery and in reaction from its lingering, post-freedom trauma. But does not 'referent' apply to the black and brown people in the post-colonial Third World? I am not concerned by the 'attribute of oppression/paranoia'. Is this an ineradicable characteristic of Third World blacks? Is it a diminishing characteristic? Increasing? Impervious to changing social, political and economic conditions? There can only be a relevant and comparative psychology if we can reasonably assume that human nature is universal and that people can perceive other people in a non-paranoid manner, and that they can reach others emotionally although, perhaps, at a less intimate and informal level than one might wish and be familiar with. Yet, paradoxically, Dixon and Foster do not see that 'empathetic understanding' may exist across collective boundaries. The methodological question is how to create a true cross-cultural or comparative psychology that explores 'empathetic understanding' - escaping from the inverted ethnocentricism that assumes too unquestioningly that we are imprisoned within our own cultures and suspicious of others.

The Third World Contribution

An exclusively Third World psychology would cut off a vast segment of humanity and seal it into its own world, which is as racist in its implications as the most overtly Eurocentred psychology. It is equally invalid. My position is that there is as wide a variation within Third World peoples as within peoples in the urban-industrialised world. There is a wide, indeed, probably total, psychological overlapping between the Third World and the rest of the world. The historical experiences and socioeconomic changes that have affected all communities in our brief human history - and continue to influence hitherto untouched communities - make a scientific psychology a psychology of change. Yet, change is rarely directly addressed in mainstream psychology. The contribution of the Third World is to compel psychology to apply its theories and techniques to the universal phenomena of change. The contribution is positive, creative, and likely to generate a new and realistically comparative cross-cultural psychology. There are two broad possibilities of the Third World contribution.

The Importance of Symbolism and Ritual

All peoples, whether Third World or Western, dwell in a 'forest of symbols'. All peoples 'pride [themselves] on being realistic, pragmatic, rational...' (Stein, 1985). But this reality exists in terms of their own collective definitions. The individual and collective working realities of everyday life - the myths of the past and the hopes and expectations of the uncertain future - may be far from the rationality that most psychologists feel themselves competent to investigate. Psychoethnology is bolder. Turner (1967), for example, has beautifully and sympathetically described the forest of symbols that define the world of the Ndembu of East Africa. The Ndembu live in a colourful environment that is rich in trees and plants which offer them the resources of survival. But survival is emotional no less than physical. The objects with which the Ndembu live together with their natural qualities, acquire qualities, meanings and emotional colouring. These qualities are as powerful determinants of Ndembu behaviourand experience as the natural qualities themselves. The objects of the Ndembu world differ from the same objects as perceived by their non-Ndembu neighbours - to say nothing of enquiring social scientists! The objects are embedded in rituals and evoke deep, symbolic inner significances and relationships with the Ndembu. The *mudyi* tree is more than a tree. It secretes a milky white juice if it is cut. The tree and its life-fluid are used in rituals and symbolise an astonishing variety of things and relationships. It is not surprising that it may represent the mother's breast milk which extends to the social activity of nursing the baby and the mother-child relationship. More difficult to appreciate intuitively for the non-Ndembu is that it also symbolises the abstract (but far from immaterial) pattern of matrilineal descent.

A psychology relevant to the Ndembu would be inadequate and thin if it failed to appreciate the rich texture of the Ndembu people's cognitions and interpretations of the objects in their world. Development studies too often ignore these considerations. A proposal, for example, to exploit the natural resources of the forest and to destroy the *mudyi* tree for its fruit or timber would provoke an emotional and social disruption and no amount of compensation could recreate the shattered community, which is held together by the web of meaning and belongingness spun from this real but magical tree.

A more recent example is from my experience. In the late 1970s a social anthropologist and I were consulted by a government about the possible consequences of moving villagers to clear space to build a new federal capital city. A new site for the village had been offered, discussed and apparently accepted. Monetary compensation had been paid. The villagers had materials for their new houses and transportation for the move. All seemed well, but the villagers refused to move at the appointed time, despite the authority's pleas and threats. It was not surprising. The planners had shifted trees and boulders to the new site to give the villagers a familiar environment. But the trees and boulders were not simple trees and boulders. They were also the homes of the ancestors who had not been adequately consulted and were, therefore, annoyed. The trees and boulders belonged to the ancestors. Their descendants lived in a world in which the past and the present were equally real and inextricably intertwined.

Even Westerners have not totally torn the present from the past, nor have phantasy and the symbolic been abolished. But few Western psychologists seriously acknowledge such potent, if intangible, variables. The symbolic and emotionally ambivalent qualities that are latent in many relationships influence much human cognition and perception. The psychometric, experimental and narrowly positivistic methodology of mainstream psychology is ill-fitted to investigate these most significant motivations. In the late 1990s, a century since Wundt and James founded modern psychology, it is high time to emerge from the constraints of an immature psychology.

Although Stein (1985) has pioneered in exploring the interactions between individuals and the symbolic milieux that they have created, this theme has not (as far as I am aware) been applied to the problems of socioeconomic development. It is typical of this hiatus in the centre of contemporary psychology that the imaginative text of Bock (1988) - a study of continuity and change in the study of human action - has only one five-page section about psychology and cultural change in a text of 215 pages. There is very little discussion about the relationships of the social psychology of change and development with the symbolic world that has been created and that must itself change if socioeconomic development is to evolve. Naturally, we do not live exclusively in a world of metaphor and symbols any more than we live solely in a network of relationships and social structures. But Bock, Connolly and others who confine their analyses to the latter and ignore the former, offer an inadequate account of the resistance to change and what facilitates it.

One of the most thoughtful contributions to the debate 'Can there be a psychology for the Third World?', exemplified how mainstream psychology is indifferent to the complexity and density of the worlds in which development in the Third World takes place, (Connolly,1985). Connolly pessimistically argues that 'much suffering is an irremediable part of the individual human condition', despite the massive achievements of the technological and scientific revolutions of this century. He, therefore, argues that the competence of psychology is limited in scope, although valuable as far as it goes, but it does not go very far. The massive problems that arise from the economic, social, political and technological changes in the Third World, the changes and conflicts of ideology, epistemology and life-space are, implicitly, beyond the reach of psychology. He, therefore, favours the same piecemeal approach in the Third World that has been successful in limited professional areas in the more industrialised world. Microtheories, microskills and microtechniques must be applied to the analysis or amelioration of microproblems. Western psychology avoids questioning the assumption that 'much suffering is irremediable'. A relevant psychology, rooted in the Third World, will note that the area of the irremediable has erratically but notably shrunk. It will examine the consequences of the meeting of the scientific metaphor with other metaphors. It will take heed of how the nature of the web of metaphor and myth changes in all communities. The changes have both harmonious and dissonant aspects - a relevant psychology examines the precise cognitive processes at work in different social-cultural contexts and in different individuals.

The Importance of Spiritual Enrichment

The Third World contribution will reform psychology to include as central topics the more spiritual and dynamic aspects. Western psychology has evolved as a technologically sophisticated discipline within a materialistic socioeconomic system. It has been almost wholly behaviourist in orientation and psychometric in technique.

But there have always been alternative movements within psychology. Since the beginning of the century, psychoanalysis has kept alive the interest in the complex emotional states that influence our behaviour and colour our experience. And, by its interest in the irrational, psychoanalysis has kept alive the study of unconscious motivations that influence our behaviour, relationships and sense of self. More recently, cognitive psychology has revived the interest in the processes of 'adjustment', although these are often difficult to quantify. For example, Kagan and Segal (1988) in their mainstream survey, describe the contemporary trend of modern psychology. It is 'cognitive, referring to all the ways in which we learn about our environment, store the knowledge in memory, think about it and use it to act intelligently in new situations...to help us think, understand and solve problems'. Western psychology is increasingly a study of these processes. It is less and less a catalogue of supposedly measurable categories such as intelligence. Western psychology is now not impervious to insights from humanism, psychoanalysis and many striking developments in psychobiology. It has the beginnings of a new identity as 'the science of mental life, both of its phenomena and their conditions' (James, 1950).

Little of the Third World is intensively urbanised and industrialised, and spiritual values have not been buried beneath the materialist values of Western urbanism. Few observers of the Third World fail to be struck by the creative, artistic and spiritual spontaneity of mental life which even poverty only partly suppresses. It is disappointing that even the 'radical' advocates of a Third World psychology write as though they were oblivious to the cognitive, artistic and spiritual effervescence that characterises many aspects of life in the post-colonial Third World. The Third World psychologist needs more than the simplistic, politicised Western psychology of, for example, Moghaddam and Taylor (1986).

The main thrust of Moghaddam and Taylor's reasoning centres about the consequences of the 'exportation of the social sciences'. They argue, contrary to Connolly, that there has been a considerable and harmful exportation. The harm arises from the incorrect perception of Third World societies. Western psychology has been divorced from the needs of the vast majority of people in Third World countries, who are part of the traditional sector of dual-sector societies. Psychologists are (with few exceptions) isolated from the traditional, rural sectors. The peasantry is ignored and psychology is developed within the urban-industrialised sector. It is, therefore, directly or indirectly for the benefit of new economic organizations and more closely linked with metropolitan psychology and values than to the values and problems of the Third World. It is argued that the role of psychology is both limited and distorted by sharing and encouraging the scientific and cultural subordination of the Third World. The Third World cannot be culturally liberated until its scientific subordination has dwindled and it has begun to create its own values in response to its own collective needs, aspirations and values.

Moghaddam and Taylor make much of the tendency to 'see all things Western as superior and necessarily better than anything comparable from the developing world'. This reverence for things Western includes psychology in its behaviourist and psychometric forms. They argue that Connolly is typical of many Western psychologists who assume that, if we apply Western psychology to Third World problems, it will be as intellectually profitable to the West as it will be economically profitable for the people of the Third World, or, as critics believe, as profitable for elite groups in the Third World.

What, then, should psychology be doing for the Third World? Moghaddam and Taylor see psychology as problem-centred but not limited to Western methodological purity. They believe that psychologists actively learn from the indigenous people as equal partners in the development of psychology. They insist that psychology must be politicised so that it may 'deal with the question of how feasible it is to implement a given type of psychology' and to test psychology's suitability to indigenous needs and values.

Moghaddam and Taylor (1986) propose six guidelines to a relevant psychology, but do not go far enough in exploring how these guidelines can be enriched by asking how Third World contributions may not merely complement but transform them. The criteria are self-reliance, needs responsiveness, cultural compatibility, institutional feasibility, economic suitability and political practicality. Not all are likely to be familiar to the average psychologists, even if they are working in the Third World, because few are aware of the political implications of their psychological research and probably fewer still recognise that their subjects are people too.

The psychology of self-reliance is, I believe, the most crucial problem for psychologists in creating a relevant psychology. Fanon (1986) was preoccupied with the problem of how to encourage a self-reliance in peoples whose colonial experience daily demonstrated their political and social impotence. Post-colonial Third World peoples still must acquire a healthy sentiment of self-reliance. Self-reliance depends upon growing up in a society that encourages it by providing many and varied experiences of autonomy. On a social level, this may include the growth of pride in the spiritual and cultural sides of life - it is possible to be economically poor but have a cognitive and emotional life that is rich in significance for the community. Poverty and political persecution obviously depress the spirit. The Third World context can teach Western psychology how varied are individual and collective resistances to hostile societies. It can more positively suggest questions that are largely ignored by Western psychology about how adversity may be transformed by individuals into the construction of an alternative worldview. Parin and others (1980) have analysed the tendency of groups to respond to stress by regressing to more childlike or primitive types of emotional bonding. Their research suggests the broad question about ways in which the different patterns of childrearing prepare individuals to deal with the anti self-reliant roles of adulthood. How do children learn that they are distinct individual identities despite the oppressive and often claustrophobic and alienating circumstances in which they are raised in many societies?

The Third World peoples' struggles to make sense of changing social and cultural worlds, and to establish a satisfactory sense of self-reliance suggests a question that Western psychology has barely touched. What is the emotional price that is paid for resisting authority and for attempting to establish our individual and emotionally satisfying personal boundaries?

Government Policymaking and the Individual

Western psychology works within a traditional pattern of seeking the determinants of behaviour - patterns of association between events that suggest patterns of cause and effect. There are such dizzying changes occurring throughout the Third World, and there are such varied collective and individual responses to the changes, that Western psychology's simple search for causes is arguably out of place. Is inevitability a false philosophy? In the Third World, it may well be. Both classical and operant (or instrumental) theories of conditioning are too tidy and deterministic, and too static, and are unable to make sense of the human propensity to respond to novelty. I am not convinced that people react to social circumstances passively because the complexity of social circumstances permits them to do little else but to respond. It seems truer that individuals often respond to the unpredicted with unpredictable understanding.

Popper (1988) has long held the view that a narrow and strict determinism does not apply to humanity. At the World Congress of Philosophy, he declared that 'the world is no longer a causal machine. It can now be seen to be an unfolding process, realizing possibilities and unfolding new possibilities'. The unpredictability of change in the Third World is a challenge to psychology to explore the cognitive techniques with which we plan and create possibilities, deal with the uncertainties of change and search for meaningful consistency in a world in which consistency is not always, nor even often, apparent.

The Western theory that seems most sensitive to the problems of change at both an individual and collective level is psychoanalysis. Popper's view is consistent with the 'determinism' of psychoanalysis, which is based upon the not unreasonable suppositions that there is a meaningful continuity between childhood and adulthood, and that the individual's emotional and social development in childhood continues with adult social behaviour and attitudes. Both Popper's view and the philosophy of psychoanalysis are directed to how the filaments of consistency may be distinguished within the muddles of individual and collective life. The psychoanalytic oppositions - conscious versus unconscious, rational versus irrational, creativeness versus destructiveness, love versus hate, sociability versus privacy - are together a system of metaphors that illuminate many (if not most) of the darker corners of the human mind. But how does this apply to the problems of the Third World?

Psychoanalysis is permeated by the theme of how social relationships and structures both shape individual lives and are variously interpreted, and reacted to, by individuals. As long ago as 1921, Freud was exploring the tense and complementary relationships of individuals and society in *Group Psychology and the Analysis of the Ego*. He wrote:

> In the individual's mental life someone else is invariably involved, as a model, as an object, as a helper, as an opponent; and so from the very first, individual psychology, in this extended but entirely justifiable sense of the words, is at the same time social psychology as well. (Freud, 1985)

Freud might have added that the someone else might be lover, oppressor, or alter ago. These relationships are relationships that may satisfy or dissatisfy the individual; they may enrich or frustrate; liberate or constrict. They may nourish individual narcissism or enable the individual's gratification in affiliation with others to flourish. No nation-state through its government and administrative system has yet investigated how their policies either liberate or constrain the individuals who constitute the nation-state. No government seems to have the remotest awareness that policies affect people in both their social relationships and their individual wants, needs and goals. In the Third World, the readiness with which ideological positions and policies are switched, as emergencies come and go, blinds government to the possibly harmful effects of their policies. And neither governments nor the people are emotionally prepared, either consciously or unconsciously, to cope with the uncertainties that are created by society or by society's sometimes ill-advised interference with nature.

Society lives by phantasy as well as by reality. One aspect of phantasy is what the future might be. Education to deal with the uncertain future, to cope with the collective and individual fantasy life may at present be fanciful, but cannot much longer be ignored.

Hartmann (1964), discussing the concept of health, considers the fundamental issues of adaptability and freedom. All peoples have a limited capacity to adapt to change. This capacity depends upon structural factors, upon individual ego strength and upon the nature and strength of the unconscious and irrational drives that motivate the individual. The other issue, freedom, is not the traditional philosophical problem of Free Will versus Determinism, but the practical problems of the extent to which, and in what ways, individuals and collectives are free from anxieties and irrational drives? To what extent are they free to perform their daily tasks, and what, if any, emotional satisfaction do they derive from them? The human child's long period of immaturity can socialize the child to be free and adaptable. Socialization is not necessarily a training for subordination and helplessness. A relevant educational and developmental child psychology could gather the mass of comparative material that relates patterns of child socialization and adult personality, and maybe tentative findings might emerge about how certain patterns and policies are liberating and others are not.

Freud himself, concluded his speculations about the future of the human condition with the hope that where Id was shall Ego be - if civilization survives. The psychoanalytic message to the Third World might be, therefore, to introduce no policies unless they might strengthen the Ego, and to introduce none that strengthens the Id. Alas, the makers of policies are no more rational than the rest of us.

Rethinking and Refeeling Psychology

Paradoxically, both mainstream psychology and its politicised critiques are only partially correct. The insistence on meticulous methodology is essential. We can also agree that there is no psychology that is either ethically or politically totally neutral. However, both are limited approaches that conceal the unspoken assumption that the Third World is helpless, and psychology is either utterly irrelevant or feeble. Three examples illustrate these two views.

Biesheuvel (1958), while Director of The National Institute of Personnel Research (South Africa), was involved in the assessment, selection and training of Africans then being integrated into an urban-industrial socioeconomic system.   His two research aims were 'to gain an understanding of the behaviour of African peoples' and to test 'the general validity of psychological hypotheses concerning human behaviour'. Biesheuvel seemed little concerned with human experience!   Not surprisingly in those politically insensitive times, he considered that 'African research programmes should... be preferably directed towards the measurement of limits of modifiability of African behaviour and towards a definition of the environmental factors that determine those limits'.   This static and pessimistic view persists in those theories that doubt the capacity of people in the Third World to adapt themselves to Western industrial organization, or to adapt Western industrial organization to Third World needs.

The defeatism of self-styled radical critics usually bluntly asserts that Western psychologists 'mismatch First World psychology and Third World problems' (Jordan, 1985), or 'psychologise' Third World economic, political and social problems (Mehryar, 1984).   Both types of argument lead to the view that psychology is impotent at best, and evil at worst, because (according to Jordan) it is a factor in 'the creation of perpetuation of poverty'.   But why, if psychology is feeble and irrelevant should it contribute to anything or need to be actively rethought?   Why if, as Jordan complains, psychology is one of the invalid 'voluntarist theories of change' should psychology have the slightest concern in policy issues?   There is no way to destroy another's philosophical assumptions without exposing oneself to counterassertions that are no more objective and testable than one's own. The debate is time-wasting and irrelevant.   Connolly argues that the 'failures of western psychology and its inadequacies are...not a cause for despair or despondency but a challenge'.   I shall now boldly present the elements of a committed psychology.   I shall not trouble myself with speculations about the possibility that I have a latent colonial mentality, nor whether I am trying my readers' patience by bemoaning the theoretical impotence of the social sciences.

Relevant Psychology is Social and Dynamic

C. Wright Mills contends that the social sciences are about the nature and significance of milieux. Psychology, one of these sciences, investigates the many environments within which people live and to which they respond. At times, the responses are passive and accommodating; at others, they are active and the environment is modified and assimilated to individual needs, wants and goals. Individuals, however, always behave in a specific yet changing life-space - resisting its constraints and utilising its opportunities. Individual and collective needs, wants, goals and phantasies define our perception of the environment which is, therefore, never neutral nor totally external to individuals. A mainstream experimental and positivistic psychology - a politicised psychology - is equally bound to understand the interaction between the individual and the sociocultural.

The milieu or the environment is not a thing like a plough or a railway system. It is a changing relationship between a people and their ploughs and their railway system - what they make with them, and what they fear, love, respect and expect of them. This position pushes mainstream psychology toward questions and issues that it has been reluctant to face. This social psychology - committed and challenging - is already creeping into mainstream psychology (Gergen, 1975), and although Lewin's plea for relevant psychology is now of historical importance, his dynamic, cognitive position has reappeared in the form of a more interactionist position. Society and the individual are increasingly seen as a unit.

There is a convergence between the radical and sociological criticisms of mainstream psychology and mainstream psychology itself. They all denigrate psychology as a humanity by reducing its scope. The pioneering psychoanalyst Otto Rank wrote in a study of psychology and social change that 'the tendency of our times to minimise the importance of all psychological explanation of human behaviour seems indicative of the failure of our rationalistic psychology [and sociology] to account for the increasing power of irrational forces operating in modern life' (Rank, 1958). By 'irrational' Rank referred to 'powerful ideologies' that appear to be uncontrollable because they have deep emotional roots underlying their manifest cognitive and intellectual content. Racism is an example of such an ideology.

The convergence is a paradox: 'social integration is largely, if not overwhelmingly, achieved by psychological process' (Stein, 1985). Even the socially erratic transition from colonial dependence to post-colonial independence has been created and experienced by individuals. Those individuals have been influenced as much by wishful thinking and their unconscious feelings and attitudes as by the realities of economic, political and social problems.

One crucial psychosocial problem of independence that illustrates the paradox is identity. Motivating many political conflicts and misunderstandings are such questions as: 'Who are we, the Utopians? How do we differ from our neighbours? Are we one people or many? Are we one family of peoples, or many competing families thrown together by the accident of our colonial past?' Connolly (and others writing from within the mainstream and radical perspectives in psychology) ignore this fundamental problem of identity. I believe that until the nation-states in the Third World acquire a sense that they are communities, then economic and technological innovations are doomed to benefit one section of the state; thus, the seeds are sown for a vigorous growth of secessionist or regional fragmentation or conflict. Because few countries have succeeded in creating a paramount sense of identity, cultural fragmentation tends to become highly politicised and unstable.

Therefore, in explaining social problems, psychologists must never forget that individuals are variables too and that it is insufficient to confine research and understanding to the behavioural level. Thinking and feeling that one is a member of a society means both learning that one belongs to it and feeling accepted by it. The culture and society about which one learns is not a network of events and relationships as solid and unambiguous as the pyramids. Cultures and societies are interpreted, understood, loved, feared and even hated by individuals whose peculiar relationships and socialization refract their sociocultural perceptions. Little Muyunda and little Sikota live within the same culture. But what is this 'sameness'? The external and superficial definition of nationhood, ethnic membership, even of family, kin and village membership and their behavioural and emotional demands, is far from identical with Muyunda's and Sikota's inner, personal and idiosyncratic defences against the anxieties and frustrations of their lives. Society and culture are often muddled. Relationships are often unsatisfactory. Our socially defined identity does not always foster our self-esteem.

Let us return to the forest of symbols to examine in detail how these convergences and conflicts between sociocultural and psychodynamic views suggest a new direction for understanding the human problems of surviving emotionally in a changing world.

Psychology in the Forest of Symbols

Western psychology has tended to be more at home with describing human skills and the measurable aspects of personality, and finds faintly raffish the concern with the unmeasurable and subjective conscious and unconscious feelings of identity. Yet, unless individuals live in a world in which they can mature from helplessness to self-determination, that world will probably be stagnant or even regressive. I agree with Winnicott (1974) who has argued that 'the fear of breakdown' or of failure is a major factor in inhibiting individuals from dealing rationally with their world. Individuals are unconsciously vulnerable to two kinds of fear of failure. Some people fear the breakdown of ego-organisation - they struggle to deal with the sense of having no meaningful identity, or they resist an imposed identity. The imposed white masks of colonialism have sometimes distorted or damaged the black faces that they conceal. Other people fear the pains of reality and resist growing up and having to accept the demands of adult responsibility in both cases. Winnicott's patients tended to regress to the emotional relationships of childhood and repeated, in those relationships, the contradictions of love and hate that characterise childhood. As children, less is expected of them than of adults and, if they are fortunate, they may be protected emotionally where adults are left exposed. But, as children, they are more emotionally vulnerable than adults are expected to be. In the Third World unsettling fears of failure exist collectively as well as in individuals, and they converge and exacerbate each other.

Durkheimians would describe the economic, social, and political uncertainties, deprivations, and conflicts of societies struggling to develop a practical, working sense of being a society. The economic and political relationships of the Third World with the donor nations have done little to reduce these uncertainties to emotionally bearable levels. For individuals, there are deep uncertainties about how to cope with the plethora of problems and the unpredictability of their social, political and economic worlds. The emotional problems of independence are many. Not least is vulnerability to the fear of feeling that one's society is weak and is perceived as such by the powerful outside world. Colonization, slavery and other forms of exploitation, damage individuals and societies alike. Individuals are socialised into learned helplessness - they learn to depend upon helping hands. These hands, however, often do not help but strike indifferently or angrily. The expectation of helplessness is accompanied by expectations of erratic help. Panic results from living in situations and relationships that are unpredictable and uncontrollable. Individuals are forced, individually and collectively, to create emotional defences against a destructive world. Sometimes these defences are positive, anticolonial sentiments are generated and political movements are formed. At other times, however, groups retreat regressively into a quasi-family with emotionally and culturally closed boundaries. Internal security and fear of failure is bought at the price of isolation from wider and, therefore, stronger loyalties. The problem of the Western world and of the Third World is the dissolution of community. The Third World also faces the resistance to change of communities that are motivated by insecurity and that limit the growth of wider-ranging social sympathies and loyalties. Declining villages and swelling cities create vast problems.

For development studies, three aspects of the fear of national failure and sheer survival seem to be particularly important:

1. There is a fear of the annihilation and death of the society with its emotional and social bonds corroded by the acids of ideological and technological change. Many communities in the Third World oscillate uneasily between a sense of defeat and self-pity and an extravagant sense of self-reliance and rejection of the need for outside help. The realities of economic, social and political problems are grave. They are not solved by the capricious shifting from superficial euphoria to deeply rooted self-doubts. The fear of annihilation is often unconsciously expressed by a search for the political magician who will radically restore the society's former vigour and purity, renew its collective sense of purpose and expel the evil forces of corruption. The dramatic nature of grand political gestures by would-be saviours are fundamentally attempts to postpone the death of the society and are often strongly infused with depressing omens of the terrible fate of the society if the saviour fails to save. Another attempt to deny annihilation is the angry rejection of bits of society feared as worthless or as evil. Self-torturing and hypercritical punishment or destruction of 'worthless' individuals, groups or ways of life, lead to suicidal economic and social policies that lead to the very weakening of social bonds that is feared.

2. There is often a sense of inner emptiness, both individually and collectively, expressed in sentimental regrets for bygone times and long past glories. More significant are widespread expressions of feelings of alienation and of complaints that the society offers nothing to the masses while providing wealth and power to the elites. There is a manic flight from the overwhelming problems of society into a numbing defeatism. No one would deny the reality of many problems, because poverty and drought or flood are tragically real, but much social policy degenerates into manic, meaningless diversions - masquerades that give the sensation of accomplishment but that are rooted in desperation. An obsessive concern with forms of government and systems of economic and social organisation and an illusory sense of reassurance that is fostered by yet another paper new world, breed and increase a sense of emptiness. Failure to overcome failure deepens the feeling of impotence, and impotence destroys the consciousness of an inner confidence, competence and self-esteem.

3. V.S. Naipaul has cruelly described the world of 'the mimic men'. The mimic men run those countries that have nothing of their own. They do not exist to provide a permanent sense of satisfactory belonging and meaningful activity for the masses but for external symbols of power and wealth. These symbols are owned and manipulated by the elite, but they are vicariously enjoyed by the masses. The country of mimic men (and women) exists by mimicking the ways of life of more successful countries. The mimicking nations have names, flags, heads of state and nominal, legal independence, but little else. A sense of emptiness pervades them, and they are characterised by ambivalence toward the mimicked countries which are blamed and repudiated, resented for their influence yet, nevertheless, mimicked.

Of course, the outside world does exist. It is the world with food, shelter, education and security. It may even be perceived (erroneously) to have an enviable sense of community. This world demonstrates what the deprived country lacks and is a reproach and a source of envy not unlike a distant and wealthy relative. There is often an unhealthy deterioration that moves from regrets that 'We have no collective ego, no identity' to 'We don't want *your* collective ego, your identity, now that colonialism has passed by'.

The unconscious and ultimate surrender is: 'But the ego that you show us, your success and your wealth, though they may be terrible and alien to use, may be the best that we can effectively mimic'.

The Third World, because of the overwhelming burdens of reality, is always dangerously close to increasing the risks of real social breakdown by the fear of breakdown. Reality is bad enough. There is, alas, no realistic reason to expect that the Third World can be any more certain than the rest of the world of finding political and social leaders who are able to meet the challenges and soothe the anxieties of a reality that is often interpreted as malignant - and with some justification. But there is nothing so deeply rooted in the sociology of the Third World that it is condemned forever to flee to empty mimicry from painful reality. An African friend asked me rhetorically: 'Why must the Third World be so anxious to build a bubble-gum world?' Winnicott would perhaps reply that a mimicked identity is a substitute for a badly damaged one. The spurious identity and sense of belonging of the bubble-gum world symbolises success, power and economic autonomy. The West can never break down! It is secure and predictable - established. It has long had nationhood and a history of overcoming the turmoil of war and economic and political failure. The mimic men and their mimic societies display 'flight...from internal reality' (Winnicott, 1975) - the inner reality of learned helplessness and disappointments. Politics become daydreams of wealth, of phantasies of power and status. But daydreams do not for long check the depression that is caused by a surfeit of the burdens of reality. T.S. Eliot observed that 'Mankind cannot bear much reality'. When reality is too much to bear, mankind retreats into phantasy. The life experiences of many Third World people fail to offer them a world where a realistic sense of self-determination is possible. Confidence in the predictability of situations, relationships and values is frequently, erratically shattered. But 'a personal continuity of existence' (Winnicott, 1966) is an essential condition of healthy, emotional maturity and, if the development of a sense of continuity and integrity is denied to the growing child, it will not be easily developed in adulthood. If societies promote fears of breakdown, of impotence and of bewilderment, then the capacity to deal with reality is diminished. It is crucial, therefore, to interpret social relationships and systems on both the realistic, pragmatic level and on the level of unconscious phantasy about that society and its relationships. Winnicott (1966), as a clinician, explored the experiences of children in coming to terms with reality and persuasively argues that children's styles in dealing with emotionally favourable and unfavourable experiences will influence how they deal with them in adulthood.

Two areas of adjustment to reality are, I believe, central to the problems of development - achievement orientation and the opposing sentiments of optimism and pessimism. Weiner (1974) is one of many psychologists who stress the importance of the orientation toward either failure or success. This orientation is seen on both individual and collective levels and seems to depend upon two sources. First, do we perceive causes to be within our control or outside it? Do we, therefore, feel that we must rely upon our own efforts for success or that we are the pawns of some sort of fate or superhuman agency? Second, how predictable are the causes? To what extent and in what way can we influence them? A major part of religion and of magic is the attempt to influence causes that are perceived as beyond normal human control and, thus, in need of specialist intervention.

The relevance of these considerations is easily seen in everyday life and on both a supernatural and social level. For example, in many Third World societies, it is important to have 'long legs' or access to influential relatives if one is to succeed. Similar contacts are not unknown in the industrialized world! If we believe that we have no such access and that we are, therefore, doomed to fail, then we are likely to be failure oriented. If, on the contrary, we have such access, then we are more likely to grow up optimistic and success oriented. We live in a changing and an imperfect world where virtue is not as frequently rewarded as one might wish. If children learn that they are members of a success-oriented group, then they are more likely to succeed than if they are brought up in a failure-oriented group. The ignored question in psychology and sociology is: how do individuals and communities compensate for the built-in encouragement to failure? Alas, often by withdrawing into a supernatural world or into political fantasies in which their virtue *is* rewarded.

A relevant psychology is, therefore, a developmental psychology that focuses on the paths that children find through the forest of symbols. I have suggested that optimism or pessimism, defeatism or a sense of competence are acquired through relationships and may be realistic or unrealistic. Few psychologists who work in the Third World have tried to unravel these complicated aspects of growing up. Almost none have tried to relate patterns of childhood optimism and pessimism to the orientation of adulthood. Children use adults as their models of success or failure, which are intermingled in most adults. I have been unable, however, to find any research into the precise areas of optimism and pessimism in studies of the Third World, so there is little but intuition to guide the student of the Third World about what patterns of child socialisation and education might increase rational realism and optimism. Individual children have their own needs for success and their own fears of failure, however, so they will unconsciously or consciously select models of adult behaviour or phantasies about them. Children, too, may consciously or unconsciously oppose adult influences and, in so doing, they are opposing the social and cultural values and practices of which adults are the models. Children, thus, hew from the raw human material of family, kinship and other primary groups their own meaningful cultural experience and orientation toward their world. This experience may be happy or unhappy. It may lead to children's developing an orientation toward success and failure that is characteristic of their society - or it may not. It often leads to the tense, often violent, confrontations between the younger and the older generations. The older generations assume or openly claim that they have earned the right to a monopoly of authority and wisdom and, therefore, of the opportunities for success. But those who are assumed or asserted to be destined for subordination and failure consciously or unconsciously resist. Slaves, members of inferior castes, women, certain 'ethnic' or minority groups may be imprisoned throughout their lives in a failure-oriented position. For these subordinated groups, technological and economic development is inconceivable unless it is associated with liberation from their lowly status and, thus, a little explored consequence of technological and economic development is the disruption of many authoritarian relationships. Behind many sociopolitical conflicts of the Third World - and the others - is the unconscious, symbolic warfare between the generation of authoritarian fathers and their subordinate, but rebellious, children.

Elements of a Relevant Psychology

The elements of a relevant psychology cohere about the emotional, developmental and irrational-unconscious social-psychological aspects of psychology that are now largely ignored. If any one aspect be crucial it is identity or the self. The major psychological dilemma of the post-colonial and post-slavery period is that of the restoration of the self (Kohut, 1977). The dilemma is how to restore the self without either retreating into a mythical past or adopting an equally mythical and facile 'Western' identity.

The Western and the Third Worlds have been haunted by the questions: 'Who am I?','Who are my people?','What type of people are we?','What is our nature, our uniqueness?' The factors that facilitate the development of a sense of collective and individual identity, and those that inhibit it, are at the heart of a relevant psychology. I wonder whether identity is a problem that did not exist in pre-colonial times. One of my students once explained passionately during a debate: 'I am *not* an African! I am *not* a Nigerian! I am *not* a Hausa! I'm Danladi Umaru! *That's* who I am!' I doubt if even a decade ago so powerful a defence of the integrity of the self could have been made to an audience without being met with silent or stormy outrage and incomprehension. In the late 1980s such a statement vibrated with significance. Yet, I do not doubt that an inner ambivalence about identity in the Third World troubles many introspective younger people who feel that they both belong to the Third World and to the increasingly influential Western. This ambivalence is delicately evoked in Act Four of *The Tempest*. Prospero, the magician prince, has given orders to his sprite Ariel, who acknowledges his orders and asks: 'Do you love me, master? No?' To which Prospero replies: 'Dearly, my delicate Ariel.' Prospero continually promises Ariel his freedom and continually postpones it. Continually Ariel demands his freedom, yet never rebels and, in the end, is touchingly reluctant to leave his beloved, yet resented, master. His master is - or seems to be - reluctant to let him go.

The restoration of the self is, I believe, a psychopolitical problem for both the Third World and the Western. Mehryar (1984) and Jordan (1985) smother the point in tendentious political cotton wool by insisting that if psychologists analyse Third World problems, they are indulging in irrelevant 'psychologising'. The questions of development - of wealth and poverty - are, of course, economic, political and technological, but why do we yearn to abolish poverty and insecurity? Surely only to liberate people so that they may individually and collectively develop emotionally satisfying identities and a sense of a worthwhile self. Mehryar and Jordan (and most self-styled radical critics) write as though the Third World were not populated by people. They 'externalise' individuals by reducing them to mere images of sociopolitical constructs.

One of the most powerful motivating forces during the struggles for independence has been the rise of black consciousness or other ethnic-based parties and movements. All Third World peoples - Africans in South Africa and those scattered by the diaspora - have fought to restore their collective sense of self. This, I believe, is far more than an effective emotional resistance to colonialism or other forms of discrimination; nor is it only a response to racism or to the deeply disturbing effects of cultural and political change. It is an active assertion of identity and, as with all assertions of identity and selfhood, it is emotionally ambivalent.

The belief persists commonly in the Third World - often manifestly, but sometimes unconsciously - that the emotional legacy of colonial mentality inhibits the growth of an independent national sense of identity. Dividing and ruling had emotional results beyond their administrative outcomes. Many countries are still oscillating between past and present. There may be an obsessive search for emotional roots of a collective selfhood, for a myth of origins, for a utopian past. Such a search can be dangerously regressive however. If a community is too obsessed by searching for a past that has never existed except in the collective imagination that needs it, this obsession prevents the group's developing a contemporary, forward-looking sense of self. I doubt the emotional wisdom of encouraging a determination to adopt uncritically the ways of the Western World. The Western World's diminishing sense of community, its widespread alienation, its harmful hierarchical structures and the consequent racism, sexism and economic inequality, are better avoided than mimicked.

Both regressing to a mythical past and trying to profit from the West have similar dangers: communities are drawn from the realities of change and of self-determination. The 'exhumation' of the past is as unrealistic as the 'group phantasy according to which people are scrambling for belonging and security' (Stein, 1985), by claiming the identity and *raison d'etre* of different worlds with their own problems of *anomie* and insecurity.

Writing of the Western World, Lasch (1985) remarks that 'identity has become uncertain and problematical...because [people] no longer inhabit a world that exists independently of themselves'. I wonder whether the Third World has begun to experience a similar problem with the weakening of village and other local or regional emotional ties? Once a sense of identity and of belonging was firmly rooted in and constrained by life in small, localised, clearly defined social units that are easily imagined and identified with. Children were socialised to be sensitive to the boundaries of these units and so their place in their social world was unambiguous. Children learned who they were, to what groups they belonged and what behaviour was expected of them. They grew sensitive to relationships both with their contemporaries and with their past.

The social boundaries, however, are now beginning to dissolve and to become ambiguous - the Third and Western Worlds. On a cultural level, the Western World is being influenced by the Third World. Technologically, economically and politically, the Third World is more and more tightly integrated within the Western World. Collective views of identity and selfhood are changing and are increasingly tinged with inconsistency and conflict. Individual and collective definitions of the self are losing their sharpness and conflicts result. Moreover, the universal and primitive conflicts between age and youth, the sexes, the individual and the collective, have acquired a new and growing intensity in the Third World. These conflicts are more and more openly directed to the strivings for individual identity in societies in which the collective constraints persist to conflict with the growing influence of opportunities and constraints that arise from outside the Third World. It is unfortunate that the behaviourist and psychometric psychologists have not yet turned their attention to the methodologically difficult questions that arise from these problems.

It is surprising that in the section of his book entitled 'The Liberation', Asante (1987) does not discuss the self or identity. Yet in the 'Afrocentric discourse' he proposes three fundamental themes of which one is 'human's relationships to their own being'. The three pages on 'personalism' are a Blakean rhapsody to mankind's harmony with nature and to relationships. Asante writes that 'The African finds energy and life in the midst of persons...Ours is pre-eminently a tradition of remarkable encountering with others...I know myself only in relation to others...' Later, he makes much of the notion of 'possession' by the gods of Africa. Africans search actively to achieve harmony with their collective experience by becoming possessed by the collective gods, by music and dancing, rhetoric and prayer. The Western 'logical positivist tradition' that dominates Western thought and relationships for Asante starkly contrasts with African spirituality. Unfortunately, I feel that Asante's romantic views are uncomfortably close to the romantic racism of, for example, Mannoni (1956) and Jung.

Relevant Psychology is Anti-racist

One of my Nigerian friends commented with some bitterness: 'this undead colonialism is self-colonialism'. The residual colonial mentality is a preoccupation of many Western psychologists. Even those who are concerned about sharing psychology with the Third World have tended to be unaware of the racist implications of constructing a psychology of the

Third World that assumes - or openly asserts - that dominated peoples remain unyieldingly dominated, self-colonised and dependent. Although overtly racist psychologies are less influential than they were twenty years ago, the latent racism of such psychologists as Jung and Mannoni has not vanished. A relevant psychology, therefore, must counter these views that influence Western immigration policies and are dangerously divisive in the Third World.

Mannoni (1956) practiced as a psychiatrist in Madagascar and generalised from his experience to the Third World. He argued that there are two basic personality types - the dominator and the dominated. He applies this theory to colonial situations where the colonised people have a need to be dominated and the colonisers (nearly always Europeans) have a corresponding need to dominate. This becomes a symbiotic relationship. Collectively and individually social relationships develop that are analogous to sadomasochistic relationships. Indeed, the violence of some master - servant relationships is very close to sadomasochism. Mannoni criticises the economic interpretations of colonialism as inadequate. The colonist is not simply seeking profit; he is greedy for psychological satisfaction. This, Mannoni suggests, imprisons the colonist in the colonial situation that satisfies his inner needs to dominate others. Profits are frequently sacrificed for the sake of emotional satisfactions, because an economically more profitable system might well have educated and trained the colonial people, although this would raise their status and enable them to feel independent. According to Mannoni, however, the dominated people demand independence but, when they receive it, they readily return to sociopolitical systems that are as hierarchical and authoritarian as the colonial regimes.

Certainly the history of colonialism has been marked by perverted sexual and sadistic behaviour by colonists - both individually and collectively - that in other situations would probably have been regarded as pathological. The colonised peoples have often been stigmatised as immature or even subhuman creatures who exist only to be exploited for profit and emotional satisfaction. *Robinson Crusoe* and the hundreds of stories of adventure and exploration have consciously or unconsciously been used by Europeans as vehicles for the baser phantasies of power and domination. There are a mere handful of stories in which a non-European is treated as an equal. One of these is Samuel Johnson's *Rasselas, Prince of Abyssinia*, which was written as a moral essay in 1759. Prince Rasselas expounds what is probably Johnson's own philosophy of life and is far from being portrayed as a 'noble savage'.

Mannoni believes that the European restlessness and the collective impulse to find people to dominate is related to sexual guilt and frustrations. Guilt and frustration are transformed into manic flight - the mad itch to explore and to exploit the significantly named 'virgin' lands. The colonised peoples are emotional scapegoats onto whom unconscious guilts can be projected. The colonised people are felt to be wild, unpredictable, sexually attractive, yet forbidden, malevolent (and to be feared), yet childlike. This primitive is a projection of the coloniser's own wild, unpredictable restlessness, malevolence, childishness and sexuality. In Jungian terms the colonised peoples symbolise the dark side of human nature - a dangerous side that both attracts and repels. Further, the individual is subordinate to the 'collective' or 'racial' unconscious: this is a mythical entity, the origins of which are lost in an archaic nature that distinguishes one people from another. So, for example, blacks are distinguished from whites, Jews from Aryans, the colonisers from the colonised, because of their collective unconscious.

The hidden agenda of white racism is that the peoples of the Third World are locked in dependency relationships and are, therefore, slow to change - if they can significantly change at all. This latent racism is, however, abated by a psychoanalytic approach to personality development, in which insights from cultural anthroplogy are integrated. In all societies there are 'key integrative systems' (Kardiner and Ovesey, 1951). Human beings share the same basic psychobiological needs and characteristics, which only appear superficially to differ in different cultures, because to develop from an asocial infant to a socialised adult entails the same developmental tasks in all societies. Underlying cultural differences, there may be recognised similar emotional sensitivities - needs for self-esteem and social respect. Although the opportunities and constraints of one community differ from those of another, there is a universality of human emotions that belies the glib racist assumption that there is more than one kind of human being. A realistically relevant psychology has, therefore, to search for the universals as a corrective to those psychologies that overemphasise the superficial differences between communities.

There is of course, more than one version of the integrative systems. I propose the following because I think that they are arguably fundamental:

1.   In all societies the human infant is helpless and needs care, nurturance and protection. The quality of care varies: in some cultures it is erratic, in others it is consistent; in some it is given

reluctantly or with hostility, in others it is given freely and with pleasure. But the tendency of all infant care is to make dependency in infancy a motivation for relationship in adulthood. The dependency relationships described by Mannoni are not, therefore, peculiar to the colonised people. Establishing a sense of independence in adulthood is an emotional problem in all communities.

2. In all societies relationships between children and adults are reciprocal; infants provoke adults to relate to them. Adults are more or less individually responsive to their infants. The norm for relationships in a community may be warm, open, honest and intimate, or they may be chilly, distant and wary. There may be emphasis upon cooperation and reward, or upon obedience and punishment. In no society can there be so deep a mutual sense of distrust between children and adults that no socialisation into society's norms is possible.

3. Children's sibling relationships shape adult relationships. The norms within families of controlling or sublimating rivalries and aggression, co-operation and competition, ways in which the younger generation defers to the elders or unites in silent opposition to them, have never been described and related to problems in larger social units.

4. We need to know far more than we now do about what holds societies together and what stimulates conflict and disintegration. No society is without conflict between groups and individuals, any more than families are. Some families seem to be so preoccupied with their internal rivalries and conflicts that there is little emotion remaining for the betterment of the family. Indeed, some families thrive on rivalry and conflict which are their *raison d'être*. Likewise with societies: an outsider may despair at the emotional extravagance of societies locked in draining civil wars or where exhausting poverty exists side-by-side with an ostentatious wealth. How, we must ask, do societies (from the family to the nation-state and beyond), socialise their members so that potential conflict and disintegration is sublimated into action that permits cohesion to continue - until the disintegrative latent conflicts can no longer be

contained? All societies are a network of constraints and of acceptable relationships, which both shape socioeconomic development and are influenced by it. The interaction between existing and changing patterns of integration and disintegration in Third World societies has barely been recognised as the urgent problem that it is.

5. Influencing the social systems and relationships are the beliefs and attitudes of members of the community. We ignore the reality of the phantasy worlds inhabited by the many different groups within a society: young and old, females and males, urban dwellers and rural, believers in different religious or philosophical systems, those identified with Western values and those who reject some part or all of them and the rich and the poor. It is dangerously simplistic to describe any society as though it were one more-or-less uniform unit without its internal divisions that development often exacerbates.

It is peculiarly puzzling that social scientists have almost totally neglected the arts, crafts and traditional techniques of societies. Herskovits (1949) wrote that '...art is to be thought of as any embellishment of ordinary living...any manifestation of the impulse to make more beautiful and thus to heighten the pleasure of any phase of living that is so recognized by a people'. He even writes of 'the aesthetic drive' and was eloquent in the tradition of many earlier cultural anthropologists who interpreted dance, oratory, storytelling...as activities that forever remind the observer that a functional and pragmatic view of social life is an impoverished view. Beyond the degree of technical virtuosity in inventing or elaborating a dance, making a raffia house or decorating dwellings, the content of artistic and creative activity says much about the emotional preoccupations of society. Besides, much creation and construction is collective, bringing people together and symbolizing comradeship, whether it is temporary or prolonged. The fears, hopes, anxieties, complex emotions, phantasies and group relationships within a society are as real in their artistic expression as they are in the 'real' world.

Radin and Herskovits have described the American Indian interest in the 'trickster-transformer', and the elaborate creation myths of the South East Pacific are as well known as the universal myths about families of supernatural animals or humans. These phantasy worlds are more than fancy. Bettelheim (1986) has analysed those myths of and about childhood that we call fairy tales, and has shown how the fears and wish-fulfillments that they contain are related to everyday fears and preoccupations. The fairy tale, according to Bettelheim, is one expression of the 'existential predicament': 'the psychological problems of growing up - overcoming narcissistic disappointments, oedipal dilemmas, sibling rivalries; becoming able to relinquish childhood dependencies; gaining a feeling of selfhood and self-worth and a sense of moral obligation...' People in the Third World, as in every other world, must bring order into the chaos of emotional, personal life and into the relationship chaos of social life. Bettelheim has distinguished more than thirty fairy tale themes, the most common of which is 'the struggle for meaning' in life. In the Western and the Third World our identity and relationships are dramatically transformed. Fairy tales present children with emotional and relationship problems, offer symbolic solutions and encourage them with happy - or fairly happy - endings. Similarly, many artistic activities reveal emotional and social problems and offer hope, relief and control of the more destructive emotions and relationships.

Conclusion

A relevant psychology for the Third World is, therefore, not irrelevant to the Western World. Too much of contemporary psychology is accurate but limited, far distant from what motivates men, women and children in their everyday lives. But the attempts to construct a relevant psychology for the Third World must be sensitive to the dangers of a pitying 'inverse racism which is racism, nevertheless. Bruckner (1983) warns bitterly:

> Take care! Throughout the argument about the current term 'Third World' there is a current controversy: that of the mental space that we reserve for the future for non-European peoples. When we speak about the Third World as though it were a hospice, it shrinks the psychological horizons of our fellow human beings. It disqualifies four billion people from future generations. (L.B.'s translation)

Can there be a psychology relevant to the Third World? Yes! It should be a psychology with no covert racism. It must be, therefore, a psychology that is addressed to the emotional and social problems of growing up in all worlds. Fanon (1980) has, from the Third World, attacked those simplistic descriptions of the world as though it were composed of black people and white. Such descriptions may be emotionally comforting and politically motivating, but they are a mystification of reality. Fanon pioneered a psychology of the Third World and rejected any suggestion that this could be based upon stereotypes: there is no justification in lumping together as a few undifferentiated masses the billions of people whose experiences and emotional and cultural resources differ. The diversity and complexity of the Third World is as essential a characteristic as its post-colonial struggles for economic, political and emotional independence.

Psychologies of all worlds must rectify the simplicities of those mainstream exercises that blandly ignore the complexities of individuality and of human society. There are many worlds within the Third World in which billions of individuals strive throughout life to make sense of their experiences and to express their feelings about them. A relevant psychology must be far more enterprising in studying the dilemmas of emotional, cognitive and social survival. Relevant psychologists will have to abandon part of their scientific detachment and substitute for it an all too rare empathy and identification with the world's (euphemistically termed) underprivileged.

Relevant psychologists must begin to examine historically their professional philosophy and practice. Is psychology meeting the challenge of the times? On whose side is the profession? What is the profession doing to break out of the 'thick membrane of technocracy, which deflects any questioning in advance, indeed, rules out the possibility of questioning, the "pure, value free and scientific" pursuit' (Kovel, 1988) of a committed, humanistic and practical psychology?

References

Abdi, V.O.(1975), 'The Problems and Prospects of Psychology in Africa', *International Journal of Psychology*, vol. X(3), pp. 227-234.

Ardila, R.(1983), 'Psychology in Latin America Today', In M. R. Rosenzweig and L. W. Porter (eds), *Annual Review of Psychology*, 1982, vol. 33, Palo Alto, Calif: Annual Review Press.

Asante, M.K.(1987), *The Afrocentric Idea*, Philadelphia, Pa: Temple University Press.

Bettelheim, B.(1986), *The Uses of Enchantment: The Meaning and Importance of Fairy Tales*, Harmondsworth, UK: Penguin Books.

Biesheuvel, S.(1958), 'Objectives and Methods of African Psychological Research', *The Journal Of Social Psychology*, vol. 47, pp. 161-168.

Bock, P.K.(1988), *Rethinking Psychological Anthropology*, New York: W. H. Freeman.

Bruckner, P.(1983), *Le Sanglot de l'Homme Blanc: Tiers Monde, Culpabilité, Haine de Soi,* Paris: Editions du Seuil.

Connolly, K.(1985), 'Can There Be a Psychology for the Third World?' *Bulletin of the British Psychological Society,* vol. 38, pp. 249-257.

Dawes, A.(1988), 'The Notion of Relevant Psychology with Particular Reference to Africanist Pragmatic Initiatives', *Psychology in Society,* vol. 5, pp. 28-49.

Dixon, V., and Foster, B.(1971), *Beyond Black or White,* Boston, Mass: Little, Brown.

Fanon, F.(1986), *Black Skin, White Masks,* London: Pluto Press (original edition 1967).

Gergen, K.J.(1978), 'Toward Generative Theory', *Journal of Personality and Social Psychology,* vol. 36(11), pp. 1344-1360.

Hartmann, H.(1964), 'Psychoanalysis and the Concept of Health', in H. Hartmann, *Essays on Ego Psychology,* New York: International Universities Press.

Herskovits, M.J.(1949), *Man and His Works,* New York: Alfred A. Knopf.

James, W.(1950), *The Principles of Psychology,* New York: Dover Books.

Jordan, J.(1985), 'And a Psychology of the First World?' *Bulletin of the British Psychological Society, vol.* 38, pp. 417-418.

Kagan, J. and Segal, J.(1988), *Psychology: An Introduction,* San Diego, Calif: Harcourt, Brace & Jovanovich.

Kagitcibasi, C.(1982), 'The Relevance of Social Psychology for Development', Paper presented at the *6th International Congress of the International Association for Cross-Cultural Psychology,* Aberdeen, TX, July 1982.

Kardiner, A. and Ovesey, L.(1951), *The Mark of Oppression,* New York: Meridian Books.

Kohut, Heinz.(1977), *The Restoration of the Self,* New York: International Universities Press, Inc.

Kovel, J.(1988), *The Radical Spirit,* London: Free Association Books.

Lasch, C.(1985), *The Minimal Self: Psychic Survival in Troubled Times,* London: Pan Books.

Mannoni, O.(1956), *Prospero and Caliban: The Psychology of Colonisation,* New York: Praeger.

Mehryar, A.H.(1984), 'The Role of Psychology in National Development: Wishful Thinking and Reality', *International Journal of Psychology, vol.* 19, pp. 159-167.

Moghaddam, F.M. and Taylor, D.M.(1986), 'The State of Psychology in the Third World: A Response to Connolly', *Bulletin of the British Psychological Society, vol.* 39, pp. 4-7.

Parin, P. et. al.(1980), *Fear Thy Neighbour as Thyself: Psychoanalysis and Society among the Anyi of West Africa,* Chicago, Ill: University of Chicago Press.

Popper, K.R.(1988), reported in *The Times,* London, August 25, 1988.

Rank, O.(1958), *Beyond Psychology,* New York: Dover Books.

Stein, H.F.(1985), *The Psychoanthropology of American Culture,* New York: The Psychohistory Press.

Stein, H.F. and M. Apprey(1987), *From Metaphor to Meaning: Papers in Psychoanalytic Anthroplogy,* Charlottesville, Va: University Press of Virginia.

Turner, V.W.(1967), *The Forest of Symbols,* Ithaca, NY: Cornell University Press.

Weiner, B.(1974), *Achievement Motivation and Attribution Theory,* Morristown, New Jersey: General Learning Press.

Winnicott, D.W.(1966), 'The Location of Cultural Experience, *International Journal of Psychoanalysis*, vol. 48, pp. 368-372.

Winnicott, D.W.(1974), 'Fear of Breakdown', *International Review of Psychoanalysis*, vol. 1, pp. 103-107.

Winnicott, D.W.(1975), 'The Manic Defence', in D. W. Winnicott, *Through Paediatrics to Psychoanalysis*, London: Hogarth Press.

2 Social Science in Africa: Problems and Prospects

Introduction

The aim of this chapter is to examine the delicate relationship of social science in Africa to the political, social and administrative context. It is argued, in contradiction to the defeatist views of, for example, Mehryar (1984), that social scientists do both their profession and their societies a disservice if they surrender the study of social problems to politicians and administrators.

Social Science and Social Policy

Few, if any, African societies have escaped traumatic economic, political, social and technological changes since Independence. As a result, values and practices, organisations and institutions that once suited a community's needs, now collide with innovations, often with unpredictable and socially disruptive consequences (Bloom and Amatu, 1983; Uchendu, 1977). These interactions may be initiated from within Africa or introduced from outside, but, in either case, their consequences, both short-term and long, are hard to predict and even more difficult to moderate.

Social policies are designed in an ideal world to deal with the consequences of change. Marshall *et al.* (1978) have analysed the two fundamental questions which guide them, and although they wrote about the more industrialised urbanised societies, where the social sciences have a longer history of co-operation with government, their questions apply equally to Africa. First, what are the concealed and open theories of social justice that are used by government to justify their policies? Second, what does government know, or believe, to be acceptable to the communities or groups that will be affected by these policies?

In Africa, even in formal constitutions there are scanty signs that governments recognise the need to articulate either question. On the contrary, despite the widely differing social and political systems in Africa,

40

a few assumptions about the nature of society, and hence of justice, seem common to governments:

1. A strong tendency to authoritarian and hierarchical government, with which is associated a suspicion of participatory democracy.

2. A conflict between lip-service to the idea of national identity and the lively persistence of 'ethnic', linguistic or smaller regional groups.

3. The pervasive influence of the extended family and the 'ethnic' group as the dynamic and cohesive force behind wider economic, political and social organisations. The growth of a small wealthy class has barely touched this influence. Rather it tends to reinforce it.

4. There is male domination or even male monopoly of power and influence in many sectors of society. In particular, there is little or no effective sharing of political power by men with women. Father or elder brother rules! There is not yet even one female head of state in Africa and only in Mozambique, Angola and among South African Africans have women been encouraged to take a significant part in political activity, despite their part in the struggle for Independence as, for example, in Ghana.

What governments know or believe to be acceptable to the citizens equally depends upon the assumptions held by governments about the mechanisms of consultation. Mechanisms that were practical and acceptable to nations of villagers are no longer adequate. There are few leaders who, like Nyerere, Gowon and the young Nkrumah, have understood the necessity to maintain an emotional rapport with all the communities within the society. Now, even their efforts would be inadequate or inappropriate as new constituencies have grown up. Many new economic, political and social interests have been taken up by new groups, old power groups based upon older interests have lost influence. No one can predict the future clearly, except that many observers note that power is increasingly urban-based.

Rein (1976) considers three further issues:

1. How, if at all, do the administrators of policy take into account
the need to harmonise individual needs, wants and goals with social
goals? Do administrators take seriously such harmonisation, or do
they brush it aside with arguments about 'common good' being
paramount? For example, when the Nigerian government was
planning the new capital, Abuja, there was some consultation with
the local people who were going to be dispossessed about their
wishes and needs for a new settlement. But there was no question
about the decision to build the new capital, although many
Nigerians were sceptical of its necessity and resentful of the huge
expenditure. It may be asked if social scientists are concerned about
the fundamental *ethical* problem or if, and how, such harmonisation
of individual and social needs may be maximised. In Africa the
social sciences have tended to shun such questions.

2. Rein asks if social scientists should challenge the administrators
or governments that employ them.

3. He further asks if they should be 'moral critics', moving beyond
the conventional limits of 'pure' and 'applied' research to question
the very foundations of the ethical soundness of the policies whose
consequences they study empirically.

The social sciences have nowhere in the world had no struggle in
asserting their independence. In Africa, as elsewhere, social science has
never been encouraged to explore the fundamental conflicts of their
societies. Vested interests, inside government and the most powerful
economic groups, do not care to have their positions challenged, even by the
indirect challenge of showing the consequences for the wider society of their
limited perspective. In Africa there is an additional taboo that arises from
the shame of admitting that in post-Independent countries the economic and
political inequalities, the maladministration and political violence (and many
social problems), are less and less plausibly blamed on the inadequacies or
even mischief of colonial administrations. In 1998 the governments of 1998
are responsible for 1998's problems! It grows less and less acceptable to
youth to blame yesterday's white governors when today's brown ones are
often manifestly no better.

Rein argues that the central question of social policy is to investigate, as fully as techniques permit, the needs, wants and goals influenced by policy decisions. A politically sensitive issue follows. Although it is technically possible to monitor the effects of policies in which governments are unused to scrutiny and challenge, even detached professional monitoring is unwelcome. Monitoring challenges the very root of authority: that government, father, knows best what the people, the children need, want and *ought* to want. The inexperience and instability of many governments, the weakness of administrations, often with too few experienced and trained professionals to run them, are understandably sensitive to scrutiny and evaluation. Barren and irrelevant policies abound because of the severity of Africa's economic, social and political problems, with which no existing administration or infrastructure is strong enough to cope. The record of African governments in accepting the *bona fides* of critics, even those of unexceptionable moderation, has been unworthy of the continent's need for criticism. Few countries have never closed down educational institutions, arrested academics and students, nor shackled the media. Alas, social scientists are not famous for their boldness!

Rein argued that social scientists and policy makers should 'try to question the orthodox and established pattern, trying to discover where it is vulnerable and what alternative approaches are required'. Commendable advice. But unless the educational and political systems and the mass media are free and encouraged to criticise society, there will be little or no incentive for debate to take place. Too often every questioning, especially by younger people, is perceived as a potential rebellion, and education is controlled by starving it of funds and of the stimulation of contact with the wider world outside Africa.

The deeper motives of both the orthodox and the *soi-disant* radicals are equally suspect by the truly independent critic. Those who zealously criticise, reject or seek to destroy the orthodox, are often tainted by their own dogmatism. If they obtain power they usually become inflexibly determined to introduce and maintain a new orthodoxy. They proceed to establish on their new dogma a new rigid social structure, which will stimulate opposition and, in its turn, be torn down and rebuilt. This unstable flight from one sociopolitical system to another is to search for the one magical formula to cure all evils.

Rein assigns the role of moral critic to the social scientists, but they, like the policy makers, have their individual and collective values, beliefs and attitudes. These are rooted in both individual experience and in class and other social loyalties and affiliations. Perplexing questions arise about the complex of individual and social constraints, inducements, fears and phantasies that influence the political and ethical views upon which policy is ultimately based. Many a decision is permeated by the irrationalities of the policy makers' indifference, or even hate, towards group or community. In recent years the irrationalities of chauvinism in its varied forms has done much to weaken the rational elements in decision making, and nervous intolerance of the more educated has weakened many once lively academic communities, leaving no *practical* alternative to criticism from outside Africa, with all its possibilities for wilful or innocent misunderstanding and misinterpretation.

Tizard (1976) has warned of another significant distortion of thinking about policy: the conviction that 'only long-term goals are important'. This discourages 'short-term goals and indications of immediate well-being. Only when we abandon notions about the supposed or hoped for long-term prophylactic values, Head Starts and permanent cures, will we begin to examine the characteristics of the environment that contribute to immediate happiness'. By rejecting contemporary problems with the argument that they are local, trivial or temporary, and that they can only be solved when long-term, more radical policies are carried out, government ineptness and lack of sensitivity can be excused. The infallible wisdom and authority of the father can be maintained. The discontented children can be hushed.

Societies, like individuals, can be characterised as either over-optimistic or euphoric, or even over-pessimistic and defeated. The former are frenetically confident of their ability to improve everything. An ideological position, a new constitution, a charismatic leader, yet another 'War against Indiscipline' will show the route to a better world. Alas, although there have been many roads to Utopia, none has yet led a society anywhere near to that elusive destination. The pessimistic society is equally impractical. It is distinguished by the belief that society cannot be changed by human intervention. One must await the intervention of a religious or political God, or one must patiently expect a religious or a secular millenium. Unwillingness even to attempt realistic change is often associated with an obdurate determination to maintain the *status quo*, and hunger, ignorance, disease and political and social insecurity continue.

In these circumstances, social scientists (if they are at all tolerated), are in danger of becoming driven by crisis and compelled by panicky governments to find speedy solutions to insoluble emergencies. They are being blamed for their ineffectiveness when the problems are found to be more difficult to understand than governments hoped, and therefore more intractable.

Social Policy and Human Needs

In Africa we have largely wasted the opportunity to study systematically the human consequences of economic, political and social change. The opportunity to consider the consequences of ecological change, and to arrest its devastating effects before it is too late, has been almost totally ignored. Social scientists have too often been conscripted into the wasteful role of proposing *ad hoc* justifications for *ad hoc* policies, cobbling ways to save them from failure.

But must the social sciences be so wasted? Even sceptics such as Mehryar (1984) and Moghaddam and Taylor (1986) grant a limited - if highly politicised - role to the social sciences.

Mehryar's bitter and tendentious paper argues that psychology (and no doubt other social sciences) has two functions: 'by acknowledging the real cause of...poverty and backwardness' and by 'reminding (people) of the need for political struggle'. He continues by rejecting the 'Western' tradition that individuals are responsible for their actions, and observes that social scientists are 'often part of the machinery of control'. Moghaddam and Taylor plead for a psychology that rejects colonial attitudes towards 'Third World' societies.

Mehryar's paper is as value-laden as the views that he rejects and proposes nothing more practical than seeking 'a target for change...in the hearts of the ruling elite'. Moghaddam and Taylor propose that social sciences should be 'appropriate'. Appropriateness is defined by six criteria, ie; social sciences should be applied to the questions of: '(1) self-reliance, (2) needs responsiveness, (3) cultural compatibility, (4) institutional feasibility, (5) economic suitability and (6) political practicality'. The proposal of these writers is compatible with my view that an essential task of the social sciences is to remind governments and administrators of basic human needs and wants and of the many ways that they can be harmed.

One approach to the question 'What are basic human needs?' is to consider the domain of social psychology. Moscovici (1984) and his collaborators divide the field into three broad divisions:

1. The nature, formation and change of attitudes. This includes the central topics of conformity and obedience, innovation and the influence of minorities, the changing of attitudes, and continuity and change in behaviour and experience.

2. The interactions between members of groups and between groups. How are group decisions made? How are novel, creative decisions made?

3. Thought and social life, possibly the most crucial section, includes such essential questions as: how do we think in everyday life, how are events explained, to what causes are events attributed? What is the community's collective view of reality? How does it interpret such social phenomena as health and illness, childhood, occupations? How are classes of people perceived? How are language, thought and communication related?

Moscovici's domain is largely cognitive and offers an over-intellectualised view of human needs and activities. It omits another aspect of human needs, made familiar by psychoanalysis. The quality of relationships between males and females, members of different generations and within generations, of which the relationships of love, sex and aggression are fundamental, cannot be ignored.

Looking further at Moghaddam and Taylor's criteria: 'self-reliance' refers to a country's confidence in using its own resources - not 'isolationism' but 'a genuine exchange between equals' outside that society. A major psychological and sociological problem is that of shifting attitudes away from narrow, sectional, chauvinistic loyalties towards an orientation that embraces wider circles of meaningful contact, both within Africa and beyond it. Another criterion depending upon a changing psychology is 'political practicability': 'how feasible is it to implement [policy] given the political limitations existing?' The psychological and social factors that inhibit or that encourage continuity or change are modified by policies, whether or not they are taken into account. The people resist changes or accept them; they weave them into the fabric of society or that fabric is, itself, rewoven. A major problem in Africa has been the almost total indifference by government and administrators to the *sociopsychological* consequences, and hence feasibility of policies.

Social scientists could be well-placed to evaluate the extent and manner of the harm and the welfare that programmes might bring about to those directly and indirectly affected by them. The administrators and government themselves may pay the price of creating economic, political and social instability for their policies: it is arguable that sensitivity to what the people need and want might have avoided more than one deposed head of state. In moving boldly beyond their classical positivistic, hypothesis-testing and fact-finding roles, social scientists would cease responding to the questions: 'Professional independence good or bad?' They would be responding to a more difficult question: 'Professional independence - what is the price for selling it to governments by tacitly refraining from looking into what policies mean to the people, how they feel about them and how they might respond to the damage done by them?' Berry and Lonner (1975) include papers that discuss social problems as they were perceived both by administrators and by 'those administered'.

But asking 'the administered' challenges the nervous arrogance of those 'who know best' and who readily assume the mantle of authoritarian infallibility in societies where most people are politically ill-educated in the values, attitudes and practices of participatory democracy. Moreover to put such a challenge, however tactfully presented, raises the disturbing question of the social psychology of political failure in Africa. Broadly, the failure is closely related to the authoritarian conservatism of many social institutions and groups, so that criticising authority is emotionally equivalent to criticising the elders or the father, and by extension, is equivalent to opposing the mores of the family. The political socialisation within the family is rarely one that encourages participatory democracy, including both sexes and all age grades. An imposed loyalty to the father and the group exposes the group to considerable emotional distress and confusion if the father fails. If sibling rivalry becomes uncontrollable, the most bitter of strife results.

In evaluating the effectiveness of policy it is not too difficult to devise criteria that are rational in the administrators' eyes. It is far more difficult to devise criteria that are psychologically deeper. 'Effective' must lead to the continuation: 'and desirable for whom? with what positive and negative consequences for the people affected? with what consequences for social psychological cohesion, stability and happiness?'

How Shall the Professions be Scrutinised?

It is almost banal to note that the applied social sciences are as exposed to bias and professional opportunism as are most other human activities. Yet the acceptance of a collective self-scrutiny by the profession is far from widely accepted. For example, two recent discussions of applied social sciences, Argyle (1980) and Cherns (1979), fail even to mention the problems of professional scrutiny.

Scrutiny is of two kinds. Firstly, it may refer to the status of a profession in a society at a given time. Secondly, it may refer to the biases and opportunism of a profession in relation to its institutional masters. At its most blatant, research and its implications for policy may be little more than sophisticated justifications of the political *status quo* and current ideology, either because a profession tacitly accepts its privileged position in society, or because it is more or less openly playing the tune called for by its masters.

In Africa, even more than in more industrialised-urbanised continents, there are too few social scientists who are committed to studying applied problems. Yet the problems proliferate, and social scientists may be tempted to go beyond their narrower competences. They are thus exposed to the impatient disenchantment of their society, or rejected by it when it is found that they may be a little more wise than the administrators. The professions may then attempt to assuage a collective sense of guilt by justifying its methods and principles, pleading for more resources for better research. But if they are given more resources, governmental control and scrutiny will be more intense, independence more difficult to achieve, and the professions become even more weak and ineffective. Within the professions strain and conflict grows: some maintain detachment as the ideal, others advocate open political commitment to the *status quo*. So either the profession may claim over-energetically that it has solutions to society's ills, or it grows so modest about its competences that it leads government to doubt that it is competent to advise anything.

Action-research competes for resources with research into fundamental problems, and to the extent that the former are favoured and defined by governments, the social sciences become increasingly unsuited to explore the broader implications of research or to generate debate about the nature and functions of their discipline. Moghaddam and Taylor (1986) refer to the 'question of how feasible it is to implement a given type of [social science]...given the political limitations existing in a country'.

Feasibility is likely to be differently perceived by government and by social scientists. One of the most delicate tasks of the latter may be to educate government to be more sensitive to what it is possible for the social scientist to do, both *qua* detached scientist and committed citizen.

Thus Africa's many compelling and urgent social problems press social scientists and governments to waive fundamental research. Instead, social scientists are driven to seize any opportunities to fund applied research, hoping that more basic or theoretical research and debate may become possible when times are more propitious. There is no certainty that this willl occur. Meanwhile, the laity might become more familiar with the scope and limitations of social science research. But even this will not occur unless social scientists are more active in entering into dialogue with administration. The professional social scientists in Africa have been less active in using the prestige and influence of regional and international bodies to educate their governments. Instead, too often, an opening address by a Minister is followed by governmental silence or no lessening of chauvinism and ideological suspicion.

Mace (1973), discussing psychology, held the view that psychologists 'unlike most other scientists, cannot maintain even professionally, a state of complete political neutrality'. They cannot, therefore, ignore the latent political implications of their work. This applies to all social scientists. Consider, for example, seven of the major social problems affecting Africa:

1. The influence on traditional values, beliefs, ideologies, information and skills of values, etc., originating from outside Africa.

2. The creation of wider, national, regional and Pan African loyalties and identifications out of communities with intense, local loyalties.

3. Communication in societies that are multi-lingual, multi-cultural and composed of few educated and many uneducated people.

4. Migration from rural to urban areas, resulting in grave distortions of traditional economic, social and political organisations.

5. The creation of academic, vocational and professional education,

suited to a rapidly changing Africa.

6. The selection and training of workers in new occupations, trades and industries, including the largely neglected and inappropriately skilled women.

7. The development of workable economic, social and political organisations and institutions.

These seven issues encompass innumerable theoretical and empirical questions that have barely been touched. It is, however, difficult to imagine a satisfactory report on any aspect of any one issue without its implied favoured position from which policies might be drawn. Yet there are few indications of an emerging, indigenous social science in Africa, the concerns and questions of which differ significantly from the present ones, rooted in Western assumptions and values.

Bruckner (1983), however, in his disturbing book *Le sanglot de l'homme blanc: Tiers Monde, culpabilité, haine de soi*, warns against assuming that different cultural and social patterns are *lived* by different types of human beings. He warns: 'Take care: running through this contemporary term, "Third World", is a symbolic conflict in issue: that of the psychological space that we reserve in the future for non-European people. To speak of the Third World as though it were a hospice, is to shrink the psychological horizons of our contemporaries. It disqualifies four billion human beings as a future generation'. It is sociologically and psychologically meaningful to contrast two major divisions of mankind: the Western, industrialised and rich, and the Third World, rural and poor. It is sociological and psychological nonsense to treat these divisions as immutable. It is methodological nonsense if the social sciences in Africa fail to borrow from the universal body of social science methods, principles and findings whatever may be relevant to understanding the universal problems of change and conflict.

Africa's Unique Problems?

The previous reflections apply to both the more and the less technologically advanced societies, and the problems of non-African professional social scientists are shared by their African brethren. But there are problems that are more acute in Africa - and, perhaps, in other parts of the Third World.

Probably the gravest problem experienced by social scientists in Africa is the ignorance and suspicion of both administrators and the general public about the role and function of the social sciences and of their responsibility towards society. Professional detachment is often misinterpreted as implying indifference to social problems. Social scientists are seen as civil servants and loyalty rather than 'to speak truth to power' (Wildavsky, 1979) is their principle duty. Caplan *et al.* (1975) studied how social science knowledge was used in the U.S.A., and found that senior executives ranked the contributions of social sciences in the following descending order of importance: (1) sensitising policy-makers to social needs; (2) evaluation of ongoing programmes; (3) structuring alternative policies; (4) implementing programmes; (5) justifying policy decisions; and (6) providing a basis for choosing among policy alternatives. The effectiveness of all of these contributions depends upon power's readiness to listen to truth and to act upon it. It also depends upon truth's capacity to avoid speaking too softly, too obscurely and too hesitantly.

But professional independence and outspokenness is practicable only where the political and social structures and ideologies permit them. Or, at the least, do not hinder the growth of organisations and discussions of ideologies that challenge the status quo. In Africa, sociopolitical structures, both traditional and modern, do not readily accommodate the more-or-less encapsulated, self-regulating professions that Western societies are accustomed to. Such independent organisations are essential if development is to succeed. They are, however, emotionally intolerable in societies where social and political life are intimately and closely regulated and often subordinate to the demands of family, kin and region. Deviant organisations, like deviant individuals, are only with difficulty tolerated until roles are evolved for them. Professionals thus have conflicting emotional loyalties, for they are too tied into the family, kinship group, 'ethnic' or even linguistic group. They, too, are pressured to use their skills and influence to benefit those individuals and groups to whom they have a social obligation beyond their professional. It seems that professional independence will remain vulnerable until societies develop in which social mobility is common.

However, even if the professions try to distance themselves from control by administration, they are then often accused of creating a professional mystique and an unjustifiable privileged position. The professions are exposed to both accusations in both socialist and capitalistic

countries. In capitalist countries, the professions may be unable to avoid
being associated with elitism within an inegalitarian and hierarchical social
system. Similarly, in socialist countries there are established elites with
which the professions may be driven to associate themselves to extend their
political influence and thus their independence.

Problems of Detachment

Two policies have commonly been adapted to escape the accusations of
elitism and to extend independence from political influence:

> 1. The standards of entry to the professions are modified to
> encourage more and a wider range of entrants.

> 2. The profession may intentionally seek to be involved in debates
> on policy and in decision-making.

In Africa, the medical profession has struggled to avoid diluting the
standards of entry, though it is doubtful if it has anywhere succeeded as far
as it would wish. Law, on the other hand, has almost traditionally become
closely linked with the political and administrative establishment, often time-
serving the political extremes of 'Left' and 'Right'.

The professions may become conservative pressure groups of the
'Left' or the 'Right', and their declarations of professional neutrality are no
more than rationalisations, concealing their partisanship for an ideological
position or their allegiance with a power-elite (Horowitz, 1965). Thus a
close attachment to the government of the moment and a sensitivity to
ideological whims, drives the social scientist further and further from being
able to offer expert and independent advice. The politically unacceptable
truth will not be told. The harmful consequences of policies will be
concealed.

The predicament of the social sciences is, therefore, threefold: how
can a balance be made between (1) a professional contribution to
understanding and solving social problems, (2) professional integrity and a
high standard of expertise and (3) the open accessibility of the skills and
findings of the social sciences to all those concerned with them - both policy
makers and those affected by those policies? The balance between these
three is unstable, but it may be less so if governments become more

confident that detached, professional criticism does not necessarily conceal political ill-will or latent opposition.

Bitensky (1976) has analysed pessimistically the frequent failure of social scientists to apply their skills, arguing that the fundamental reason is that they are so nervous of political risks that they retreat into 'a state of aimless methodologism'. Cuff and Payne (1984) deal head-on with this nervousness. They assert boldly that there is no choice for social scientists who seek to do something about social problems. They cannot avoid operating 'as social reformers, as politicians, or as citizens'. But the political risks in Africa are great, not because of the power of government, but because of its underlying weakness. There are double dangers for the social scientists: they have to put themselves at risk in the task of educating their masters, and when they comment upon policy. Becker (1967) has warned social scientists that whatever they may do, or refrain from doing, a question that they must always pose to themselves is: 'Whose side are we on?' All social scientists favour some groups and ideologies and disfavour others. They are more likely to gain and retain their independence by demonstrating their allegiance to a scientific approach to social problems, and if they refuse supinely to succumb to the pressures and constraints of government and administration. 'Whose side are we on?' In the long run it has to be the people who will still be in need of social sciences when the temporary government has gone. Social scientists have a duty to maintain, openly or covertly, the subversive and essentially political activity of providing signposts to the routes through the quicksands of political fears, bigotry and ideological euphoria.

Does the international recognition of a professional organisation protect its independence? Two conflicts can arise between the international professional network and national, political considerations. Firstly, the internationally acceptable level of professional training and practice may be politically unacceptable: governments have insisted on the lowering of professional standards to raise the numbers of professionals. Professionals have, moreover, been forced to participate in ethically objectionable practices. Lawyers, for example, have drafted and administered unjust and repressive laws. Writers have lied persuasively for their governments. Social scientists have collaborated in the planning of mass-movements of population. Yet often social scientists have actively opposed tyranny, criticised governmental folly and inefficiency, suggested notions of an alternative society. The last has not come from the direct and open collective decision of a profession, but from individual members or minority groups who are indirectly supported by the profession's collective - if sometimes tarnished - standards.

Secondly, professional associations have been tempted to seek political advantage by adopting ritualistic 'anti-expatriate', 'anti-white', 'anti-foreign' or 'ethnic' prejudices.   Rational policies of recruitment, training, teaching and research are thus subordinated to the irrationalities of the current political ideology and prejudice.

However, the position of the social science associations within an international system, sharing international values and a sense of the commonality of human, social problems, may demonstrate that the problems of society are solved by neither supporting the *status quo* nor by encouraging the revolutionary itch to build society *de novo*.

Africa Needs the Social Sciences

It is arguable that the less-industrialised societies, as in Africa, have an even greater need of independent social scientists than in the more 'developed' societies. In rapidly changing Africa there are desperately urgent economic, political and social problems, that governments cannot even begin to solve without adequate statistics and policy analysis.

Consider some of the major social and psychological problems. Rural communities are becoming more urbanised and depopulated, while the growing urban communities face problems of a magnitude unknown since the urban revolution in mid-nineteenth century Britain.   Societies with political organisations that evolved in small-scale and localised communities are compelled to invent, reject and invent again new forms of political and social organisation competent to deal with large-scale economic and social problems. Small fragments of polity have to devise means to adapt to national and continent wide polities. The problems of ethnic and linguistic, religious and ideological conflict have no more been solved in Africa than in Europe, and their consequences are no less tragic. The emergence of wider bases for identity have yet to be solved. The growing alienation of individuals from groups, that arises from the depersonalisation of changes in economic, political and social organisations, is destroying Africa's strong collective ethos.   Associated with alienation is the growth of 'learned helplessness' (Seligman, 1975): the conviction that one's efforts to control one's life are in vain. Africa has had too few experiences of success arising from its own efforts, and has learned a depressing sense of failure by the constant over-emphasis of the power of the West. The learned helplessness has been caused, in part, by the failure of education to encourage the cognitive skills that are required for a changing economy and society, and has been exacerbated by the persistence of authority relationships that inhibit youth and females and those of lower status from growing independent, expressing divergent and unorthodox opinions, and enjoying the exhilaration of having open minds in open societies. Political and social indoctrination is both common and suffocating.

Governments cannot, of course, be blamed for these problems. They can, perhaps legitimately be criticised for failing to maximise the discovery, education, training and employment of the widest range of skills and talents of their population: women and men alike, and of all ethnic, linguistic and religious groups that compose societies. The constant threat of crisis and administrative breakdown that haunts African states is largely the result of the failure of governments to provide opportunities for knowledge and skills to be acquired and applied, even where they oppose the current wisdom. Jaques (1955), in a study of the unconscious psychological origins of social rigidity, has shown how 'effective social change is likely to require analysis of the common anxieties and unconscious collusions underlying the social defences determining phantasy social relationships'. In particular, it is emotionally less anxiety-provoking to search for collective scape-goats to blame for social problems, than to trust social scientists to consider the realities on which problems are based, unacceptable as these often are. Administration tends to be nervously obsessed with detailed rules and procedures, rigid and oppressive, disinclined for self-analysis and self-appraisal, much less does it call upon the social sciences to assist in those necessary and anxiety-provoking, yet ultimately liberating, tasks.

There are two fundamental sociopolitical problems where the international community of social scientists could assist governments, without the latter admitting failure. Firstly, to anticipate and monitor the social and psychological tensions and conflicts that accompany the change and growth of organisations, cultures and values. Conversely, successful change might be monitored and the lessons learned from it shared with other communities. Secondly, to develop new and more effective forms of social and political participation and new organisations, to encourage the evolution of communities away from authoritarian structures and values and to direct them towards a respect for the individual and for minority, unpopular groups - a respect that few contemporary states display much concern about.

Conclusion

Even if these contributions of social science are rejected by administrations, there remain educational functions for the social sciences. They can encourage administrations to accept the relevance of the human aspects of those technological and administrative techniques that are known to direct and facilitate economic, social and political change. The social sciences may provide leadership in educating people at all levels of authority to respect the value of a 'Fourth Estate' of social scientists, free from political pressures and advocating ways of making sense of society and liberating Africa rationally from ignorance, disease, poverty and conflict.

References

Argyle, M.(1980), 'The development of applied social psychology', in Gilmour, R. and Duck, S.(eds), *The Development of Social Psychology*, Academic Press, London.

Becker, H.S.(1967), 'Whose side are we on?' *Social Problems*, vol. 14, pp. 239-247.

Berry, J.W. and Lonner, W.J.(eds) (1975), *Applied Cross-Cultural Psychology*, Swets and Zeitlinger, Amsterdam.

Bitensky, R.(1976), 'The conscience of the social scientist', *The New Universities Quarterly*, vol. 30, pp. 219-226.

Bloom, L. and Amatu, H.I.(1983), 'Nigeria: Aggression, A Psychoethnography', in Goldstein A.P. and Segall M.H.(eds), *Aggression in Global Perspective*, Pergamon Press, New York.

Bruckner, P.(1983), *Le sanglot de l'homme blanc: Tiers-Monde, culpabilité, haine de soi*, Editions du Seuil, Paris.

Caplan, N. et al.(1975), *The Use of Social Science Knowledge in Policy Decisions at the National Level. A Report to Respondents*, Institute for Social Research, University of Michigan, Ann Arbor.

Cherns, A.(1979), *Using the Social Sciences*, Routledge, London.

Cuff, E.C. and Payne, G.C.F.(1984), *Perspectives in Sociology*, Allen and Unwin, London.

Horowitz, I.L.(1965), *The New Sociology*, Oxford University Press, New York.

Jaques, E.(1965), 'Social systems as a defence against persecutory and depressive anxiety', in Klein, M. et al.(eds), *New Directions in Psychoanalysis*, Tavistock Books, London.

Mace, C.A.(1973), 'Democracy as a problem in social psychology', in Mace, C.A., *Selected Papers*, Methuen, London.

Marshall, T.F. et al.(1978), *Evaluation for Democracy*, Home Office Research Unit, London.

Mehryar, A.H.(1984), 'The role of psychology in national development: Wishful thinking and reality', *International Journal of Psychology*, vol. 19, pp. 159-167.

Moghaddam, F.M. and Taylor, D.M.(1986), 'The state of psychology in the Third World: A response to Connolly', *Bulletin of the British Psychological Society*, vol. 39, pp. 4-8.

Moscovici, S.(ed) (1984), *Psychologie sociale*, PUF, Paris.

Rein, M.(1976), *Social Science and Social Policy*, Penguin Education, Harmondsworth.

Seligman, M.E.P.(1975), *Helplessness: On Depression, Development and Death*, Freeman, San Francisco.

Tizard, J.(1976), 'Psychology and social policy', *Bulletin of the British Psychological Society*, vol. 29, pp. 225-234.

Uchendu, V.C.(1977), 'The cultural roots of aggressive behaviour in modern African politics', *Journal of Asian and African Studies*, vol. XII, pp. 99-108.

Wildavsky, A.(1979), *Speaking Truth to Power: The Art and Craft of Policy Analysis*, Little Brown, Boston.

3 Psychotherapy and Culture: A Critical View

Introduction

The main aim of this chapter is to doubt the view that Western psychotherapy (in which psychoanalysis is integral), only applies within Western cultures. It is not denied that there may be problems that can be traced to cultural conditions, but it is maintained that none of the supposed problems of diagnosis, the training of therapists across cultures, or the processes of psychotherapy differ fundamentally from the problems within a culture. A minor aim of this chapter is to examine the strengths and weakness of cultural relativism.

The question is, therefore: is psychotherapy the white man's *juju*, a culture-specific medicine that travels badly beyond its own home? I partly illustrate the chapter from my 20 years experience in West, East and South Africa, where I practised as a psychotherapist. My experience suggests that psychotherapy in Africa presented similar problems to those I met in London, and were neither more nor less difficult to solve. Psychotherapy evokes the same problems of communication, interpretation and emotional relationships in Africa as complex relationships between human beings anywhere.

Case History Examples

The complexity of these issues can be introduced by examining the emotional and social problems of three Nigerian undergraduate patients: Abu, Bitrus and Chidi.

One morning my mail included a letter from Abu, a young man who pleaded for help 'for this tortured soul'. When we met he was haggard and looked worn out. During our first meetings he gave little more information than that he felt anxious and depressed, and was so unable to sleep and eat that he felt weak and his studies were suffering. I could not discover when he first felt so depressed, but it became clear that his depression deepened when he entered puberty. Abu came from a large family and was one of the first men in his village to go to university. After we had met regularly for some weeks he began to describe disturbing dreams. Then he sent me a letter in which he confessed that his problem was that he had for some time had incestuous desires for one of his sisters.

By now Abu trusted me with one of his most intimate secrets and we could begin to work conventionally through his feelings and relationships. But I am not an African: I had to find out for myself how common in Abu's culture were such incestuous feelings and how deeply they were forbidden. More central to helping Abu was to work through with him the gravity of the incest to *him*. I had to compare his internalised guilt with the external taboo, so I had to appreciate the cultural and social influences that might have pushed him to feel so distressed and emotionally vulnerable and so socially anomalous. Abu had developed an exceptionally stringent and punitive superego. How had this come about? How could we moderate the inner conflicts between his libidinal needs and his overintense superego?

It is not relevant to elaborate the course of therapy, except to observe that I felt free to confirm his identity as a normal man by acting in a way that few African therapists would have dared. One of Abu's fears was that he was 'mad'. Toward the end of one of our meetings, I found myself asking if he had a photograph of his sister to show me. He pulled from his wallet a photograph at which I looked and then declared: 'I'm not surprised that you feel as you do about your sister. She's very beautiful'. We went on to discuss again the aim-inhibited nature of his feelings and he agreed that there was no danger that his phantasies would be carried into his active life. He felt free to accept that it was neither 'mad' nor surprising that an attractive sister could be tempting and appear in dreams, particularly since he had been a child in a crowded home where beds were often shared by the children.

Abu's distress and guilt were universal. It was expressed in terms that fitted his interpretation of, and reaction to, his culture. There is no theoretical barrier to stop me from trying to understand Abu and feeling empathy for his distress. Nor is there any theoretical reason why I should be unable to relate to him, another man, to help him overcome his guilt. Nor is there any theoretical support to ease the understanding of an African psychotherapist. Any psychotherapist might be shocked, tempted, repelled or frightened by Abu and his problem, and might experience and have to deal with a hundred transference and counter-transference situations. Both Africans and non-Africans have their individual, unconscious reactions to the different forms of incest, which are only indirectly related to their cultural experiences. We are all socialised to learn to reject certain categories of people as sexually attractive, but these categories are mediated emotionally and thus distorted in terms of the individual's own needs before they become internalised.

But, of course, culture and society consist of far more than an objectively realistic and external pattern of events, relationships and values. Even within the family each sibling has, emotionally, a different mother who arouses different emotions that are expressed through qualitatively different relationships. Whether or not we choose to reify culture and the relationships and events that compose it 'events have a sense of reality for the [individual] whether they coincide with external events or not...What is commonly described as an historical event is composed of the actual happening and assumptions about the meaning of the happening' (Novey, 1968, p. 41).

For example, Bitrus described dramatically the custom of his village whereby children were sent by their parents to relatives or friends who said that they 'needed' a child. The child was cared for in return for its services. This was culturally acceptable and is common practice in Nigeria. Bitrus, however, interpreted this as an arbitrary rejection and even as a man in his late 20s he talked bitterly about the six mothers with whom he had lived before he was eight. He depicted a rootless childhood in which, although he rarely lacked a bed or food, he rarely felt loved and wanted.

The case of Chidi was an even more complicated interaction of individual and sociocultural factors. One afternoon my office door burst open and three students rushed in, holding hands. The middle student was talking loudly and excitedly to an invisible audience while staring into the corners of the ceiling. His head was bound in a large and roughly tied bandage and his shirt was bloodstained. I was told his name, but when I spoke to him he replied incoherently. The phrases that I understood were erratically punctuated by nonsense. Gradually I learned that he spoke faultless English.

The first meeting was inconclusive and unsettling. Chidi looked and sounded deeply disturbed: I doubted that it would be possible to reach him while he was in this condition. How could he be protected and cared for? The two students who accompanied him and knew him well were unafraid and promised to look after him. While I talked to his friends and tried to talk to him, Chidi wandered about the room picking up, examining and replacing objects; when he was offered food, he accepted it but toyed with it and seemed to be unaware of what it was. He left the room without warning and his friends told me that he had been shouting wildly in the library and the refectory. Students had been frightened and an angry man had struck him on the head with a knife.

The student friends protected and cared for Chidi: they stopped him from wandering off the campus and had his wounds treated by the university's medical services. Surprisingly, he was not offered psychiatric help. During the semester, Chidi often sat in my office and visited my home. On campus he was clean but dishevelled and continually addressed his invisible audience. He always smilingly greeted me and often tried (without success) to hold a conversation. After I became accustomed to his sitting in my office chatting with his familiars, I felt that I was accepted as a protector. Chidi seemed to approve of my office and house as safe shelters. I then began tentatively to encourage him to talk about his 'angels', and he began pointing to them. He told me that they discussed his future with him and Chidi revealed that he, a history student, was being urged by them to become an aviator. As Chidi came to trust me he invited me to share his discussions. I explained that I was unable to hear the angels, but that I agreed to converse with them if he assisted me and if he thought that this would help him to clear what he began to describe as his 'confusion'. So we proceeded for more than a year. A practical result of our triangular relationship was that the angels agreed not to engage Chidi in loud conversation when I or my visitors were busy.

Three interrelated questions now seem appropriate:

1. Was Chidi suffering from a schizophrenic disorder?

2. Were there sociocultural factors that might make sense of Chidi's behaviour? How might they interact with his individual psychic needs?

3. Was Chidi's behaviour influenced by my being white?

First, *prima facie*, it seemed that Chidi might be schizophrenic. His disturbed behaviour appeared first in his early 20s and caused a rapid and striking deterioration in his ability to care for himself, to relate to people and to function competently as a student. His reality testing was significantly impaired, although it was not wholly damaged, and because of this his cognitive processes were sometimes bizarre. However, even when he was most preoccupied by his thoughts and his angels, he was unfailingly gentle and considerate. If I was very persistent he could, for short periods, be diverted from the angels and engage in short, rational conversations. After I had known him for about three months, Chidi revealed glimpses of insight: 'I'm so confused', he would announce apologetically.

It was impossible to categorise Chidi's behaviour, even when it was at its most bizarre because of the uncertainty of the 'schizophrenia hypothesis as generally encountered. Instead, we are directed to a competing hypothesis: that schizophrenia is a moral judgment and like all moral judgments is conditional upon time, place and person, and upon identifiable social features of the persons who declare the moral verdict' (Sarbin and Mancuso, 1980, p. 1).

I had to ask myself if there were any identifiable and significant features in Chidi's life experience that might explain his behaviour. One obvious observation is that Nigeria's unsettling social, political and economic conditions affected all Nigerians. Yet, although all Nigerians lived in a world of emotional uncertainties, only some responded by behaving in a bizarre and unacceptable manner. Moreover, many Nigerians have experienced disturbing family relationships. Further, why was it only some of the students who felt so frightened or affronted by Chidi's behaviour that they came close to murdering him? Why was it that other students accepted his eccentricities and were caring and gentle?

If sociocultural factors label individuals as disturbed, then Nigeria must be a very fragmented culture to permit such a range of judgments and responses. It was also a mystery that nurses and doctors had failed to judge Chidi's behaviour as so odd, and the man as so helpless, that he needed psychiatric care.

Second, were Chidi's family relationships so deeply disturbed that they might explain his preoccupations and disorientation? In what ways was his idiosyncratic behaviour related to idiosyncratic emotional development? Or, had he responded idiosyncratically to family relationships that were common in his culture? A more complicated question asks: how did he transform his personal phantasies and emotional states into behaviour that was patterned by, and meaningful, in his culture? It is most likely that a combination of all these considerations is involved.

Third, in what way was Chidi influenced by my identity as a white

English male old enough to be his father? From time to time Chidi appeared to identify me with Winston Churchill. Did Chidi perceive me as Winston Churchill and, if he did, what apects of Churchill did he transfer to me?

Gradually, Chidi and his friends let me know enough about his childhood to make sense of his disturbed behaviour. In the early 1960s, shortly after Nigeria became independent, Chidi's father was sent to England to be trained as an accountant. He had been a lowly clerk in the civil service and was not well educated, but there was a dearth of professionally qualified civil servants and he was chosen to go. He returned with a low-grade qualification and an exaggerated respect for English customs, values and dress. He was, for example, described as always wearing a dark three-piece suit and a black derby. He was both a practicing Christian and an active member of a local, indigenous religion. Chidi was raised to respect and emulate the English, their skills and ways of life yet, inconsistently, he had to obey the social and religious customs of his village.

Chidi was highly intelligent and entered the local university as a student of European history, where he did well. But shortly before he entered university, his father abandoned his Christian beliefs, took a new wife and ejected Chidi and his mother from their home. Chidi lost his family, was forced to fend for himself and was emotionally devastated.

Chidi's angels were not simply his own phantasy that personified his fear, anger and bewilderment. In his part of Nigeria, the ancestors and other supernatural beings commonly punished the wicked, interceded with authority or gave advice and comfort. The father who had evicted Chidi and his mother behaved like many another Nigerian (and non-Nigerian) father. But did the English behave like this? Chidi thought, or wished to believe, that they did not. I was English, therefore I was a Churchill and a saviour. Even though I was not an angel (except metaphorically!), I was expected to collaborate with Chidi's angels to help him save something from his shattered life.

It was often puzzling to recognize how Chidi identified me and what transferences were taking place. Transference and counter-transference are always a little mysterious. The mystery is vividly expressed by Symington (1986): 'whenever two people meet there is an instant fusing so that a new being emerges...Large parts of the analyst's personality are sucked into the personality of the patient and vice versa' (p. 30). Chidi made me aware that he was identifying with my 'Englishness'. He imitated my distinctive English accent and took to wearing a white shirt, dark trousers and a tie that he let me know 'looked English'. He also added badges that he said were worn by aviators.

Identification is well known as a means to neutralise anxiety, fear and a sense of non-being. For example, Bettelheim (1970, 1980) has chillingly described how prisoners in Nazi concentration camps sometimes imitated the uniforms, mannerisms and values of their guards. In all societies, psychotherapists must understand the dynamics of identifications. These often originate in immensely complicated unconscious phantasies and draw upon both individual and collective sources. Psychotherapists must, therefore, be unafraid of asking 'questions of great provocativeness [about] the meaning of actions, their significance and intention and the subjective position they hold within the life of the person concerned' (Frosh, 1989, p. 6). In Africa, as in Europe, my patients were sucked into each others' lives and learned to perceive the 'real' individuals behind the mask of identifications. In London as in Africa, I have had to strive to understand in what ways relationships, events and identifications are related to the patient's culture and in what ways they are idiosyncratic and personal. In every aspect of our social life transferences and counter-transferences are formed, some of which are negative and others positive. Some are easier for the therapist to penetrate, but others are resistant to intuitive understanding. As long ago as 1950, Paula Heimann warned that 'it has not been sufficiently stressed that [transference] is a *relationship* between two persons...The aim of the analyst's own analysis, from this point of view, is to enable him to *sustain* the feelings which are stirred in him...in order to *subordinate* them to the analytic task in which he functions as the patient's mirror reflection' (p. 81).

The Dilemma of Cultural Relativism

The position of those who maintain or imply that psychotherapy is to a large extent or entirely the white man's *juju* depends on the arguments of cultural relativism. As its most extreme: 'counselling in Africa has to operate within a totally different cultural context from that in Europe and America' (Ipaye, 1982, p. 35). If this sweeping and inaccurate generalisation is accepted, it is very similar to racist views in which a stereotyped 'African' is contrasted with a similarly stereotyped 'European' or 'White'.

The theory of cultural relativism is based on the obvious cultural diversity of humanity. It orginated in the early ethnographic preoccupation with recording and classifying differing cultural skills, customs, beliefs, technologies and forms of economic, social, political and religious organisations. Its most persuasive advocate was Herskovits (1949), who asserted that:

> all peoples form judgments about ways of life that are different from their own...Moral judgments have been drawn regarding the ethical principles that guide the behaviour and mould the value-systems of different peoples. Their economic and political structures and their religious beliefs have been ranked in order of complexity, efficiency, desirability...Evaluations of this kind stand or fall with the acceptance of the premises from which they derive. But this is not the only reason. Many of the criteria on which judgments are based are in conflict, so that conclusions drawn from one definition of what is desirable will not agree with those based on another formulation. (p. 62)

In its strongest form, cultural relativism implies that cultures and societies can only be understood and evaluated in terms of their own values. Therefore, an outsider cannot accurately and sensitively observe a foreign culture or society. If this position is correct, then only an insider could effectively practice as a psychotherapist. But in a weaker form, cultural relativism implies no more than that a psychotherapist can practice effectively only if he or she is sensitive to the values and relationships of a foreign culture - which position I accept.

The anthroplogist Roheim was cuttingly critical of cultural relativism. He (1969) asserted that 'the idea that all nations are completely different from each other...is a thinly veiled manifestation of nationalism, the democratic counterpart of the Nazi racial doctrine...The slogan of cultural relativity is...a reaction formation: "You are completely different, but I forgive you", is what it amounts to' (p. 362). He further maintains that if one is content to try to understand and evaluate a culture or a society within its own scheme of values, it is probable that no more than a superficial and preconscious interpretation will be carried out. To achieve a full understanding of a culture it is necessary to examine *in detail* the defence mechanisms, sublimations and patterns of repression by which individuals deal with the tensions and anxieties of becoming 'civilised'.

Herskovits linked cultural relativism with the anti-ethnocentric and anti-racist positions that were a notable feature of American anthropology in the 1920s. It was also influenced by attacks on 'primitivism' and supported the view that there was no justification for the term 'primitive'.

The egotistic cultural superiority of the West could only be demonstrated (and that doubtfully) during the very brief period when complex, capitalistic economic organisation was based on a highly sophisticated machine technology.

Relativism and antirelativism are still live issues. Geertz has devoted many professional papers to attacking antirelativism, though even he (1984) admits that relativism is 'yesterday's battle cry' (p. 263). His position seems to be that Benedict's and Herskovits' pleas for cultural relativism were pleas for tolerance for alien or foreign cultures, in the belief that it was all too easy to evaluate unfamiliar cultures and societies pejoratively.

Geertz (1984) contrasts relativism and antirelativism:

> What the relativists, so-called, want us to worry about is provincialism - the danger that our perceptions will be dulled, our intellects constricted and our sympathies narrowed by the over-learned and overvalued acceptances of our own society. (p. 265)

On the other hand:

> What the antirelativists, self-declared, want us to worry about...is a kind of spiritual entropy...in which everything is as significant, thus as insignificant, as everything else. (p. 265)

As so often in the social sciences, polarised positions conceal assumptions that are not starkly opposed. It can be admitted that cultural differences exist, and that they influence individual experience, values and behaviour. But it cannot be denied that there is a psychobiological unity of humanity. Developmental processes, both emotional and cognitive, follow remarkably similar patterns regardless of the individual's culture. The therapist therefore has to solve difficult questions at the outset of working with each patient: are there cultural factors that might distort my understanding of this patient and complicate my relationships with him?

Are there cultural factors that might cause or contribute or shape her condition? How far, and in what ways, are there sociocultural conditions that are specific to the patient's personal life experiences and his responses to them? How does the patient value different elements of her cultural and social worlds? The therapist could ask similar questions of herself. Therapists, of course, like any other collection of individuals, will have their personal sensitivities and insensitivities. It would be nonsense and unrealistic to assume that only 'insider' therapists are sensitive to culturally specific conditions and the patient's attitudes toward them. Moreover, there is no reason to assume that cultural factors are, *in themselves*, responsible for individual differences in sensitivity and interpersonal skills. Some African therapists are intuitive and have sophisticated interpersonal skills, but some are not. This is equally true of non-Africans.

The relativist positions are also open to psychodynamic qualifications: even Herskovits (1949) admitted that culture is a psychological reality. It is also a psychological construct. The relationship of the individual to culture is complex. Individuals interpret and evaluate the elements of which their culture is composed. They have feelings about it, believe parts to be true and others parts to be false or doubtful. They understand some aspects and are puzzled by others. For example, it may or may not be correctly reported that maternal-feminine myths are stronger in some Indian cultures than in some Western. Hindu boys have to respond to the myth of the powerful mother in culturally appropriate ways that may influence their adult attitudes towards females (Kakar, 1989). But it is individual Hindu boys who make the response. Some boys respond negatively, some positively and some are emotionally neutral about the myths. Some boys are emotionally disturbed by their responses and may need psychotherapy. Other boys will not. For some boys, their cultural experience is supportive, meaningful and emotionally satisfying. For others it may be damaging, inhibiting and unhappy.

Psychoanalysts, for example, Winnicott (1967), have asked: where is culture? Does it exist in its own right, or is it a psychological construct, an experience that is shared by a community of individuals? Winnicott has raised doubts about 'the location of cultural experience' that are ignored by cultural anthropologists and by many sociologists. Throughout life, individuals strive to harmonise their inner psychic life and its realities with the external cultural and social realities in which they are living. Cultural experience, or the reconciliation between the individual's internal and external realities, is located in 'the *potential space* between the individual and the environment (originally the object). For every individual the use of this space is determined by *life experiences* that take place at the early stages of the individual's existence' (Winnicott, 1967, p. 371). The baby learns about the external cultural world through the intensity of his interactions (positive and negative) between the 'me' and the 'not-me' objects that he experiences. During earliest infancy the mother (or other intimate carer) mediates between the baby and the external world; consequently 'the deprived child...has an impoverishment of capacity to experience in the cultural field' (p. 371) because the potential space cannot be trusted to provide satisfying objects. The empty or unsatisfying potential space is, therefore, filled by the individual's own imaginary objects or those borrowed from whatever or whoever is a substitute for the mother.

Personal trust, interpersonal predictability and reliability are the emotional bases of an individual's sense of cultural continuity. Emotionally disturbed behaviour is caused by a *'breakup* of whatever may exist at the time of *a personal continuity of existence'* (Winnicott, 1967, p. 369). Individuals construct, as best they can, a working system of their culture and social worlds out of the relationships that they experienced in infancy. If they are fortunate, their personal and cultural spaces coincide and they experience an unbroken world. There is, unfortunately, no certainty that individual infants will experience reliable and emotionally satisfying relationships from which to construct a cultural and social world.

The interaction between individual uncertainties and cultural is illustrated in the life of Innocent, who consulted me about his persistent depression. Innocent approached me in a respectable bar in a small, remote town in South East Nigeria, introducing himself as a civil servant. It emerged that he was only a junior prison officer. He soon offered me an elaborate account of how his mother's sister had married a Greek and that therefore he had Greek cousins. Innocent was anxious to persuade me that he felt close to his 'racially' ambiguous cousins. His own family was poor and broken, his education was meagre, but his intelligence and stylish speech made it easy for him to masquerade as highly educated. For example, he claimed that he was qualified to enter university, and he carried well-written letters, purporting to come from influential people, in one of which he was informed that he was free to proceed to specialise in 'any of the fields in Human Anatomy from any university of your interest'. Innocent soon discovered my profession and, uninvited (not uncommon in West Africa), visited my house to ask me to treat him for depression, panic attacks and a variety of somatic disorders. Despite Innocent's agreeable social manner, I often felt that he was emotionally cold and unable to form deep and lasting relationships. He was, indeed, only able to fabricate a bearable everyday life by maintaining phantasies about his identity and childhood. He also had perfected a smooth persona that enabled him to exploit relationships in order to sustain his fragile sense of being in control of his life. His boundaries between reality and unreality, both personal and social, were uncertain, but in Nigeria's erratic and anomic society he could live unchallenged within his personal aberrant space (see Bloom, 1982).

Individuals and Social Change

Like individuals, cultures and societies change; some structures, relationships and values change more than others. There is, therefore, some degree of disharmony or conflict between the changing elements. Individuals live in the interior of a sociocultural kaleidoscope and are continually driven to accommodate to change. Some social changes are accepted, others are rejected, all are interpreted by the individual (as far as may be possible), to meet his or her needs, wants, goals and drives. Individuals respond to change with an almost endless variety of emotions, interpretations and identifications, and the roles that they occupy, the relationships that they form, reform and abandon, are the medium of the individual's changing and often unconscious identity.

Humans have a striking capacity to deal with the ambiguities of a prodigious variety of cultures and societies. It is not the cultural and social uncertainties that are responsible for emotional disturbance, but rather the *interaction* between (1) the individual's capacity for understanding and tolerating social and cultural change and (2) those *specific* sociocultural elements that force upon the individual an awareness that personal continuity is 'breaking-up'.

Individuals search endlessly for emotional security and a sense of identity in the universal and endless sociocultural changes in which all humans live. If society offers adequate and appropriate support and security, then most individuals can contain their insecurities. If individuals fail to find a supportive environment that satisfies them as individuals, then they may experience emotional disturbance. In Africa, as elsewhere, there are similar interactions between individual and social uncertainties. The essential task of a psychotherapist is to enter the patient's life space in a fragmented social-psychological world: I see no reason why this should be more or less difficult in Africa than elsewhere.

Individuals, therefore, have continually to make choices that, in our imperfect world, rarely reconcile personal drives and social patterns. But choices are also made collectively: in all societies individuals are defined in many arbitrary ways, for example, by their sex or age. Moreover, there are those with power and authority and those with little or none. There are the economically secure and the insecure. There are, moreover, more clearly individual groupings: the mavericks and the conventional, the emotionally sensitive and the insensitive, the more and the less intelligent, the creative and the uncreative - and many more. Societies accept specific individual qualities and reject others. Individuals have some qualities that are valued and others that are rejected. Individuals, therefore, have to nurture their self-respect and narcissism as well as they are able and in whatever ways their societies permit. Individuals in all societies are forced to be devious in order to protect their identity. The patient is often a person who can no longer tolerate the strains of the deception.

The 'Normal' and the 'Abnormal'

Relativism is on stronger ground when it is argued that the terms 'normal' and 'abnormal' can only be understood within the frame of reference of a specific culture. The weakness of this view is that it exaggerates the flair of individuals to understand each other. Even if it is admitted that understanding a culture involves understanding what is specifically defined by that culture as acceptable, meaningful and predictable, it is not also admitted that *some* degree of understanding is impossible. The question in every case is: to what extent and in what areas of life can understanding be gained by an outsider? 'It is possible in principle to transcend our culturally determined beliefs. And the possibility is also there of indefinitely refining our capacity...to gain greater knowledge' (King-Spooner, 1990, p. 27).

Individuals retain their own emotional needs even when they are incompatible with the values and norms of their society. To define the "abnormal" therefore entails the delicate operation of penetrating beyond superficial values and norms to the patient's personal world. But what is the culture within which individuals maintain their personal world? Are there, for example, secret personal worlds occupied by women and by children that I, an adult male, can only enter if I am invited? Why is it that only some individuals surrender to mental illness while others fight for mental health? (see *Freedom from Ghetto Thinking*, Bettelheim, 1990).

A partial answer to Bettelheim's question is hidden in the mysteries of individual development. Individuals make their own efforts to transform external worlds into internal meanings and develop their own manner of handling the emotions that the meanings agitate. 'It is essential...to clearly distinguish pathological private constructs of meaning from normal [shared] cultural constructs' (Hammond-Tooke, 1975, p. 31).

It has been maintained that the divergence between African and non-African ideas about the causes of illness is so wide that 'Western' notions about the 'abnormal' are inappropriate in Africa. But which Africans and which non-Africans are being contrasted? For example, do the educated and the noneducated, the urban and the rural differ? Do those who have been exposed to Western medicine differ from those who have not? It is claimed that the African universe, unlike the Western, is personalised and that events are caused by human-like gods, by the ancestors and other supernatural beings. It is reasonable to examine contrasting beliefs about causation, but it can be doubted if they are strictly dichotomised in any society. It seems more probable that all societies include a wide range of beliefs, some materialistic and science-oriented and others not. Many individuals probably move from one frame of reference to another. What, for example, could be less rationalistic than the hostility to modern medicine of some fundamental religious sects in the U.S.A. and in Europe? Perhaps 'we should avoid caricatures of both primitive and modern mentalities and should not represent Westerners as thinking scientifically all the time when scientific activity is a special one practiced in very circumscribed circumstances. One must compare like with like, our everyday thought with their everyday thought' (Tambiah, 1990, p. 92).

In psychotherapy it is, therefore, essential to assess specifically which worlds of ideas are meaningful for the patient. It is probable that most patients, like most psychotherapists, live in worlds in which different notions of science and the 'normal' and the 'abnormal co-exist.

Whatever the individuals' culture of ideas, the therapist cannot avoid the task of understanding the needs, drives and goals of the specific individual who *lives* the culture. In the words of Bastide (1950):

> We must...distinguish the manifest content from the latent ideas of neurosis. The manifest content is provided by society, but it is animated by the libido. [The social and the libidinal] are two different phenomenological orders. They mingle as the waters of two streams intermingle, but which spring from different sources: One arises in human drives and the other in the interpenetration of human consciousness. (p. 184]

In other words, 'through culture we objectify our inner fears...Culture is the *container* for all our unfinished emotional business' (Stein, 1985, p. 11). This thesis emphasises the interaction between the personal and the social: the emotionally disturbed live in a culture, but that culture is interpreted in terms of their unconscious emotional conflicts and anxieties, their fixations and regressions. The culture forbids, permits or sublimates the individual's emotional conflicts. But the repressed conflict and anxiety continue to complicate the individual's social life. If, however, our theory of the abnormal reduces individuals to little more than passive elements of society, then we are employing magical thinking to counter the wild forces of the libido. Such an uncomplicated and fearful reliance upon culturological argument implies an attack on individuals and individuality. I am optimistic that psychoanalysis may 'breathe life and soul back into the human sciences in an environment where the external forms and structures of social life...threaten to become oppressive, reified and empty' (Scaff, 1990, pp. 97-98).

The puzzling interactions between the normal and the abnormal, and between the individual and the cultural, have been convincingly described by Lou Andreas-Salomé (1987), who observed that 'in most of Freud's writing, civilised man appears as a sadly domesticated savage, and his sublimation by the aid of his repressed savagery assumes an essentially negative quality - drive and culture being contrasted like the inner and outer value' (p. 56). The paradox is that neither culture nor the individual ego can exist without the other. 'The ego, which is manifest in culture, must find in it directly the forms in which it will fully discharge its instinctual energy. For culture does not only confront the ego; it also expresses its own individually developed development' (p. 56). Freud was fascinated by the shifting relationships between the so-called normal and the abnormal. In his *Gradiva* book (Freud, 1907) and four early essays on creativity, he explored the common ground between literature and psychoanalysis because 'the borderline between normal and morbid psychic conditions is, in a way, a conventional one and, in another way, in such a state of flux that probably every one of us oversteps it many times in the course of a day' (p. 65). Dreams and delusions, the 'normal' workings of the imagination and the 'abnormal' psychic states of so-called abnormality are closely related.

Culture: The Dangers of a Latent Racism

My argument implies that an overemphasis on the autonomy of cultural and social factors can lead to a tacit collusion with racist arguments. At its most gross, there is a concealed 'racism' in such assertions as that only African therapists can work with African patients, only whites can treat whites, only women can treat women. Then why not: only children can work with children? If it is platitudinously maintained that 'people are different because they experience different situations ... [We] forget that they are people. To find our common humanity we need not search for what it is to be common but for what it is to be human' (Miller, 1989, p. 4).

The weakness of culturological and sociological positions is that they ignore that Africans, women, the old, or any collection of individuals that is for any reason *regarded* as a group, are people. The modish ethnopsychiatric approaches fail to appreciate the intricacies of the integration and interactions between individuals and their social and cultural worlds. Individual emotional problems are lost from view in sometimes too glaringly obvious cultural and social problems with which individuals have to cope. It is, moreover, tempting to search for sociocultural exotica and ignore the universal human being. An African's depression feels the same as a non-African's, a woman's feels the same as a man's. Even though depressions are experienced by individuals living within a local reality, the suffering individuals have to develop their individual defences to ward off both internal and external threats to their ego integrity.

Four publications exemplify the overemphasis on cultural differences between Africans and non-Africans: Brownell, de Jager, and Madlala (1987), Bührmann (1984), Ipaye (1982), and Ezeilo (n.d.).

Writing from South Africa, Brownell et al. (1987) maintain that:

anthropological research in recent years has clearly shown that health service programmes of technologically advanced societies cannot simply be transferred to developing societies without taking specific cultural factors into account... and in particular [in catering for mental health], the educational psychological needs of particular ethnic groups. (p. 34)

Most of this paper describes the methods and philosophy of traditional healers and compares them with Western medicine. However, it ignores the defensiveness of traditional healers whose collective interests are served by maintaining the myth that Africans are culturally distinct from whites. This view colludes with *apartheid* psychology in which Africans are still stigmatised as unurbanised, largely illiterate, primitive, and unready to share the benefits and burdens of urban and technologically developed society.

But as long ago as 1964, Bloom noted that:

in barely one generation in South Africa there has been a development of urbanisation comparable to what took more than a century to accomplish in the U.K. Africans are speedily ceasing to be a rural people and are becoming a predominantly urban, landless proletariat... Despite the considerable social and physical isolation of the Africans ... contact is nevertheless maintained with the 'modern' world. (p. 941)

A moderate view is taken by de Jong, who was for many years a psychiatrist in Guinea-Bissau (West Africa). In Africa, as elsewhere, there are many medical philosophies and practices. There is, therefore, sometimes a conflict between Western and traditional philosophies in their diagnosis of illness. Therefore, to understand mental illness it is necessary to adopt 'modern currents in anthropology, which focus on an encounter with other cultures as a dialectical process, thereby enhancing Western scientific discourse and possibly formulating criticism concerning one's own society' (de Jong, 1987, p. 199).

Individuals, like societies, may have a mixture of orientations to medicine generally and to mental illness specifically, so that according to their orientation a traditional or a Western healer might be more appropriate. It must not be too readily assumed that in Africa the causes of mental illness are always claimed to be magical or supernatural, the result of bewitchment. For example, in 1964, in a South African sample, it was found that even the traditional healers (the *izinyanga)* favoured a plurality of causes. Psychosocial, physiological, and supernatural causes were named. A typical account of a young and uneducated man said that 'the causes are worry, bewitching, and poverty. It is worse now than it used to be, because there is a lot of frustration and poverty among our people; the cost of living is high and yet our people are not earning enough to meet their needs' (Bloom, 1964, p. 93).

A patient may even resist traditional beliefs in the supernatural. For example, I was treating Emeka for his severe and persistent depression. During a public holiday he went home to his isolated village to stay with his mother, with whom he had a stormy and ambivalent relationship. He returned surprisingly elated, smiling and with sparkling eyes. He told me (and the story was confirmed) that he had been tricked into accompanying a group into the interior of the forest, where he was accused of being a witch and of causing his mother's physical illness. Emeka's life was in danger, but his presence of mind was commendable. He retorted that if he *were* a witch, then he was going to bewitch his accusers. He was then allowed to pass unharmed to the edge of the forest, where he was safe. Emeka's bravery enabled him to release himself from his unhappy and claustrophobic family, as well as village relationships and beliefs.

Bührmann (1984) also writes of the 'two worlds' of the traditional

Africa and the Western world, as though they were totally isolated from each other. Her book implies that the 'two worlds' are populated with men and women with totally different and sharply opposed philosophies, motivations, and values. One world is 'the Western world which is primarily scientific, rational, and ego-orientated, and the world of the black healer and his people, which is primarily intuitive, nonrational or orientated towards the inner world of symbols and images' (p. 15).

In an earlier paper, she sought an answer to the question: 'why are certain procedures of indigenous healers effective?' (Bührmann, 1979); but she fails to consider why certain procedures are ineffective. Nor does she ask why some patients make use of traditional healers and others prefer Western healers. Yet others may use both traditional and Western medicine. Which are the crucial variables: the patient's educational level, urbanisation, the accessibility and cost of different kinds of healer, the nature of the illness, or experience and sophistication? Africans, like non-Africans, inhabit individual life spaces, which mingle a variety of ideologies, values, and norms. Africans are not the only human beings who think and feel intuitively, irrationally, symbolically, and imaginatively. Nor are they alone in being frustrated and angered by the distress caused by their cultures and societies. Moreover, they are not alone in responding to their frustrations, fears, and anxieties by seeking salvation or revenge in religion, magic, or witchcraft.

Even African psychotherapists seem reluctant to accept that witchcraft beliefs can only be understood within the context of the interactions between the patient's individual experience and social and cultural conditions (see, e.g., Ipaye, 1982 and Ezeilo, n.d.). Ezeilo, in her review of the problems of psychotherapy with African patients, holds that a 'belief in the preternatural and the supernatural causes seems to be shared by both educated (Westernised) and uneducated Africans ... This seems consistent with the African's belief system in external causation of his/her illness. This absolves him/her of responsibility for the aetiology of the problem' (p. 3).

The irrational, unconscious distortions of reality and the growth of magical (and quasi-magical) beliefs are universal, because every individual copes, both rationally and irrationally, with the problem-filled world. Psychotherapists and patients confront a universal quandary: how can social pressures and uncertainties be disentangled from individual phantasies about them? A sensitive psychotherapist, moreover, must continually question whether the patient's magical fears and beliefs are exciting unconscious responses in the therapist.

Both the therapist and the patient have beliefs that are shaped by their culture and society, but their unconscious origins are intensely personal. Social beliefs are elaborated by individuals. We develop conversion symptoms, form symbolically significant relationships, and exploit cultural and social norms to act out our unconscious dramas. Our social behaviour is permeated by innumerable transferences and by all the irrational, emotional colouring of our interpersonal relationships. In addition, repression and resistance, interpretations, the resolution of transferences and countertransferences, the interpretation of dreams, and other products of the imagination and the unconscious have never been confined to patients at 19 Berggasse. The smouldering anger of a paranoiac may be transformed into witchcraft or accusations of witchcraft, but there is no limit to the social forms that it can adopt. The repressed returns and explodes in symptomatic formations in all societies at collective and individual levels.

Another view that overrates cultural and social factors is that African patients report somatic symptoms rather than emotional distress (e.g., Ezeilo, 1982). I found that many more students complained of these symptoms before examinations or in response to a family or financial crisis. It was usually possible, however, to move from the somatic to the emotional, and unlike Ezeilo (and other writers), I see no justification to regard this somatisation as unusual. Nor does it create 'problems of assessment and diagnosis for the clinician whose ethnic background and orientation differs from that of the Third World client' (Ezeilo, n.d. p. 3). A psychoanalytic orientation would sensitise a clinician to suspect if somatic symptoms were screening emotional problems. For example, Felix was a university freshman who consulted me about his 'pains in the chest' and asthmatic attacks. I assured myself that he had had medical investigations and that there were no organic causes for his illness. Despite his breathlessness, Felix had a flair for oral rhetoric that I envied. During one of our meetings it struck me that he was both gasping for breath and delivering an eloquent indictment of his parents. He accused them of neglecting and rejecting him in early childhood so that he was compelled to care for himself. There was no way to check if this was true, but it was *Felix's* truth. His anger literally choked him, so that he had to struggle to utter his invective against his parents. He was also punishing himself severely for his anger.

It is often claimed that the extended family relationships in Africa are so distinct that they are obstacles to psychotherapy. Uzoka (1979, 1980) and MacPherson (1983) argue that the persistence of kinship ties offers family members a community that is closer, more intimate, cohesive, and supportive than the family in Western and urbanised societies. Uzoka urges clinicians to appreciate that the extended family has beneficial human relationships that the nuclear family lacks. He writes (1980) that 'the significant difference between African notions of family and Western attitudes may lie in the extent to which primordial feelings of attachment are openly acknowledged and utilised' (p. 856). He denies that technological development necessarily depends on the nuclear family and predicts that the extended family may survive urbanisation and industrialisation as it has in Japan and Korea. Bott and Hodes (1989) claim that Africans are so closely defined by their kinship group that group or family therapy might be more appropriate than in the less communalistic ethos of urbanised societies.

This emphasis on the communal exaggerates its emotional advantages, and minimises (or even ignores) its disadvantages: the extended family can be as claustrophobic as is the nuclear family. It is a major developmental task for children, in both the extended and the nuclear families, to form emotionally satisfying ego-boundaries. A major problem in psychotherapy is to recognise the patient's struggles to break out of the collective, family boundaries in order to find his or her own identity. I have often been reminded with varying degrees of intensity: 'I'm not only an African! I'm *me!'*

But whether the family norm is nuclear or extended, there are only a few types of relationship that individuals can form, and these are essentially in their emotional foundations. Psychotherapists investigate the quality of interpersonal relationships and the patient's phantasies about them, and have therefore to penetrate the concealments of the social forms of the family. Besides, every family is its own microworld with its own emotional norms. Some families are democratic and others are authoritarian; some are emotionally close but others are distant; some warm and others cold. In extended as in nuclear families, children experience both stable and unstable relationships and must cope with loving and caring, rejecting and punishing, siblings, aunts and uncles, and a host of relations and family friends. Some children are favoured; others are rebuffed. A parent might make emotional demands on one child and be indifferent to others; children identify with adults and with their siblings in many ways. Some families establish emotionally satisfactory ways of solving conflict and rivalry, but other families live in little battlefields. In some families the development of sexuality is tolerated, but in others it is feared, resented, or hated. Unconscious incest phantasies are powerful in some children, but for others they barely exist. Some families succeed in keeping out the world. In others the children are socialised into accepting or even welcoming the outside world. Therefore, a major psychotherapeutic activity is to expose the emotional and social relationships that constitute the social psychology of a specific family. The psychotherapist has to recognise intuitively the specific unconscious attractions, rejections, and conflicts that motivate the members of the patient's family.

Problems of Communication

'Spontaneous thoughts occur to the analyst at all stages of his work. But it is the spontaneous communication of a new idea that evokes a spontaneous reaction in the patient and gives to both a feeling of a constructive session which will lead to further development' (Klauber, 1987, p. 33). Good therapy will break through the cultural and linguistic constraints that inhibit communication. I doubt if difficulties in communication are inescapably a peculiar characteristic of psychotherapy across cultures.

Communication is both verbal and nonverbal - for example, gestures, bodily posture and orientation, and facial expression. Even a mediocre therapist should be sensitive to the nuances and ambiguities of the patient's emotional signals, whether they are individual or derived from cultural norms.

For example, a patient named Ofem was once accusing me angrily of neither understanding Africans nor sympathising with them. Yet while he was verbally attacking me he was holding my hands. I felt my anger rising at the unfairness of his accusations, and after a few minutes I gripped his hands tightly, forcing him to try to draw them away. "Look at your hands!", I ordered. He looked down, then glanced at my face and grinned. It does not demand an uncommon sensitivity to interpret some of his feelings about me *as an individual* and me *as a white man*. His anti-white, anti-colonial eloquence was external and concealed his personal trust: you do not hold the hands of someone whom you hate. But was he not also transferring onto me his ambivalence about his powerful and dominating father - a typical father in his culture - a father who is trusted yet resented, a friend yet a rival?

It is dangerous to exaggerate cultural strangeness and allow oneself to be distracted from the dynamics of the individual patient. But another fundamental question is ignored by those therapists who overemphasise cultural factors. Who, it should be asked, consults a Western-trained and orientated psychotherapist? Surely, only those patients who are partly or entirely Western in *their* orientation to the causation and cure of emotional disturbances? Therefore the therapist and the patient may need to initiate therapy by exploring what *for the patient* are the relationships, values, emotional constraints, identifications, and anxieties crucial in the patient's own judgments and feelings about the culture. The patient may need to escape from specific bonds of values and relationships of the culture. Does not this apply to patients in all cultures? Further, in what ways and how deeply repressed are these bonds? What are the patient's expectations from therapy? What are the specific areas of emotional relief or sense of liberation that are expected from therapy? How does the patient struggle with mothering and fathering relationships, and how do they affect transference and counter-transference situations?

Ade, for example, consulted me about his 'bad chest' and his depression. The 'bad chest' proved to be a psychogenic asthma that responded to psychotherapy, but the depression was persistent and began to ease only when he felt free to talk openly, directly, and passionately about the 'primitiveness' of his village. In the village he was an anomaly - he disbelieved in witchcraft and the supernatural. He was uninterested in making the swiftest possible buck. He was urban, 'modern', a natural scholar - and there was no place for him in the small, closed world in which he was raised. He had no alternative but to escape geographically. But could he escape emotionally? His attitudes toward his parents, siblings and the villagers who cared for him when he was a child were ambivalent. On one hand he was grateful for the financial care and the protection. On the other hand he felt that he had to escape from the people who failed to understand and accept him for his own personal qualities. Ade's self-punishing guilt arose from the tangled loyalties and love-hate relationships, which were his response to the impossible demands that his social situation posed for his sense of identity.

It is significant that many of the films that are now coming out of Africa deal with similarly complex situations. For example, *Finzan* is a film from Mali (West Africa) about a song and dance ceremony that is performed only by exceptionally brave men. The film portrays and praises the bravery of two most unusual women, who rejected the traditional ways of their people about circumcision and widowhood.

The languages of action and speech are tentative or experimental. When we attempt to communicate with another person, we cannot be certain that our message will have the cognitive and emotional effect that we intended. Psychoanalysis, 'the talking cure', is a linguistically complicated method of translation that has the aim of enabling a communicator and a recipient to share ideas, feelings, memories, and dreams.

Bruner (1990), a cognitive psychologist, has described language behaviour in terms that are close to psychoanalysis: 'Language is acquired not in the role of a spectator but through use... The child is not learning simply *what* to say but how, where, to whom and under what circumstances' (pp. 70-71). In addition, 'social understanding ... always begins as *praxis* in particular contexts in which the child is a *protagonist* - an agent, a victim, an accomplice' (p. 85). If we add to these mainly cognitive tasks, the communication of emotions and the contents of the unconscious, Bruner could be writing from within psychoanalysis.

An earlier pragmatist philosopher (Lewis, 1956) wrote that:

> we are able to understand one another because - for one reason - a common reality is presented to us. But so to put it is to reverse the order of knowledge. We have a common reality because - or insofar as - we are able to identify, each in his own experience ... and particularly by that part of behaviour which serves the end of co-operation. (pp. 110-111)

Words and actions make it possible for us to share the dream world of those other people with whom we share a common reality because we are similar humans.

Freud took the study of communication and language far beyond questions about the development of the nature of language and language skills. Psychoanalysis is concerned with the many ways that language both conceals and reveals the individual's feelings, intentions, and expectations. Even though language and communication constitute social behaviour, individuals behave in terms of their own cognitions and emotions. Words are given life when they are understood as *belonging to* the patient as well as to society. The psychotherapist may 'hear' the words but fail to 'hear' the background noises of the patient's world by which the words are given life. It is not difficult to be correct in a dictionary sense, yet to be emotionally in error. Therapists may think that they are speaking the same language as the patient, yet they may be feeling different worlds. If we are sensitive we can learn our personal communication insensitivities. For example, an African patient once said to me: 'You don't treat me like Musa, but like an

African!' Was this praise, irritation, or bewilderment? Was it Musa's plea that I begin to relate to him as the individual Musa? The reported words indicate little. Musa's tone of voice, demeanour, and the context of the conversation signalled that he was protesting (unjustly I felt) against my lack of respect for his individual identity and problems. It also revealed what he personally (and not as a Nigerian or an African) felt that he needed from our relationship.

In psychoanalysis the primary 'common reality' is the dyad of therapist and patient. A competent therapist *learns* what an individual patient is really communicating. Sometimes what is communicated can be directly related to the broader social reality; sometimes 'reality' is directly related to the patient's idiosyncratic and constructed social reality. In psychoanalysis, more than in other personal relationships, 'events are "understood" to mean more than they ostensibly "say", by being fitted into patterns of behaviour [and emotions] which make sense to us' (Segal, 1985, p. 27). What makes sense depends both on our superficial social learning and our deeper (and often unconscious) emotional needs.

Toward a Psychotherapeutic Orientation

Psychotherapy in Africa still lacks a model and philosophy. The broadest survey, Erinosho and Bell (eds., 1982), ends with three pages of recommendations that totally ignore the central features of economic, political and social change and go little beyond advising psychiatrists to bear in mind tradition and culture. It is curious that there seems to be no research to establish if psychotherapists experience the problems that are impressionistically described in Ezeilo (n.d.) and in Erinosho and Bell (eds., 1982), nor are there attempts to create appropriate models for Africa that are not merely non-African.

Davis *et al.* (1987) have offered a 'taxonomy of therapist difficulties' that would be a valuable basis for research in Africa. Nine types of problems were reported by therapists in this study. Therapists may: (1) feel inadequate or incompetent; (2) fear that the patient is being harmed by therapy; (3) feel blocked, uncertain how to go on with therapy; (4) feel unable to form a relationship with the patient because there are obstacles to reaching the patient emotionally; (5) feel threatened and in need of protection; (6) fail to keep their personal lives out of the therapeutic situation; (7) be confronted with an ethical problem and be undecided how to solve it; (8) feel that both therapist and patient are 'trapped, hopeless', locked in a therapy where no progress is apparent; and (9) feel that a patient is 'actively impeding' the progress of therapy.

Any of these difficulties may affect psychotherapy in any culture. A competent therapist can learn the cultural and individual forms in which they might emerge. Professional associations and discussion groups should be sensitive enough to offer therapists support and advice when they experience difficulties. It is disappointing that Ezeilo's paper has only one page on 'training', which says nothing about how therapists can be helped to develop a transcultural sensitivity. Ezeilo approves her own university's course in 'Ethnopsychiatry', but like many of such courses, it is confined to describing the externals of behaviour and says nothing about the psychodynamics of the therapist-patient relationship. A weakness of an 'ethnopsychiatric' approach is that gives an insensitive therapist a rationale for avoiding questions about the therapist's role in society. For example, writing of psychotherapy in South Africa, Spitz *et al.* (1990) write that 'in exceptional circumstances, so-called pathological defenses may be the only ones that enable an individual to survive and cope' (p. 25). A therapist would be insensitive and useless if he would shun helping a patient to cope with the psychic suffering that is caused by political and social assaults on individuals. Would Ezeilo and Lambo (1978), for example, collude with a patient's fear of bewitchment, or would they help the patient to resist this fear? In a patriarchal society (as are many African societies), the therapist cannot avoid asking questions about the extent to which power relationships are wholly or partially responsible for a female patient's malaise. The next question is: how does the therapy help to strengthen the patient's resistance to power?

Winnicott (1988) considered the types of material that are dealt with during psychoanalytic psychotherapy, and his approach integrates individual and social material:

> The stuff of the analysis (child or adult) can roughly be classified into types:
>
> (1) External relationships as between whole people.
>
> (2) Samples of the inner world and the variations on the theme of a phantasy life placed either within or without.
>
> (3) Intellectualised material in terms of which work can

be done, but this work needs to be repeated in another
form with feeling in it in the transference relationship.

4)   Material principally indicating the structural
weaknesses of the Ego, and the threat of loss of capacity
for relationship, and the threat of unreality and
depersonalisation. (p. 89)

Psychotherapy is, thus, emotionally and cognitively active and the
therapist and the patient interact to bring together, as harmoniously and
creatively as possible, the patient's internal and external worlds. Some
psychotherapists might judge that the crucial problem is the 'threat of
unreality and depersonalisation'. It may therefore be as essential to deal
with real threats from the external world as with the equally real threats
from the unconscious. Many social and cultural circumstances that are ego-
destructive are internalised: from the family, socioeconomic class, ethnic and
other socially defined identities, even age and sexual identity. Inevitably
'the analyst is lassoed into the patient's illusory world. He is more involved
in it, more victim to it than the average social contact' (Symington, 1986a,
p. 262).
        But the analyst may also be lassoed into the patient's reality world.
If the patients appear to believe in witches or feel victimised because of
their sexual identity, the therapist must either avoid being lassoed or work
with the patient to free them. The decisive question is: how real is the
belief? Is it a convenient symbolisation of the patient's personal phantasy
worlds? Or is there an external reality that corresponds to the patient's
beliefs? In therapy patients should find an emotionally and ideologically
safe base from which to explore and assess their emotional, intellectual, and
social existence. The therapist has a moral obligation to patients to
encourage, strengthen and free them so that they may re-feel and revalue
their lives. Patients do not cease to be individuals in therapy: they have the
right to be enabled to face individual and collective, realistic and phantasy
dangers and so to reorder their expectations of society that they can the
better resist society's damaging intrusions.

Psychotherapy and Freedom

The central aim of psychotherapy is to free the individual from the repressed
and the irrational, and from depersonalising and isolating relationships.

Individual freedom is blocked both by the individual's idiosyncratic perceptions and by the social, political and economic constraints within which all people have to live. Freud was mildly hopeful that the passions of the Id would eventually be not only controlled but replaced by the rational Ego. If this is ever to come about, it would have to happen both in individual and collective life.

Human freedom is therefore denied from two directions. It may be denied by those who minimise the power of cultural and social influences in causing neurosis and simple unhappiness. It may be denied by those who minimise individual autonomy. In reality, cultures and societies are created by, and are composed of, individuals. Individuals live communally, although they do not lose their individual transferences, identifications, and unconscious motivations. A central problem for psychotherapists is to probe how a specific culture and society facilitates or discourages freedom by how individual behaviour and experience are manipulated and valued.

Psychotherapists are citizens too - they cannot avoid their own emotional echoes of their patients' fight for freedom within society's maze of constraints and openings. No psychotherapist can evade a quasi-political role; perhaps a cryptopolitical role is more accurate. But a caveat is necessary, because 'the high narcissistic gratification that a person gets out of seeing his or her own ideals realised in the external world [contributes] to an identification with those-tragically afflicted' (Parin, 1985, p. 73). There are obvious dangers in emulating the Wilhelm Reich of the later 1920s and early 1930s.

It is now widely accepted that 'psychoanalysis has only recently shifted its emphasis from the study of the individual in conflict with society to the study of the individual within society' (Michels, 1988, p. 181). Michels' statement has totalitarian implications, but it remains true that the therapist and the patient are in a joint social enterprise, the dynamics of which are energised by standing outside of the wider society. Therefore, to argue with Ezeilo (n.d.) that in Africa 'client-therapist expectations are at variance', (pp. 6-7) begs questions about the *specific dissonances* between therapist and patient expectations at the outset, during and at the end of therapy. It begs other questions about the *specific consonances* that arise from the joint social enterprise of dealing with a society in which the patient is ill at ease.

It is disturbing that Ezeilo (and other psychotherapists in Africa), uncritically assume that African beliefs in magic and witchcraft are an insurmountable barrier to Western psychotherapy. I assume that these writers are exempt from these beliefs. They nowhere explain how they became exempt, nor they do they ask if other people are nonbelievers. Psychotherapists accept professional defeat too easily if they shun patients who are trapped in social or political beliefs that deprive them of freedom. Patients come to therapists to be helped to liberate themselves from irrational and unconscious obstacles to freedom. Does Ezeilo want to condemn Africans to be forever helpless and obedient to irrational forces, individual and collective?

If psychotherapists uncritically accept their (and their patients') beliefs, they deny that their patients' and their own beliefs (social, political, moral, or religious) are legitimate materials for analysis. In therapy there is always the danger that patients and therapists may slide into colluding with each other's beliefs, and that conventionally narrow techniques may fail to uncover this tacit collusion. If the therapist is 'a prisoner of this patient's controlling impulses' (Symington, 1986a, p. 255), or if therapist and patient are imprisoned by their controlling beliefs, then therapy is unchallenging - it is failing to explore ways in which the patient's life space can be enlarged. We often forget that cultural and social myths and relationships are unconsciously used to express the patient's internal wishes and conflicts. The content of psychotherapy is 'a product of the inner phantasy life in interaction with first the mother, then the mother and the father, siblings, and finally the whole social environment' (p. 267). Beliefs do not float freely like clouds; they are firmly lodged in the individual's psyche.

The psychological problem of freedom is, therefore, twofold. It is necessary to be sensitive to the intellectual and emotional development of the patient's beliefs and the therapist's response to them. It is also necessary to appreciate the significance for the society of the patient's beliefs. I am, perhaps, too bold in arguing that sometimes the therapist is right to support the patient's beliefs and to reject society's. What sort of therapist can limit therapy to the understanding and relief of symptoms? Even classical psychoanalysis has to deal with moral, political and social values. Hartmann (1960, p. 54), for example, distinguishes three aspects:

> First of all, the genesis, the dynamics, the economics of the patient's imperatives and ideals . . . Second, we meet the problem of the confrontation of his attitudes with the codes of his family and, more generally, of the culture he lives in. There are, third, the personal moral valuations of the analyst with respect to the material presented in analysis.

I would extend Hartmann's third aspect to include the analyst's valuations of the wider culture and society.

Therapists and patients have the difficult task of increasing the patient's *'responsible causality* [so] there is an empathic relation between the person and his or her inner and outer world' (Symington, 1990, p. 105). The analytic process 'turns the blind forces within and without and makes them part of me and me part of them' (p. 105), and this happens when individuals can respond actively to their internal and external worlds. In all cultures, psychotherapy has the immensely difficult task of strengthening patients so that they may transform themselves from victims of society into autonomous people.

References

Andreas-Salomé, L.(1987), *The Freud Journal*, London: Quartet Books.

Bastide, R.(1950), *Sociologie et Psychanalyse*, Paris: Presses Universitaires de France.

Bettelheim, B.(1970), *The Informed Heart*, London: Paladin Books.

Bettelheim, B.(1980), *Surviving*, New York: Vintage Books.

Bettelheim, B.(1990), *Recollections and Reflections*, London: Thames & Hudson.

Bloom, L.(1964), 'Some psychological concepts of urban Africans', *Ethnology*, vol. 3, pp. 66-95.

Bloom, L.(1982), 'Lying and culture: A West African case study', *J. Psychoanal. Anthropol.*, vol. 3, pp. 175-184.

Bott, D. and Hodes, M.(1989), 'Structural therapy for a West African family', *J. Family Therapy*, vol. ll, pp. 169-179.

Boyer, L.B. and Boyer, R.M.(eds) (1993), *The Psychoanalytic Study of Society: Essays in Honour of George D. and Louise A. Spindler*, Hillsdale, N.J.: The Analytic Press.

Brownell, A.J.J., de Jager, A.C. and Madlala, C.F.M.(1987), 'Applying first-world psychological models and techniques in a third-world context', *School Psychol. Internatl.*, vol. 8, pp.34-47.

Bruner, J.(1990), *Acts of Meaning*, Cambridge: MA Harvard University Press.

Bührmann, M.V.(1979), 'Why are certain procedures of indigenous healers effective?' *Psychotherapeia*, vol. 5, pp. 20-25.

Bührmann, M.V.(1984), *Living in Two Worlds: Communication Between a White Healer and her Black Counterparts*, Cape Town, S.A.: Human & Rousseau.

Davis, J.D., Elliott, R., Davis, M.L., Binns, M., Francis, V.M., Kelman, J.E. and
Schroder, T.A.(1987), 'Development of a taxonomy of therapist difficulties: Initial
report', *British J. Med. Psychol.*, vol. 60, p.109.

De Jong, J.T.V.M.(1987), *A Descent into African Psychiatry*, Amsterdam, The Netherlands:
Royal Tropical Institute.

Erinosho, O.A. & Bell, N.W.(eds) (1982), *Mental Health in Africa*, Ibadan,Nigeria: Ibadan
University Press.

Ezeilo, B.N.(n.d.), *Psychotherapy with African clients: Problems and prospects*, Nsukka,
Nigeria: Department of Psychology, University of Nigeria.

Ezeilo, B.N.(1982), 'Somatisation of psychological distress among Nigerian undergraduate
medical outpatients', *Psychopathologie Africaine*, vol. 18, pp. 363-372.

Freud, S.(1907), 'Delusion and dreams' in Jensen's *Gradiva,* Standard Edition, vol. 9,
pp. 7-96. London: Hogarth Press, 1959.

Frosh, A.(1989), *Psychoanalysis and Psychology*, London: Macmillan.

Geertz, C.(1984), Distinguished lecture: Anti antirelativism, *Amer. Anthropol.*, vol. 86,
pp. 263-278.

Hammond-Tooke, W.D.(1975), 'African world view and its relevance for psychiatry',
Psychologia Africana, vol. 16, pp. 25-32.

Hartmann, H.(1960), *Psychoanalysis and Moral Values*, New York: International Universities
Press.

Heimann, P.(1950), 'On countertransference', *Internatl. J. Psycho-Anal.*, vol. 31, pp. 81-84.

Herskovits, M.J.(1949), *Man and His Works*, New York: Knopf.

Ipaye, T.(1982), 'Some cultural factors in counsellor functioning in Nigeria', *Brit. J.
Guidance and Counselling*, vol. 10, pp. 34-43.

Kakar, S.(1989), 'The maternal-feminine in Indian psychoanalysis', *Internatl. Rev. Psycho-
Anal.*, vol. 16, pp. 355-362.

King-Spooner, S.(1990), 'The fictional nature of introspection', *Brit. Psycholog. Soc.,
Psychother. Section Newsletter*, vol. 8, pp. 19-29.

Klauber, J.(1987), 'The role of spontaneity in psychoanalytic therapy, *Illusion and
Spontaneity in Psychoanalysis*, eds. Klauber et al., London: Free Association Books,
pp. 22-34.

Lambo, T.A.(1978), 'Psychotherapy in Africa', *Human Nature*, vol. 3, pp. 32-39.

Lewis, C.I.(1956), *Mind and the World-Order*, New York: Dover Books.

Macpherson, S.(1983), 'Mental illness in the Third World', *Mental Illness: Changes and
Trends*, ed. P. Bean, New York: Wiley, pp. 445-465.

Michels, R.(1988), 'The future of psychoanalysis', *Psychoanal. Quart.*, vol. 57,
pp. 313-340.

Miller, R.(1989), 'Critical psychology: a Territorial Imperative', *Psychol. in Society*,
vol. 12, pp. 3-18.

Novey, S.(1968), *The Second Look: The Reconstruction of Personal History in Psychiatry
and Psychoanalysis*, Baltimore, MD: Johns Hopkins University Press.

Parin, P.(1985), 'Freedom and independence: On the psychoanalysis of political
commitment', *Free Association*, vol. 3, pp. 65-79.

Roheim, G.(1968), *Psychoanalysis and Anthropology*, New York: International Universities
Press.

Sarbin, T.R. and Mancuso, J.C.(1980), *Schizophrenia: Medical Diagnosis or Moral Verdict?* New York: Pergamon Press.

Scaff, L.A.(1990), 'Modernity and the tasks of a sociology of culture', *History of the Human Sciences*, vol. 3, pp. 85-100.

Segal, J.(1985), *Phantasy in Everyday Life*, Harmondsworth: Penguin Books.

Spitz, S. et al.(1990), 'The torture goes on: the psychology of restrictions', *Psychology in Society*, vol. 13, pp. 17-26.

Stein, H.F.(1985), *The Psychoanthropology of American Culture*, New York: Psychohistory Press.

Symington, N.(1986), *The Analytic Experience*, London: Free Association Books.

Symington, N.(1986a), 'The analyst's act of freedom as agent of therapeutic change', *The British School of Psychoanalysis*, ed. G. Kohon. London: Free Association Books, pp. 253-270.

Symington, N.(1990), 'The possibility of human freedom and its transmission (with particular reference to the thought of Bion)", *Internatl. J. Psycho-analysis*, vol. 71, pp. 95-106

Tambiah, S.J.(1990), *Magic, Science, Religion and the Scope of Rationality*, Cambridge: Cambridge University Press.

Uzoka, A.F.(1979), 'The myth of the nuclear family', *Amer. Psychol.*, vol. 34, pp. 1095-1106

Uzoka, A.F.(1980), 'The African child and the dilemma of changing family functions: a psychological perspective', *African Social Research*, vol. 30, pp. 851-867.

Winnicott, D.W.(1967), 'The location of cultural experience', *Internatl. J. Psycho-Anal.*, vol. 48, pp. 368-372.

Winnicott, D.W.(1988), *Human Nature*, London: Free Association Books.

4 Cultural Fragmentation and Mental Distress

Introduction

In contemporary Nigeria, whether it is seen as one collective culture or as a cluster of many cultures, there are cultural themes and sociopolitical stresses that give rise to mental distress. I do not use the term 'mental illness', because that can lead to sterile controversy. Only an exceptionally captious critic would object to the proposition that there are many pressures and conflicts in Nigeria that are likely to discourage positive mental health.

This chapter is partly based upon the impressions of a psychologist who has been teaching psychology and practising as a psychotherapist and counsellor in Nigerian universities for some eight years and is also based upon research reported in Bloom and Amatu (1982) and Bloom (1978, 1982, 1982a, 1982b), so that a total of over 100 autobiographies and nearly 100 essays on 'anomie' have been studied, all of which were collected from university students with no more precise focus required of the writers than to write about their own experience of growing-up, and to ignore the formal material of textbook treatments. No doubt the sample is too highly educated and therefore neither representative nor random. But it is arguable that students are at the very focus of the conflicts of a changing society, and that the stresses that they experience are likely to be experienced by other sectors of society as they become embedded into the tensions of change.

And one caveat: it is not my argument that contemporary Nigeria is a 'sick society, nor is such a position necessary. Mental distress is encouraged or even forced upon people - collectively or individually - by many sociopolitical factors; but one may be moved, even humbled, by the many emotionally balanced Nigerians in a society that is far from encouraging emotional stability.

The essential problem that Nigerian children have to solve is how to accomplish Erikson's fundamental life-task: that of achieving a sense of 'Basic Trust' towards oneself and towards one's fellows. Erikson (1959) and Jahoda (1985) regard Basic Trust as the foundation of a healthy personality and it is the theme of this chapter that there are so many institutionalised experiences of helpless-dependency, presenting the child with feelings of anxiety that persist into adulthood, that a healthy sense of self-reliance and self-esteem is only acquired with difficulty.

By 'Basic Trust' Erikson is not referring to what a lay-person calls 'confidence'. 'Basic Trust' is a naïve and mutual relationship between individuals who have learned that others are consistent, benevolent and caring: that one can trust one's 'outer providers', but that one can also rely upon the capacity of one's own powers to satisfy one's urges and needs. 'Basic Trust' is associated with an optimism about the real world and the world of dreams, that giving and receiving are dependable qualities of human relationships. But a sense of confidence is not sufficient: many a child or adult is trusting without having confidence in its powers and without a sense of optimism. Many a child or adult is sufficiently strong and confident to get what it wants but has no accompanying sense of trust, nor the ability to make reciprocal relationships.

Marie Jahoda (1958) has approached the related problem of defining successful adjustment to society, by adopting a model of mental health that comprises six factors which, taken as a whole, parallel but go beyond Erikson's 'Basic Trust' Jahoda suggests that mental health is positive and is not reducible to the absence of psychopathology. Mental health includes: self-confidence, self-esteem and the ability to use one's strengths and limitations; growth or self-realisation; the developing capacity to use one's potentialities; resistance to stress; a sense of autonomy, or of independence from social pressures, and the ability to choose for oneself so far as society permits it; empathy or social sensitivity; the ability to form relationships in work, love and recreation, together with the ability to master the social environment to achieve such relationships. The underlying theme of Jahoda's and Erikson's formulations is that the mentally healthy individual is striving to become a self-confident yet socially sensitive individual, neither crippled by a low self-esteem nor crushed by an over-constraining society and culture.

Describing her work as a psychoanalyst in Ahmedabad, India, Mrs. Kamalini Sabhai has described two typical psychiatric problems: the young male who is anxious, afraid of a strict father, unable to make independent decisions; and the 'first-generation learner' who comes from an illiterate family and breaks down under the pressure of social change (Dinnage, 1981). These are indeed the root-problems of difficulties about identity experienced by young people growing up in a rapidly changing society - an 'identity vacuum' is created by the dissolving of traditional, agrarian roles, statutes and values that it takes time to fill by urban-industrial life.

Nigeria, like India, is undergoing considerable social stress. There are massive cultural and social transformations occurring, in which the relationships of caring for others and being cared for are in confusion. Growing up is difficult if one does not know what sort of a world one is growing up into. If also one is uncertain of one's relationships with people, then neither of the broad factors of socialisation are effectively predictable. Erikson's view of the successful development of identity, is that it can only be accomplished when the child's experiences and relationships lead to a 'successful alignment of the individual's basic drives with his endowment and opportunities'. The ego is cumulative, and is developed with the continuity of the feelings of sameness and familiarity where the sense of ego has a positive meaning for one's fellows. The child accrues a sense of self-esteem and self-respect from his relationships, where the developmental process takes place within a sociocultural reality that is understood and is experienced with a sense of accomplishment.

A Segmentary Society

The sociocultural reality of contemporary Nigeria is close to that which Durkheim (1933) described as 'segmental, in which the society is divisible into 'quite small compartments which completely envelop the individual', often on a clan base, and increasingly the structures enjoy a lesser degree of interdependence. The segmental society tends to be anomic: the sense of collective consciousness and communion is slight, the individual becomes isolated because society is unable to integrate the individual with society generally but encapsulates the individual in a tiny islet of claustrophobic neighbourhood and kin in a sea of strangers. Moreover, economic and social activities are intensely individualistic, class conflict, is common and a multiplicity of often-conflicting moralities is stronger than the sense of collective unity - a unity that is difficult or impossible for the individual to imagine. It is a world in which it is more and more difficult to feel at home except in a small collectivity, in which therefore most people are strangers and in which, as urbanisation and industrialisation take away many of the functions of family, family and neighbourhood only give the illusion of familiarity and cohesion.

All societies, it is true, have their segments and their hierarchies, but it is striking that these constraints are so continuously and anxiously discussed and experienced in Nigeria. It matters very much in one's everyday living that one's age, sex, ethnic affiliation, family and kinship connections are of the right kind to permit the individual to accomplish what needs to be accomplished. Above all, wealth and the influence and power flowing from wealth, define who one is, what one may do, and what one may as well forget about trying to do.

The preamble to the Nigerian constitution laudably refers to the need to create a unified people, implying that the people are not, now, united. Because the economic and politico-social systems actively drive Nigerians to define themselves in segmentary terms, it is difficult to perceive oneself as an individual Nigerian: one is forced to perceive oneself as defined by the momentary, situationally functional, identity.

In developmental terms this has the effect of socialising the individual into learned helplessness: it is only possible to cope with the demands of everyday living by allowing one's identity to be absorbed by a group. The tacit power or influence of a group to which one belongs is a strong determining factor in whether one succeeds, or fails, in getting what one wants. If one is confronted by an alien group, or by a person with more group-power than that of one's own group, then there is little or no personal or individual power upon which one can depend. The sociopolitical message runs: 'Help me, I'm an Ibibio...like you'. 'Help me, I'm your cousin, and you are my rich and powerful relative'. 'Help me, you have got magical powers'. Society teaches the individual that one is worthless, incompetent and feeble. It is psychologically ominous that already the legitimated sociopolitical segments, that is, local states and Local Government Areas, are characterised by paranoic suspicions and prickliness, and show few of the open and welcoming qualities of healthy self-confident and trusting egos.

The sociopolitical system appears to be rapidly converting Nigeria into a society in which everyone is an 'expatriate', and in which there are, therefore, strong social pressures to feel anxious about membership of a particular segment, to be prone to respond suspiciously and aggressively towards other people of different segments, and to be uncomfortably aware of being 'different' from one's fellows.

Authoritarianism

The notion of the F (authoritarian) scale has been in the literature since Adorno (1950). It is my impression that the nine major personality variables are encouraged by Nigerian sociopolitical pressures, at least among the more educated of the population.

The variables are: conventionalism; authoritarian submission; authoritarian aggression; anti-intraception; superstition and stereotypy; power and toughness; destructiveness and cynicism; projectivity and sex. Authoritarianism is a strong and pervasive quality: both the tendency to accept the authority of the in-group and the tendency to stigmatise in moralistic terms those who are unconventional or critical of authority. There is a marked preoccupation with power and toughness: the comment: 'What Nigerians need is a strong leader' and the praise of military heads of state as 'strong leaders' illustrate the search for a dominating father-figure to bring his unruly offspring into order. There is an increasing tendency towards destructiveness of both human and natural resources, accompanied by a cynical disregard for the value of being human, and of the need to preserve the world for the succeeding generations. The destructiveness in the human sphere is indicated by the indifference to improving the low level of such basic needs as water, power, education and public health, so that many people are allowed to live in discomfort, ill-health and ignorance. Destructiveness in the sphere of natural resources is indicated by the indifference to improving and preserving the natural world, so that forests have been destroyed, slums created and the basic ecology of huge areas irreparably damaged. There is a tendency underlying much decision-making and many official relationships, to ignore (at the least), or (at the worst) positively to disparage human considerations, that often touches upon moral sadism.

An approach to the understanding of authoritarianism is that of Erich Fromm whose analysis of *The Fear of Freedom* opens with an analysis of freedom as a psychological problem. Freedom, according to Fromm's analysis, is a specific kind of social relationship of individuals to one another, in which 'the longing for submission and the lust for power' are subordinated to co-operation with others and the development of individuality and self-consciousness. One refuge from the burdens of social and economic uncertainties and change and from the burdens of growing up is to become bound to what Fromm describes as a 'magic helper': a magic helper enables the group or the individual to escape from freedom into a personification of the protecting parents. 'An inability to stand alone and to fully express his own individual potentialities' (Fromm, 1945), drives lonely, unconfident, untrusting, and unspontaneous people into searching for dependency relationships that may lead them into loyalty to a so-called charismatic leader, or to an organisation such as a sect, political party, a religion or a philosophy, that will provide the answers to doubts and some reassurance against insecurity.

Fromm describes how the social, political and intellectual dissolution of the Middle Ages in Europe caused emotional insecurity that indirectly encouraged the proliferation of 'magic helpers' in Europe in individual or collective guises. There are cogent parallels between the sociopolitical situation in contemporary Nigeria and the breakdown of the security of the Middle Ages in Europe as described by Fromm. In particular, the dissolution of the bonds of traditional rural communities, and the replacement of simple and convincing explanations of the nature of society by complex and often contradictory moral, religious, and philosophical assumptions about the changing world. The very rough winds of the adult world in Nigeria are too strong for many people, and for many communities an authoritarian shelter from the anxieties of everyday life, although ultimately spurious, is temporarily and immediately alluring.

Nigeria is characterised by many strongly authoritarian relationships and values, in which punitive and protective elements are mingled. Much social and administrative practice swings unpredictably between over-protection and over-control at the one extreme to repressive, sometimes vindictive, punitiveness at the other. The response of society to young people, for example students, is a cogent example. Students are effectively inhibited from experiencing the need and the opportunity for independence and maturity in their work, their lives and in the practice of shared, mature responsiblity: 'Here are your hostels!' 'Here is your food!' 'Here is how you must behave!' 'These are the things you must learn!' 'This is what you must believe!' The latent message from society is that if the students want to be good children then they will be obedient and passive children. The reward will be that they will graduate and probably will get jobs and join the army of other good children in the wider society - hedonistic, uncritical - and wasted. But if students question the conditions in which they live, the content of their studies, or the nature of the relationships with their teachers, and if they retain sufficient sense of independence to question the quality of the society into which they will pass after their graduation, then the repressive mechanisms of society operate. These mechanisms are not simply the raw crudities of police assaults, rustications and 'kangaroo courts', but the more menacing knowledge that unless one conforms, one's economic, personal and social future may be ruined irretrievably.

Nigerians, both young and old, therefore become caught in a constant tension, because of the interaction of Authoritarianism with not infrequent bursts of collective and individual anarchic rebelliousness. The learned-helplessness, the heavy social and emotional penalties for resisting authority, the rewards for obedience, together combine to shift the locus of control away from the self and onto others - mother or father, the family, the government, international companies, expatriates, richer countries, other ethnic groups. Yet, despite the ubiquity of authoritarian controls, there are contradictory exhortations to be responsible, independent and mature. The double-bind message from society is that although one should be independent and self-directed, this kind of behaviour is dangerous because society will repress such temerity for its supposedly disruptive and 'destabilising' (the latest cant word) effects. Stylised exhortations are accompanied by institutionalised bullying!

The society is authoritarian and punitive for another reason: it is a society often close to bursting into anarchic reaction against the prevailing authoritarianism, so that even a minor shift of the locus of control towards the individual and away from the elders, authority and the many self-imposed quasi-parents is perceived as threatening. At all levels of social and political behaviour, there is a tendency for 'authority' to treat people as potentially naughty children and no one is free of the emotional anticipation of a beating - actual or metaphorical - by authority.

One potentially dangerous result of the tension between never ceasing to being treated as a child while always being commanded to be an adult, is that the search for a saviour, for a loving, accepting and understanding father and mother, diverts individual and collective attention from the political task of examining the roots of the emotional conflicts that are generated by society. There can be little success in reducing conflict until its emotional causes are rationally examined. Hero worship, moreover, in a country apparently blessed with few heroes (and fewer heroines) encourages those with meretricious qualities of leadership strenuously to offer themselves as saviours. But, as coup after coup in many countries in similar straits has shown, saviours fail again and again because sociopolitical instability can only be reduced when emotional stability is generated naturally, within a benign society in which a feeling of belonging to society does not clash with the equally pressing human need to be independent in a environment that can be trusted.

Aggression

Relationships that provoke anxiety frequently generate frustrations that tend to create hostility and aggression. Much of Nigerian everyday life is characterised by a readiness for aggressive posturing, on both individual and collective levels. Even institutionalised relationships of an impersonal kind, for example, of bank clerk and customer, can expand into an aggressive conflict of wills, a confrontation of statuses, of ethnic identities, of male against female, of the apparently stronger against the weaker (Bloom and Amatu 1982). Daily life can therefore be baffling, bruising and humiliating: baffling, because one is forced to search one's conscience in case one was unintentionally the cause of offence; bruising, because one is often driven to defend oneself aggressively against abuse and humiliating, because one is made to feel that one is intruding, making unreasonable demands, without rights and without an identity worthy of another's respect.

Direct and indirect factors explain aggression in contemporary Nigeria. The most striking direct factor is the ferocious competition for highly-valued and scarce resources; status, prestige, power and wealth, which in the view of Uchendu (1977) has now become institutionalised in ethnic and class structures. Bloom (n.d.) goes further, arguing that sibling rivalry (that most destructive of all rivalries) is provoked by a socioeconomic system in which a crudely competitive ethos is intensified by 'traditional' non-economic rivalries. An indirect factor is the melting away of the traditional patterns of interpersonal relationships and mutual respect, for which few compensating new relationships have yet developed in urban life.

Earlier generations would probably have found it incomprehensible that in Nigeria, a society once deeply sensitive to community, both individuals and groups are engaged in struggling for power and prestige and are torn asunder by society's ambiguous signals, that simultaneously legitimate the struggles for power and prestige (whatever may be their undesirable consequences for the society as a whole), and inconsistently urge that one honours and is loyal to the many groups to which one belongs. Aggression appears to be widely valued for its own sake as the essential element in mastery over one's fellows. It is, moreover, intensified by its unconscious deflection towards motivating the repression of the deeper, older sense of obligation to one's fellows, becoming in the process transmuted into the apprehensive aggression of those deeply guilty for their bad behaviour. The ferocity of aggressive posturing in everyday life is as highly significant as the suddeness with which the aggression melts away. Correspondingly, where prestige and power are threatened, the ferocity of reprisals is often bewilderingly replaced by a situation in which both sides appear to have lost interest in the situation or problem that was the manifestation of an underlying conflict. Fraternal rivalry and disloyalty, as well as filial conflict are never far from consciousness and the psychocultural defences against their erupting into open aggression, individual or collective, are frail.

Identity

Basic Trust is at the root of the problems of the formation of identity, individual and social. If one's life experiences do not offer the individual a satisfying and stable sense of Basic Trust, no sense of identity can develop and the individual is in danger of growing up emotionally immature, because he is overly-dependent and socially insensitive. Much of Nigeria's psychoculture seems to encourage emotions and relationships inimical to the formation of Basic Trust, and indeed breeds what humanistic psychologists, for example Mahrer (1978), describe as 'disintegrative' and 'unfeeling' emotional states. The former include, for example, such qualities as a sense of turmoil, incompleteness, anxiety, fear and guilt and of 'being rent apart'. The latter include such less specific but nevertheless pervasive feelings as 'numbness', 'being in a fog' and 'narrowed nothingness'. Am I, I wonder, the only psychologist in Nigeria who is increasingly concerned about the growing numbers of young men and women who complain initially about a somatic disturbance that is rapidly transmuted into distress about the meaninglessness of life in a materialistic and rapacious society, where there are educational, social, economic and ideological obstacles to developing and expressing one's individuality, where there are pressures to conform that are often overwhelming, rendering individuals impotent and so feeling that they are the playthings of an indifferent or capricious society?

In brief, many young Nigerians are growing up in conditions of dire existential muddle arising, in part, from the multiplicity of changing and contradictory norms and values, and in part from the inability of the society to foster individual diversity within a sociocultural harmony. Or, as Peter

Berger expresses it in his analysis of the political ethics of social change in the 'Third World': 'Human beings have the right to live in a meaningful world. Respect for this right is a moral imperative for policy' (Berger, 1977). There is no 'cognitive map' of an acceptable reality and a desirable future to which young Nigerians can readily refer, because of the profusion of contradictory norms and of the inability of society (in general), and social institutions (like education), to generate effective concern about the future.

The proliferation of norms is compounded by the lingering belief that there is a legacy of 'colonial mentality' that inhibits the growth of a sense of an independent Nigerian identity. But it seems equally probable that compared with the contemporary and actual economic, social and political problems of everyday living, the so-called 'colonial mentality' is indeed a trivial factor, not infrequently used as a rationalisation to explain away embarrassingly perplexing socio-economic and political problems. How much longer will it be permissible to blame the the receding past for the problems of the present, without its being suggested that such a retreat from the present is, in psychoanalytic terms, regressive, even to the point of being irrational (at the very least) or neurotic? The longer that explanations in terms of the 'colonial' past persist and are believed, the more difficult it will be for a socially and emotionally meaningful sense of national identity to emerge and the more difficult it will be for individuals to emerge from the shelter of local identities such as the family, village and ethnic group. To remain fixated in the past is to remain fixated in infancy and to refuse to grow up. Infancy may partially explain the motivations of the present, but it cannot rationally be used as a justification for the present. Once a society, like a patient, has discovered the bad things that have happened in the past and has faced the shock of the discovery, neither the memory nor the confrontation can be used as an excuse to dwell forever in the nirvana of infancy. Mental health, collective no less than individual, depends upon a society's evolving mechanisms to minimise the never ending clash between the pleasure-principle and the reality-principle, however painful the enforced processes of growing up that are entailed.

To develop a sense of identity as a Nigerian is difficult. Many Nigerians are steadily compelled to become almost anything else, and have to find their sense of identity in whatever membership and reference groups that one is able to connect with, and to suffer the emotional consequences of being reduced to a unit in a segmented, atomistic world. *Anomie* is, therefore, rife. Insecurity, feelings of emptiness, of being split from one's fellows, are common and are indicated by the nationwide brooding about identity that frequently is intensive and almost compulsive. The preoccupation with ethnic and other local definition of identity is compounded by the politically-generated doubts about the nature of Nigerian identity into conflicting and tugging loyalties that show no signs of melting positively together. It seems unlikely that there will be striking changes in the economic-political significance of both the wider and narrower identities in the near future, so there seems little prospect of Nigeria becoming a 'melting pot' of identities any more than America has become one.

It is significant of the social guilt that accompanies the notion of 'ethnicity', that the term 'culture' has begun to replace the notion of ethnic identity and to acquire its own growing prominence. But it too is permeated by a strong ambivalence: it is used very loosely to describe favourably almost any kind of 'non-Western' (not even African, much less Nigerian) kind of dancing, singing, writing... that could be taken to be an expression of a cultural identity. Yet it appears to carry no noticeably deep pride nor sense of belonging, nor is it accompanied by any sensitivity to discriminating rubbish from the worthwhile. It is almost as though it is good enough that anything is good enough if its source is not too obviously from the 'Western' world! Identity through the newly-found notion of 'culture' is one more negative and restricting definition of identity. Moreover, culture (as in all societies) is a conglomeration and includes magic, superstition and the occult, hostility to innovation and to creativity, and an intense ambivalence about the relationships of Nigeria with the outside world, particularly with the western, more industrialised world. There are still active elements of culture that conflict with the rationalist-technological ethos of westernisation, but this conflict is not wholly dysfunctional, because the older, traditional culture has the positive function of providing a link with the world that is now waning. Even though that link is strained, and often appears to be the creation of the efforts and exhortations of those using the mass media, it is a temporary source of security in a changing world - a splint that the patient knows must be discarded, but is reluctant to discard.

A Role for Psychology?

George Miller (1973) has argued persuasively that the real impact of the profession of psychology will be felt 'not through the technological products it places in the hands of powerful men, but through its effects on the public at large, through a new and different public perception of what is humanly possible and what is humanly desirable'. A responsible psychologist in Nigeria, even when carrying out his professional duties, has a moral imperative to consider:

1. The human consequences of the sociopolitical system in which he is doing his job.

2. The professional duty to alleviate the emotional distress that is caused by those social conditions, although he may be unwilling to participate in action to change them.

This moral imperative cannot be hidden behind the plea that a psychologist's duty is to his profession and that this duty can only be carried out if he is professionally detached from society's problems. The psychologist by the very act of being a psychologist 'is professionally committed. Unlike most other scientists, he cannot maintain, even professionally, a state of complete political neutrality. He must report what he finds to be the case...' (Mace, 1973), even though this may offend or appear to give support to both those with radical and those with conservative social or political philosophies. (See, e. g. Bloom, 1982.)

To return to Foucault: the fragmentation of identity and the conflicts within it reflect a society's inability to confront its own conflicts. Nigeria, a society that claims to be democratic in its institutions and its values, is far from being an egalitarian, participatory democracy. Socio-economic and political goals and aspirations fail to match the actual social, political and economic frameworks. Besides, socio-economic change has proved to be too painful because it has been acutely disorientating, the future is uncertain and threatening and the past, with all its ethnicity, narrow loyalties and cosy 'familism' is still a tempting retreat.

The collective role of a handful of psychologists, of whom few are in a position directly to influence public policy, is necessarily modest in scope though it may be widespread in influence: to do all it can to assist the quiet voice of reason to be heard by more and more people. Freud consistently saw the role of psychology as contributing to the rejection of illusion and to the submission to truth. He recognised that the economic and political circumstances of people influence their intellectual and ethical attitudes, and warned that the conservatism of tradition may well resist the 'incentives of a new economic situation' (Freud, 1973) which appears to include social and political conditions more broadly conceived. Freud would probably approve of the task of our profession to be active - more active than we have been - in protecting reason's quiet and persistent voice from being smothered by the din of unimaginative conservative and radical extremes, and indeed to extend the range of that voice.

The profession is in danger of reflecting the wider society's ambivalence between 'individualistic atomism' and 'authoritarian collectivism', and is less aware than it should be of its role in evaluating and publicising the consequences of public policies which in effect veer and tack between encouraging atomism or collectivism, without regard for the possible consequences for mental health. Does one ever hear the advocates of public policies express concern, or even curiosity, about the consequences for mental health of their policies? It is, for example, never asked if policies encourage or discourage a more trusting and less suspicious communal life, or if they depress or energise people? Do policies contribute to the development of acceptable strategies for the avoidance and resolution of social conflict, both between groups, and between the individual and the group? Are individual differences in tastes and talents rewarded or punished by, for example, the ethos of the examination system? Are competence and a sense of achievement stimulated or frustrated by society?

The most urgent task of the profession is, therefore, tirelessly to point out the consequences for mental health of morbid social arrangements and political policies, and to explore, and to encourage and assist other professions to explore, ways to reduce and ultimately to eliminate the grosser harmful social **obstacles to mental health**. This does not require any more psychiatrists nor mental hospitals nor drugs. It requires a reorientation of society's concern about the individual citizen, so that the duty of society to hearten and to stimulate its members gradually becomes the standard by which policies are judged.

References

Adorno, T.(1950), *The Authoritarian Personality*, New York: Harper.
Berger, P.L.(1977), *Pyramids of Sacrifice*, Harmondsworth: Penguin.
Bloom, L.(1978), 'Values and attitudes of young Nigerians: Responses to social change', *West African J. of Sociology & Political Science*, vol. 2, pp. 99-115.
Bloom, L.(1982a), 'Socialisation and dependence in Nigeria', *J. of Social Psychology*, vol. 117, pp. 3-12.

Bloom, L.(1982b), 'Lying and Culture: A West African case-study', *J. of Psychoanalytic Anthropology*, vol. 3(2), pp. 175-184.

Bloom, L.(1982c), 'Applying Psychology in the Third World', *Bulletin of the British Psychological Society*, vol. 35, pp. 143-146.

Bloom, L.(1984), 'Psychological aspects of wealth in poorer societies', *The Journal of Psychoanalytic Anthropology*, vol.7(2), pp. 189-208.

Bloom, L. and Amatu, H.I.(1982), 'Aggression in Nigeria: A psychoethnogaphy', in A.P. Goldstein and M.H. Segall (eds), *Aggression in Global Perspective*, New York: Pergamon.

Dinnage, R.(1981), 'Going crazy in India', *New York, Review of Books*, vol. 18, pp. 52-56.

Durkheim, E.(1933), *The Division of Labour in Society*, Chicago: The Free Press. (translation of: *De la division au travail social*, Paris: 1893).

Erikson, E.H.(1959), *Identity and the Life Cycle*, New York: International Universities Press.

Foucault, M.(1976), *Mental Illness and Psychology*, New York: Harper and Row. (translation of: *Maladie Mentale et psychologie*, Paris: PUF, 1954.)

Freud, S.(1973), *New Introductory Lectures*, Harmondsworth: Penguin.

Fromm, E.(1945), *The Fear of Freedom*, London: Kegan Paul.

Jahoda, M.(1958), *Common Concepts of Mental Health*, New York: Basic Books.

Mace, C.A.(1973), 'Democracy as a problem in social psychology', in *Selected Papers*. London: Methuen.

Mahrer, A.R.(1978), *Experiencing: A Humanistic Theory of Psychology and Psychiatry*, New York: Brunner/Mazel.

Miller, G.A.(1973), 'Psychology as a means of promoting human welfare', in G.A. Miller, *Psychology - The Science of Mental Life*. New York: Harper and Row.

Uchendu, V.C.(1977), 'The cultural roots of aggressive behaviour in modern African politics', *J. of Asian & African Studies*, vol. 12, pp.99-107.

5 Ethnic Identity: A Psychoanalytic Critique

'Beware of those who prefer to individuals the idea of humanity that they have invented.'
Andre Gide (1948, p. 1290)

Introduction

In this chapter[1] I examine ethnicity and identity-formation in South Africa. I use psychoanalytic theories of some pathological aspects of narcissism to interpret how ethnic identity is an attempt to defend the self against feelings of vulnerability and inferiority that are concealed by manifest aggressive and assertive social behaviour. It is claimed that the intensity and persistence of ethnicity in South Africa is one of the results of racist ideologies and practices, and it is therefore implied that as racism is abated so will the intensity of ethnicity diminish.

Approaches to Understanding Narcissism

It is one of the paradoxes of Freud's thought that his paper 'On Narcissism' (1914) should lead to discussions of the psychology of group behaviour in *'Group Psychology and the Analysis of the Ego'*, (1921) and *'The Ego and the Id'*, (1923). Freud showed how intimately related, indeed how inseparable, were the motivations and emotional states that explain individual and social behaviour.

   Freud's basic position is that there are two stages in the development of narcissism: primary and secondary. The origins of primary narcissism are in early infancy when the baby is interested in no other world but its own body. Although in reality it lives in a world of Others upon whom it depends for its very survival, for nourishment and love, it gives little or nothing in return. Only gradually does the external world impinge upon the infant, who only gradually relates to Others with whom it can — and does normally — have emotional, affectional and libidinal relationships. Fenichel (1982) also traces narcissism back to early infancy, when the infant mistakenly seems to act as though she or he were in control of the world. The experience of early infancy creates and reinforces these feelings. From the very start of life, therefore, the infant is in contact with a world beyond the self, even though this is not appreciated until infancy begins to metamorphose into childhood. The significance of these earliest experiences cannot be underestimated:

> The individual's experiences connected with omnipotence lead to a most significant need of the human mind. The longing for the oceanic feeling of primary narcissism can be called the "narcissistic need". "Self-esteem" is the awareness of how close the individual is to the original omnipotence...Narcissistic feelings of well-being are characterised by the fact that they are felt as a reunion with an omnipotent force in the external world, brought about either by incorporating parts of this world or by the phantasy of being incorporated by it. (Fenichel, 1982, p. 40)

The original libidinal love gradually becomes love of the ego as well as of the bodily self and a secondary narcissism is formed. Others become loved as though they were part of the self, because the Others contribute to the individual's efforts to maintain self-esteem. Emotional maturity is achieved to the extent that individuals can give up the narcissistic attempt to control the significant others in their world and are free to feel independent and autonomous, no longer trapped in the contradictory ambivalence of desperately withdrawing from a world that fails to provide sufficient support for the self, or by compulsively trying to absorb the world and thus control it. Both delusions – of external threat and loss support, and internal insecurity and self-doubt – arise from the same primal, unconscious feelings of frailty.

The development of self-regard and of the ego-ideal open 'an important avenue for the understanding of group psychology. In addition to its individual side, this ideal has a social side; it is also the common ideal of a family, class or a nation' (Freud, 1984, p. 96). Collectively, just as individually, we may deal with feelings of impotence and insecurity, and with our real and phantasy external threats, by retreating behind a paranoiac, narcissistic defence. The group may, like an individual, present an ideal self that appears to be strong, assertive and integrated. But that illusory or False self may conceal a self that is unable to love, to accept and to trust relationships with others, who are perceived as nonsupportive, and therefore, threatening.

The emotional roots of adult narcissism are seen in the individual's early responses to the many and varied traumata of living. These traumata are partly caused by the relationships and stresses of one's society, but they are introjected, interpreted and experienced by individuals. Narcissism is essentially an angry withdrawal from or repudiation of relationships. It is an active process: 'a person's inner life is not a given, it is a construction. My life is ultimately my own; narcissism smothers that creation, does not allow it' (Symington, 1993, p. 124). But 'life' can, of course, make it more or less difficult to enjoy my own creation. Narcissism precludes creation other than a paranoiac interpretation of the world, because the individual's relationships are confined to what he or she phantasises can be dominated, and what cannot be dominated may be coldly rejected or angrily destroyed and is denied any independent existence in the world of the narcissist.

The *unnarcissistic* individual is not motivated by the Kleinian fear of annihilation and is not driven to project inner anger and destructiveness onto the external world as a distraction from primal anxieties. Nor does the unnarcissistic individual reject relationships with the 'life-giver': that is, 'an emotional object ... that a person seeks as an alternative to seeking himself ... the source of creative emotional action' (Symington, 1993, p. 35). The unnarcissistic individual actively welcomes relationships with the external world, and is enlivened and not threatened by Others. Not needing to protect himself from inner anger or invasive Others, there is no need to retreat behind the mask of the Winnicottian False self.

More explicitly political are the emotional bonds between leaders and the led: the led identify with the leader, making him (her) a part of their own identities. The led are relieved of their anxieties by their extreme dependence, they exclude those who do not share their leader from shared relationships, their self-love is fostered by their reverence of their leader, their aggression is readily directed towards those Others whom they see as threatening to the quasi-family, the ethnic or national group. 'In the undisguised antipathies and aversions which people feel towards strangers... we may recognise the expression of self-love – of narcissism. This self-love works for the preservation of the individual and behaves as though the occurrence of any divergence from his own particular lines of development involved a criticism of them and a demand for their alteration' (Freud, 1985,

p. 131). Freud wondered why we seize upon specific sensitivities as a provocation to group aggression or antipathy. To suggest that our group sensitivities can be traced back to historical and sociocultural situations and relationships, does little to explain their spontaneous eruption and their often long-term self-destructive quality.

Ethnicity: Sociocultural Approaches

There are two possible reasons why 'ethnicity' is so significant an issue in South Africa. Firstly, because even opponents of racist governments have often used 'ethnic' arguments to oppose racist ones. Secondly, although governments have abandoned piecemeal the glaring crudeness of blatant racist arguments, the consequences of racist policy and practice will persist until the 'new' South Africa is psychologically firmly established. Alexander (1984, p. 10) argues that 'ethnicity' is a disguised belief in 'some kind of Divine Will or biological-cum-cultural fate that allegedly "explains" why collectivities of people behave in certain ways', and which divert them from realistic political understanding and action. For Alexander the central questions about 'ethnicity' are historical. It makes neither sociological nor anthropological sense to *assume* that 'ethnic groups' are real – whatever ethnic awareness may be observed or inferred. 'Ethnicity' is an invention. It is one of the many inventions that function as defences against the historically current anxieties of the politically active members of a group. Alexander claims that studies of the emergence of 'ethnicity' in South Africa began to appear from the early 1970s, when ethnic arguments became expedient for both Africans and whites. Africans needed to mobilise political action against the dominant racist ideologies, while the latter felt that it was necessary to formulate a racist ideology that would legitimate *apartheid* separation, inequality and the cruelty employed to enforce them. It can be argued that both politically active Africans and whites were desperately and for similar reasons, rationalising their urgent efforts at building an enduring and aggressive national sentiment and identity. The tenor of Alexander's (1984) argument is that 'ethnicity' is a political construction, or a weapon in political warfare. Ethnic 'consciousness is not some kind of epiphenomenal illusion' (ibid., p. 13) that mysteriously hovers like a malignant political storm cloud. It can gain or lose salience as it is fomented and employed by political leaders. It can be interpreted only by understanding the socio-historical realities – conflicts, rivalries, stresses, constraints and opportunities – that directly and indirectly shape consciousness.

A more orthodox anthropological discussion is that of Ronald Cohen whose review paper notes that 'the terms "ethnicity" and "ethnic" refer to what was before often subsumed under "culture", "cultural" and "tribal" ' (Cohen, 1978, p. 379). The changes in official terminology in South Africa and the political terms used, illustrate how labelling both indicates and shapes social, political and economic practice. A few examples may suffice. In 1888, Rhodes declared: 'We are to be lords over them and let them be a subject race'. In 1929, Smuts was still talking of 'the natives', whose urbanisation and 'detribalisation' were causing the difficulties of 'colour problem'. The term 'race' was still used in 1948 in National and United Parties' policy statements, and in 1956 in the Tomlinson Commission Report on the economic, social and political implementation of 'Race Separation'. But the Tomlinson Report and government magazines such as **Bantu** were introducing the new term 'Bantu', which was gradually replaced by 'White' and 'Black'- later without capitals – although the so-called Bantustans divided the African population into notionally 'ethnic' groups. Insulting terms, like 'kaffir' or 'kaffir boetie', have vanished from acceptable public discourse, and even the neo-Nazi whites use the word 'African' or black.

Cohen (1978) summarises the anthropological use of 'ethnicity' as a '*series* of nesting dichotomisations of inclusiveness and exclusiveness. The process of assigning persons to groups is both subjective and objective, carried out by self and others, and depends on what diacritics are used to define membership' (ibid., p. 387). Ethnicity is no more than a 'set of descent-based cultural identifiers used to assign persons to groupings that expand and contract in inverse relation to the scale of inclusiveness and exclusiveness of the membership' (ibid., p. 387). Ethnic boundaries are therefore neither stable nor continuous, but fluctuate and change in response to shifting individual loyalties and identifications in changing political and social circumstances. Ethnicity is, therefore, a function of specific historical and social situations, and an individual's or a group's 'ethnicity' will be 'categorised according to different criteria of relevance in different situations...In one situation it may be occupation, in another education, in a third, ethnicity' (ibid., p. 388). But whatever the manifest criteria, the latent criterion is the conflict initiated by competition for scarce economic and political resources, that is, power. And 'power', a political reality, is also a complex emotional need, the origins of which are buried in the power struggles of early childhood within the family (or whatever replaces, or fails to replace, it).

'Ethnic communities' are examples of the 'imagined communities' analysed by Benedict Anderson. The 'imagined political community...imagined as both inherently limited and sovereign' is imagined because its members 'will never know most of their fellow-members, meet them, or even hear of them, yet in the minds of each lives the image of their communion' (Anderson, 1983, p. 15). They are limited because 'even the largest of them [the smallest, no less] has finite if elastic boundaries... [Also], regardless of the actual inequality and exploitation that may prevail in each, the nation is always conceived a deep, horizontal comradeship' (ibid., 16). This imagined comradeship can be dissolved by the acid realities of class and the multitude of social, cultural and political interest groups that appear and vanish as urbanisation and industrialisation create changing conflicts about power.   Anderson (1983, p. 146) ends his book by emphasising '*leaderships*, because it is leaderships, not people, who inherit' [the bureaucratic apparatus of power].   We may well be sceptical if the fervour of ethnic separatism is an adequate and rational means to combat the persecution of apartheid, nor is it an effective antidote to the understandable anger, hurt feelings and depression caused by centuries of racism. We may well be cynical about the political motives of the ill-assorted allies that emerged in the last days of the changing South Africa, who were less interested in ethnic identity than in obtaining shares of raw power.

Basil Davidson, in an historical study of colonialism and post-colonial Africa, asserts that 'the Black man's burden' has been 'the curse of the Nation-State, which was adopted as the politically expedient and 'only available escape from colonial domination' (Davidson, 1992, p. 99). He argues that in the anti-colonial struggles, a new nationalistic ethnicity had to adopt two contradictory positions. One position was to uphold traditional cultural identities to counter imported and demeaning colonial, anti-African identities. The other position was to insist that progress was only possible if new, progressive or modern identities were adopted – even if they originated in 'Western' cultures.   Sixty years before Davidson, it was observed that 'the psychology of imperialism is only an extension or development of the psychology of nationalism. The deity is an Empire instead of a nation' (Woolf, 1937, p. 258). The anti-imperialist or anti-racist psychology is in danger of deifying narrow, exclusive and politically expedient ethnic loyalties.

It is arguable that most sociocultural analyses of ethnicity go back to fears of change, of sociocultural absorption, and above all, of the perceived loss of power. Castelnuovo-Tedesco (1989) reduces the fear of change to two fundamental uncertainties, deeply rooted in the early stages of the development of identity. Change, collectively and individually, is emotionally unsettling because changing relationships inevitably arouses early, more primitive feelings and challenges the controls and defence-mechanisms that were formerly stable. Change may offer the possibility of enhancing our self-esteem, or our narcissism may be damaged. The anger and violence of the far-right and Zulu nationalism suggest that both groups fear that future political arrangements may damage their self-esteem, and both live with a past during which their narcissism was unstable and deeply unsatisfying.

Laying the Collective Ghost

The South African passive assent to many forms of 'collective mind' bedevils South Africa's politics, education and social and religious life. It is trite to state that human beings are social animals, but it is absurd and dangerous to ignore or play down that they are individual animals too. Psychoanalysts assert that a group is little more than an 'as if' category, sometimes powerfully oppressive, but always the product of the political or social imaginations of people. Groups, from the family to the nation-state, are treated 'as if' they were coherent, cohesive gestalts without factions or division, that can be understood fully regardless of the wishes, fears and phantasies of the separate individuals who *are* the group. In reality, individuals are responsible for their own decisions and actions and act individually regardless of the group norm. Thus in different circumstances individuals are more or less free to be individuals, to act in a deviant and idiosyncratic way, and to express their perceptions of, and feelings about, the group norm as it appears to relate to them – whether it be an ethnic or any other norm. Decisions, moreover, are not made by 'a group' but by an individual or individuals who, for the time being, have power or authority. Many members of a group may, therefore, do what the group 'decides' for many motives: fear, ignorance, hope, greed, love of the leaders, and so on. But, tomorrow, the conforming people may conform no longer. Even today there may be members who openly resist, and others who hide their reservations or disapproval until it is safer to openly deny or oppose the group norm.

A major reservation about the importance of group influences is that modern societies are made up of many groups, many of which are voluntary so that individuals live within a complex and dynamic web of selected, rejected and everchanging identifications. In modern societies freedom means that individuals may join and leave the groups that satisfy their emotional needs. The 'new' South Africa has already liberated children, women and men to join and to leave many groups, including ethnic groups in which they were once imprisoned and by which they were identified, setting them free to extend their social and emotional relationships. It is possible that in South Africa growing freedom from tight, imposed social groupings will be healing. If, moreover, children become increasingly free to identify with aspects of different groups, however they be defined, South African children may more comfortably develop a complex sense of enjoying multiple identities and identifications.

In brief, people are bonded into their groups, loosely or tightly, to satisfy needs on two interacting levels. On one level are the idiosyncratic needs for security, love, affiliation and sex. On another level are the historically determined needs that are no less fanciful and distant from reality than are our unconscious emotional needs. The mutual fears, aggressions and erratic relationships between Zulu nationalists, the African National Congress (ANC) and the far-right are rooted in both realpolitik and phantasy. The emotional states that prevent accommodation today between the groups, are here today and gone tomorrow. Emotional needs and the external contingencies of living are forever changing and the search for magical fathers to protect and control us is never permanently satisfied.

'Ethnic' and national identities are invented, maintained and lived by people who have their idiosyncratic, unconscious and conscious motives for this obsession. It is no adequate retort that individuals are not responsible for their society's history, culture and social structure. *Individuals* make decisions, rule out alternatives, persuade, con or bully others into superficial conformity, or possess the fleeting charisma of leadership. The collectivist obsession asserts that women, children and men are only units in the Utopian or Draconian ethnic or national identity, and are thereby deprived of two essential attributes of individuality. Firstly, the capacity to contribute their uniqueness to their society and culture. Secondly, the ability to live on individual and social levels. The boundaries between 'I' and 'other' are ambiguous and shifting, and even if – in some rarely precisely defined way – we were creations of our society, individuals are remarkably obstinate in devising and maintaining a self concept that is meaningful and emotionally satisfying, regardless of the constraints and impositions of their social life.

Identity: A Psychoanalytic Approach

The problems of identity are lifelong, and centre about their interrelated self-doubts: 'who am I?' 'What sort of a young person, woman or man am I?' 'How did I come to get that way?' All of these questions deal with the individual's needs for self-recognition and self-esteem, and the individual's answers are coloured by the earliest, and later, intimate relationships during childhood. These relationships are neither exclusively individual nor social. Our feelings of selfhood are the motivating states of knowing who one *really* is. Sharing and concealing our feelings about our selfhood is part of our self-creation, and 'depends on the beliefs we have about what we are now like: on the stories we tell about ourselves' (Glover, 1989, p. 139). We tell these stories to ourselves and to other people, and they may be motivated as powerfully by the need to conceal aspects of ourselves, as by the need to share them. These feelings cannot be reduced to membership of, and acceptance by, a social or cultural group, but may be encouraged or discouraged by society or culture. Even if individuals share a limited, narrow and specific social or cultural experience, for example, the same family in childhood, the same prison cell, the same ethnic or national membership, they tend to cling to their private feelings of singularity, of 'me-ness', or being not-another-person. In South Africa's intensely segmented society it is often a major problem of individual psychological development for children (and adults) to discover, establish and maintain their personal boundaries. In such circumstances, Stephen Frosh (1991) distinguishes three facets of the dilemma of identity.

Firstly, there can be no sense of individual identity unless social and cultural conditions make it possible for individuals to achieve an inner stability and a confident sense of personal continuity. It seems to me that Frosh underestimates the power of the *subjective* and often phantasy-based appraisal of social and cultural condition. In South Africa, for example, many whites and Africans have been living *as if* social and cultural conditions permitted personal continuity, despite the tremendous upheavals that were created by racism. In pre-Nazi Germany and Austria, many Jews lived *as if* their identity as Germans or Austrians was established and unlikely to be broken.

Secondly, there must also be stable, supportive and emotionally satisfying relationships in early childhood. It is through living these relationships that we acquire our ethnic identities. But we acquire the models for our identities indirectly and from a multitude of sources. For some individuals ethnic identity may be the most emotionally important in those circumstances where it is relevant. But for most individuals, moving in and out of the many relationships and circumstances that influence them, ethnicity may be of less or even no importance. During our childhood and adolescence we are in contact with many models from which we construct our sense of self. Moreover, the relationships that we experience in childhood are influenced by irrationality from our childhood fears, wishes, phantasies, misunderstandings and other distortions. But the adults who influence children have their own childhood and adult distortions that they communicate to children. It is difficult to see how there can be any direct and totally accurate communication, from one generation to another, of adult cultural norms and relationships. Frosh appears to overestimate the 'accuracy' of cultural transmission via adult-child relationships.

Thirdly, Frosh argues that only by examining the development of identity and the sense of selfhood, can we decide if the cultural and social worlds are a benign or harmful influence on growing children. Frosh (1991, p. 5) observes that 'the characteristic state of the self can be used as an index of the psychological adequacy of the cultural order.' He argues for an understanding of identity based upon an analysis of the positive and negative ways that our cultural and personal worlds interact to produce an account of the *experience* of what it means to individuals to be a modern person: someone, female or male, child or adult, who lives with the problem of controlling the emotional and identity confusions that are generated by the uncertainties, violence and rapidly kaleidoscopic changing social world.

In the context of South Africa's social history, the intensity of African ethnicity, and the politics built upon it, is an emotional response to white racism. One way of denying the hurtful and demeaning descriptions of being black is by magnifying the group's Zulu-ness. A people forced to deny their history by a dominating group may behave as individuals do when denied, and retreat into a phantasy collective identity, and will construct an historical myth to justify it. In our socially, culturally and economically fragmented and conflictual society, each fragment tends to strive for a narrow and emotionally defensible narcissistic exclusiveness. This collective narcissism reduces individual autonomy, and individuals have to struggle to establish a sense of individual identity and to avoid a deep sense of inauthenticity.

Fanon (1986) explores these problems in his social-psychiatric study of the psychological consequences of colonialism. There are similarities between the psychological problems of decolonisation and those o. modifying ethnicity and racism in South Africa. Frosh (1991) pleaded for an approach to the study of identity that examines the individual's account of the *experience* of what it is to be a 'modern' person. Fanon studied what it means to be a colonised person and a person who is moving out of a colonial society. He makes use of three terms: 'internalisation, objectification, and epidermalisation' (Fanon, 1986, pp. 10,11). Internalisation, is the individual's lifelong struggle to transform sociohistorical reality into a subjective reality. We live in an often threatening and confusing world and need to make sense of that world so that we can minimise the external threat. We also invent an internal reality that, to some extent, protects us from the pain of living. Objectification is the opposite effort to use one's skills, ingenuity and emotional strengths to transform reality into a less painful emotional reality. Epidermalisation is the transformation of economic inferiority and powerlessness into subjective feelings of inferiority. Much of the passion of ethnic politics seems to be similarly motivated by the reactions against the collective depersonalisation of anti-colonial movements. The crises of warring ethnic groups in South Africa are defensive responses by dispossessed, depersonalised and powerless groups that fear that today's narrow narcissism is shortly to be replaced by an enforced and wider narcissism that will leave them still powerless and stigmatised.

The history of ethnic identity is both an account of collusion with 'an illusion of benevolence' (Said, 1994, p. 19) by a ruling power, and a plea for collective recognition. But 'no one today is purely *one* thing. Labels like Indian, or woman, or Muslim, or American are no more than starting points, which if followed into actual experience for only a moment, are quickly left behind' (ibid., 407). One of *apartheid's* 'worst and most paradoxical gifts was to allow people to believe that they were only, mainly, exclusively, white, or black' (ibid., pp. 407-8). The fostered and enforced delusion that South Africans are only, mainly, or exclusively Zulu, Afrikaner, so-called 'Coloured', even children, women or men, persists almost unopposed as we limp into the newish South Africa.

Narcissism, True Self and False Self

'It may be that the spirit of the nation is a phantasy, but that doesn't mean it isn't real' (Wolfenstein, 1993, p. 284). It is real because it is ultimately founded in the emotional turmoil of the interactions of individuals and their society. Growing up means coming to terms with areas of life and relationships from which we are excluded. Individuals go through life experiencing doubts about self-recognition and self-esteem. Our phantasy and the reality of our social worlds are fragmented, because society is a far from unified, cohesive, integrated whole. 'Society' and 'culture', are more or less unconsciously introjected from the tangle of relationships that children live within. The mirror of Lacan's mirror stage is spotted, distorted and often cracked, so that an individual's image is far from perfect and undistorted.

The psychoanalytic view of identity, then, is that children *develop* identities. We are not born with or into one unchanging identity that neatly corresponds with what 'society' defines for us through the significant relationships of early childhood. Sometimes haltingly and painfully, we acquire fragments of identity that we may, or we may not, succeed in combining by adulthood into a more-or-less cohesive and coherent whole that is emotionally satisfying and serviceable for providing us with a (for ourselves) functional sense of continuity. Freud in his introduction to narcissism and his studies of how individuals and their society interact, particularly in *The future of an illusion* (1928) and *Civilisation and its discontents* (1930), demonstrated the essential tensions, conflicts and lack of correspondence between individuals *qua* individuals and individuals *qua* participants in social living.

But what is 'emotionally satisfying'? There seem to be three components, in all of which individual-society tensions are inevitable:

1. Feelings of self-esteem and self-confidence, of worthiness, of feeling wanted and belonging to other people. 'The self is relational. It is always in relation to other selves in the human community...The core of narcissism is a hatred of the relational – a hatred of something that is inherent in our being' (Symington, 1993, p. 18). Society may in reality, or in the individual's phantasy, discourage or totally prevent the relational needs of the individual. One of the most pervasive pathological aspects of ethnicity is that it enforces and shrinks the individual's freedom to relate. Individuals who are imprisoned in their imposed ethnicity or nationality are, therefore, deprived of the emotional freedom to explore the domain of feeling wanted, belonging and self-esteem. The ethnically constrained individuals live within a self-destructive

community. By narcissistically denying the worth of others, the relational is destroyed. When 'others' are denied their autonomous existence because they only exist as the narcissist defines and shapes them, that community provokes the 'others' to live by *their* phantasies to satisfy or neutralise *their* fears and hatred.

2.   Without a sense of competence that one is free and able to control significant parts of one's own life, there can be no healthy ego development. If a community lives in a ghetto or a slum it can only experience a shrivelled sense of its ability to master its physical and social environments. There can be no growth of 'competency motivation', functional play and exploration, without freedom from narrow constraints (White, 1959).

3.   Individuals need to feel secure about their identitities, to the extent that they feel assured that they will not be abolished or destroyed in the future. A conviction of self-continuity and confidence about the boundaries between self and society is an essential – though sometimes little recognised – element of emotional satisfaction.

The development of identity is active and assertive, individuals perceive opportunities and respond emotionally to what they perceive. Choice, lack of choice and emotional resonance together interact in the individual's life-long task of straining for a bearable sense of coherence and self. Imposed ethnicity and nationalism forces individuals to disown possible fragments of identity. 'If you disown part of yourself [individually or collectively], you become a victim of that aspect in other people', or, reaction-formation or projective defences are developed (Symington, 1993, p.27). The narcissism of early childhood leads to childhood's sense of omnipotence. In adult collective narcissism, there is an unconscious return to the safety of childish beliefs in one's own perfection and omnipotence, *and* thereby to the vulnerability and hypersensitivity of childhood.

Fromm (1991), throughout his *The crisis of psychoanalysis*, argues that at the heart of Freud's life-work was an exploration of false consciousness, of the fundamental human hypocrisy: the ability to manipulate individual experiences and feelings to make them appear to fit social and cultural norms. It is no banal observation that 'psychoanalysis teaches one to be sceptical of what a man *says*, because his words usually reveal, at best, only his consciousness; and to read between the lines, to listen with the "third ear", to read his face, his gestures, and every expression of his body' (Fromm, 1991, p. 192). Children do not grow up into ethnic identity: they respond with varied emotions to adults who are significant in their lives, and adults respond to them. Adults offer affiliative and friendly, or hostile and distant relationships and fragments of identity. Children absorb these fragments and relationships, interpret and transform them into feelings and attitudes about themselves and other people in the many situations of life. Children, too, form relationships with other children. Most important, children learn what is safer to repress, disguise or live in the realm of phantasy. For children as for adults, socialisation is a construction: a melange of reality, phantasy, defensiveness and defensive misinterpretation. The ethnic, and other cultures, into which we grow up are only *superficially* gestalts. They are, in reality, things of shreds and patches that we use as far as we need them, and no further:

> Ethnic identity is not necessarily an authentic identity. Individuals strive to 'feel real'. Collective narcissism is no more authentic than individual narcissism: the former is imposed by external fears and phantasies about Others. The latter is imposed by internal fears and unhappy early relationships. (Winnicott, 1965)

Winnicott's (1965) starting point is the existential doubt 'of what life itself is about'. How do individuals come to experience being alive, as beings who exist *in their own right*, distinct from their early symbiotic existence with and through a mother, and no less distinguished from the culture and society into which life has plunged them? According to Winnicott, infants need to respond to their experiences with and through a mother, and gradually, or sometimes with difficulty, discover themselves as individuals within a mother's care. Growing up thus combines feelings of union with the mother, increasing separation and self-sufficiency, selfhood and belonging. Mother and child are an intimate dyad, in which the mother's role is to appreciate the child's feelings and to respond to them in such a way that the child's strivings for independence, spontaneity and affiliation are encouraged. A healthy dyadic relationship creates a child whose *true self* is spontaneous, competent, trusting and created. But if the child's emotional signals are not appreciated, a *false self* may develop, in which compliance replaces spontaneity, conformity replaces trust, and feelings of low self-esteem and incompetence replace competence and creativity. The *false self* is doubly compliant: it may be a direct response to an externally enforced definition of the self. An impoverishing environment may freeze the individual into compliant failure. Or the *false self* may develop from impoverishing family relationships, that may themselves be imposed by social or cultural conditions. The *false self* may protect the *true self* from awareness of the external conditions that deny a sense of reality to the individual. The multiple constraints of narrow ethnicities, racism and poverty in South Africa have been formidable obstacles to the creation of *true selves*.

Similar to narcissistic egocentricity, collective separatisms like ethnicity or nationalism look 'inwardly, away from and beyond the imperfect world. And this contempt of things as they are, of the world as it is, ultimately becomes a rejection of life and a love of death... The emphasis on youth and death explains the frequent violence and horror of nationalist methods: politics is a passionate assertion of the will, but at the core of this passion is a void and all its activity is the frenzy of despair' (Kedourie, 1993, pp. 82-83). The unconscious despair is about the collective impossibility of rationally resolving the problems of the persisting past. Like individual neurotics, collectivities are unable to free themselves from their phantasies about Others, and 'one literally sees in the enemy [group] the personification of one's impulses...one deals with a split-off part of oneself personified by another...*"we" and "they" are symbiotically linked*' (Stein, 1987, p. 129). As the newish South Africa takes shape, wounded collective narcissisms are manifest and arouse self-destructive rage. It is surprising that African-white collective relationships have, so far, largely avoided angry conflict. Why? 'Adversaries who insist they cannot get along *with* one another, in fact cannot get along *without* that other to contain those phantasies about the group-self that are not acceptable' (Stein, 1987, p. 128). Three centuries during which Africans and whites could hardly take their eyes off each other and were obsessively attracted to, and repelled by, each other collectively, may have begun to develop a symbiotic relationship that is less hostile and is 'healthier' than South African whites had any right to expect.

Beyond Ethnicity and Nationalism?

The end of *apartheid* means that the 'children' have succeeded in forcing the parents to let them grow-up. The 'parents' may resent the loss of their exploitable 'children'. They may feel vulnerable and threatened by fear of the 'children' whom they can no longer torment and control, they may unconsciously even wish to transform the once-unloved 'children' into now lovable adults. But 'children' and 'parents' will have to share the same symbolic roof with out destroying one another.

South Africa seems to be passing through a period in which mourning and melancholia are oscillating with a sense of relief and a manic euphoria. It is also passing through a phase in which sibling rivalries are murderously intense. Two myths persist that no political movement seems aware of. One myth is that 'we' are the only nation, ethnic group, religion that has the answers to South Africa's problems; and the other is that 'we' are a complete, integral and distinct entity. Collectively these myths are very similar emotionally to the intensely narcissistic patient, whose therapy will fail unless the patient ceases to be terrified by the existence of other people, and learns, however slowly and painfully, that other people live in the same world and must be accepted as individuals, too. I do not know how the followers of Zulu nationalism and the far right can be relieved from living in a dreamworld in which only they live and in which they, with neurotic repetition, abolish siblings, family, home, the South Africa that is 'home' whether they accept it or reject it, by wrapping themselves in the integument of ethnicity, nationalism or 'race'.

It may be that the enforced and pinched compliance of ethnic (and other) separatisms will take a generation or more to be replaced gradually by *true self* identities as it becomes appreciated that *false self* forms of identity are neither immutable, irresistible nor rational defences against economic, political and social uncertainties and fears. Collectivities based on *false self* identities are only partially adult. Their pseudo-autonomy and anxieties can probably only be diminished as rational collective solutions are sought for the poverty, violence and damaged sense of self that are the emotional legacy of *apartheid*.

Note

1 An earlier version of this chapter was published in *Psychology in Society, (PINS)*, 1994, vol. 19, pp. 18-30.

References

Alexander, N.(1984), 'Race, ethnicity and nationalism in social science in Southern Africa', Paper delivered at *15th annual congress of the Association for Sociology in Southern Africa* at the University of the Witwatersrand, Johannesburg, 3 July 1984.

Anderson, B.(1983), *Imagined communities: Reflections on the origin and spread of nationalism*, London: Verso Books.

Castelnuovo-Tedesco, P.(1989), 'The fear of change and its consequences in analysis and psychotherapy', *Psychoanalytic Enquiry*, vol. 9, pp. 101-118.

Cohen, R.(1978), 'Ethnicity: problem and focus in anthropology', *Annual Review of Anthropology*, pp. 379-403.

Davidson, B.(1992), *The Black man's burden: Africa and the curse of the nation state*, London: James Currey.

Fanon, F.(1986), *Black skin, white masks*, London: Pluto Press.

Fenichel, O.(1982), *The psychoanalytic theory of neurosis*, London: Routledge.

Freud, S.(1914/1984), *On narcissism: An introduction*, Harmondsworth: The Pelican Freud Library, vol. 11.

Freud, S.(1922/1985), *Group psychology and the analysis of the ego*, Harmondsworth: The Pelican Freud Library, vol. 12.

Fromm, E.(1991), *The crisis of psychoanalysis*, New York: Henry Holt.

Frosh, S.(1991), *Identity crisis: Modernity, psychoanalysis and the self*, London: Macmillan.

Gide, A.(1948), *Journal*, Paris: Editions Pleiades.

Glover, J.(1989), *I: The philosophy and psychology of personal identity*, Harmondsworth: Penguin Books.

Kedourie, E.(1993), *Nationalism*, Oxford: Blackwell.

Said, E.W.(1994), *Culture and the new imperialism*, London: Vintage Books.

Stein, H.F.(1987), 'Culture and ethnicity as group-phantasies: A psychohistoric paradigm of group identity', in H.F. Stein and M. Apprey (eds) (1987), *From metaphor to meaning: Papers in psychoanalytic anthropology*, Charlottesville: University of Virginia Press.

Symington, N.(1993), *Narcissism: A new theory.* London: Karnac Books.

White, R.W.(1950), 'Motivation reconsidered: The concept of competence', *Psychological Review*, vol. 66, pp. 297-333.

Winnicott, D.W.(1965), *The maturational processes and the facilitating environment: Studies in the theory of emotional development,* London: Hogarth Press.

Wolfenstein, E.V.(1993), *Psychoanalytic Marxism: Groundwork*, London: Free Association Books.

Woolf, L.(1937), *After the deluge*, Harmondsworth: Penguin Books.

6 The Emotional Damage of Apartheid: A Psychoanalytic View

Introduction

Although the political and legal structures of *apartheid* are abolished, its emotional impact is likely to persist in both latent and manifest forms for some time to come. If it is true that the culture of *apartheid* has been at the most primitive level of development because hate rather than love or concern has become institutionalised (Per, 1992), then psycho-analysis has a responsibility to expose the unacknowledged latent effects of a social system that was intended to destroy individuality. The extent to which it succeeded - for whites as for blacks - has yet to be evaluated.

This chapter has three interrelated themes. To examine the emotional impact of *apartheid* on children and adults. I am less concerned with the obvious physical and social violence, than with the more obscure psychological effects of a social system that demeaned and diminished adults and children, imposing stringent constraints on their freedom to develop. Franz Fanon's (1986) analysis of the emotional content of colonialism seems closely related to the content of *apartheid*.

In a comprehensive review, both of theory and research, of the emotional impact of violence upon children in South Africa, Dawes (1994) adopts a cognitive, social constructivist approach and is critical of a psycho-analytic approach. This chapter complements Dawes and suggests further research that his approach overlooks.

Whether it be Utopian or not, no discussion would be complete without suggesting some institutional and attitudinal changes to strengthen the development of an emotionally new country, without which a politically liberated new South Africa is improbable.

Thematic Resumé

This chapter explores some of the emotional consequences of *apartheid* as a sociopolitical system. I assume that Menzies Lyth's (1988) model of containing anxiety in institutions applies equally to large-scale societies and that South Africa, like the authoritarian hospitals studied by Menzies Lyth, has to evolve from an emotionally anti-democratic ethos into an emotionally democratic one.

South Africa is an intensely anxious society, living with many unresolved fears and collective fantasies, much repressed anger, guilt and shame. Many black-white relationships are unstable and ambivalent. The necessary collective healing will have to go far beyond the superficial political processes of reconciliation, reparation and truth-seeking about the past - urgent though these are. As in individual psychotherapy, collective healing requires a rejection of the *fear of freedom* and the ambivalent dependence upon authority. Healing also entails the growth of a sense of autonomy, of the replacement of false self structures with more authentic self notions.

Central Issues

There are three interrelated issues I would like to address in this chapter:

1. In what ways was *apartheid* a pathogenic sociopolitical system?

2. Therefore, what emotional changes are vital in the attitudes and relationships of adults with adults, and adults with children, if an emotionally healthy South Africa can develop? How might these changes be encouraged by education and social welfare, or more broadly in political life?

3. What institutional changes might help to neutralise or reverse the anti-democratic and anti-therapeutic ethos and practices of those institutions that purport to care for children and adults?

Underlying all these issues is the problem of how to diffuse the deeply entrenched authoritarianism that permeates South Africa's social and political relationships. Leaders are seen as 'fathers', and their followers see themselves in the main as disappointed children. A young Xhosa friend expressed this to me bitterly: 'The leaders, they should show us they still love us as before and give us hope again. But now our fathers are absent in Cape Town or Pretoria (Parliament).   Once they came and talked with us in each and every place'.

In their past many South Africans, in both black and white communities, have only experienced living within a quasi-family structure dominated by powerful, punitive and authoritarian adults. Such a regressive social system encourages a longing for an illusory, idyllic and protected childhood where there are no external threats. But the price which parents demand in return for providing such protection is unquestioning obedience. As Fenichel (1982) pointed out:

> It is an old technique of authorities and educators to reply to subjects or children, who are dependent on them and are begging for protection and narcissistic supplies: You will get what you need - but on condition! If you obey you will get protection and love, which you need. If you don't obey you will be destroyed.(p. 561)

Fenichel went on to describe how a psychotherapeutic process which makes a patient dependent for the purpose of telling him to be independent is similar to an educational system that sets up contradictory ideals of submission and independence.

In South Africa there is a collective paradox which still has to be confronted, which is analogous to an unproductive individual psychotherapy as described by Fenichel. However well-intentioned the new democratic government and its policies are, there is a continuing sense that the relationships between the empowered and the powerless are still locked into anti-freedom contradictory ideals (i.e. attitudes and fantasies about power and the self).

The analogy with individual therapy may be taken further. Many patients come to the analyst suffering from a feeling of estrangement from themselves or their fellows, or of being passive bystanders to forces beyond their power, or of being in great conflict about what to do (Kennedy, 1993). In this situation the analyst (and the political leader) is too easily transformable into a magical helper who can solve everything if he chooses to (it is usually he) or into an equally magical source of impotence. After three-quarters of a century of increasingly repressive, arbitrary and racist government, it is not surprising that the recently impotent masses seem to interpret government ambivalently. The masses wish government to be omnipotent and benevolent and are therefore induced to perceive it as such. But reality soon asserts itself. The masses, like the uncured patient, become blameful and may come to hate the failed government for failing in the role of magical helper. Government knows it cannot be the magical helper and therefore it carries a burden of guilt, like the psychotherapist who cannot 'cure' the patient.

Repairing the damage can therefore be akin to the analytic process of working through those covert dependency relationships that flatter or frighten the analyst and which block the analyst from progressing towards a true emotional independence with the capacity to form relationships freely. The emotional damage is repaired when the individual moves beyond a defensive narcissism to a creative self-awareness, self-confidence and competence.

In an intensely cramped narcissistic society and culture like that of South Africa, 'repairing the emotional damage' implies recreating individuals and their relationships with society. In South Africa the sense of individuality, especially amongst black people but by no means exclusively, was effectively abolished by the flood of constraining racist laws and practices. Individual identity was replaced by an arbitrary and changing medley of imposed collective identities. Individual identity was impoverished by the endless struggle to find ways to express it within the law - and outside it. *H.*, a young Xhosa adult, put it to me poignantly: '*Apartheid* was very successful in terms of destroying and putting us black people down...I had to learn that I could prove my worth and succeed [despite] the loss of a sense of belonging'. And *A.*, aged about 20, told me: 'I know that I'm *A*. I'm intelligent. I'm gifted in many ways. I tried to compare myself with whites and was myself as an equal. I was often better, but what apartheid did to me - it made me feel inferior. I have to tell myself that I'm not inferior, but deep inside I sometimes feel inferior and I feel unsure of things with whites'.

Two Orientations: Constructionist and Psychoanalytic

In a chapter entitled 'The emotional impact of political violence', Andrew Dawes (1994) provides a wide-ranging evaluation of the major research findings from a South African perspective. While also dealing with the prevailing psychological theories of trauma, his paper disparagingly applies the term 'mechanistic' to psychoanalytic explanations of behaviour and he adopts a 'social constructivist' position, i.e. children understand themselves and their world through their social relationships and communication.

Dawes is critical of psycho-analytic interpretations of children's responses to violence and trauma. He maintains that psychoanalysis is inadequate because it: (1) adopts a 'mechanistic physical analogy...as the total truth about children's reactions to stress' (p. 193), (2) emphasises a view that psychological development is 'essentially the same as physical' and that (3) therefore the child is a passive victim of trauma and is regarded as an 'ahistorical, helpless creature' driven by early psychological development. Dawes also argues that the psychoanalytic view 'gives impetus to hypotheses...that because of their own trauma, survivors will transmit its effects to their children and even their children's children, through their child-rearing practices' (p. 193).

Dawes' criticisms of psychoanalysis are imperceptive and they provide no basis to improve research about traumatised children. Like many other academics, Dawes is content with drawing upon early Freud for his understanding of psychoanalysis, while ignoring all the major developments in the discipline - in ego psychology in the U.S.A. and in object relations theory in the U.K. to name but two. It is amazing that in the 1990s - post-Mahler, Winnicott, Klein - it is necessary to assert that children are far from being regarded by psychoanalysts as 'ahistorical and helpless'. Psychoanalysts have always understood development as an active interaction between psychic and physiological factors. Moreover, the individual psyche (with all its idiosyncracies), interacts actively with the cultural and social context as mediated via the child's relationships with peers and adults, both in reality and fantasy. The essential aim of psychoanalysis is to understand the psychic in relation to the drives as well as the social world, and the conscious and the unconscious influences that give people their individual identities and their personal techniques for making sense of their world. Moreover the argument that parents who have suffered trauma pass on their pain to their children by how they bring them up is not a psychoanalytic argument. Some parents will pass on their trauma and others will not. Some children will introject their parents' distress, some will sublimate it, others will project it and still others may be unaffected by it. Psychoanalysis has a vast theoretical vocabulary for describing the individual's response to trauma, including descriptions of those who *do* suffer trauma passively and those who do not, and how this affects the individual's adaptation to trauma. It is naive of Dawes to assert that scientists, including psychoanalysts, have carried the prevaling ideology of the child as innocent and vulnerable into the research setting. At the least, the studies of wartime and post-wartime children by, among others, August Aichorn, Dorothy Burlingham, Anna Freud and Donald Winnicott, show that children vary as widely as adults in their capacity to deal with trauma.

Dawes concludes with recommendations for studying children that are surprisingly close to what psychoanalysts do! He suggests that we spend more time talking to them so as to unravel the sense they make of things, and that we pay more attention to the way in which adults produce forms of truth and social reality for children (p. 196). Psychoanalysis would go beyond these recommendations. Merely talking with children (or adults) at a superficial ego level will not reach the phantasy world which children and adults inhabit for much of their time. Too little is known about how individual children create symbolic worlds, populated by symbolic people and monsters, and in which symbolic relationships are experienced.

The research of Swart (1990) and Straker et al. (1992) has begun, imaginatively, to investigate at some depth the psychological effects of violence. But neither study was able to investigate at the deep levels that psychoanalysis demands. We have, therefore, no research that gathers children's dreams, expressive behaviour and acting out, stories, drawings and other forms of art, and which systematically uses and interprets play and psychodrama. We still know very little about how *apartheid's* psychological turbulence and disruption distorted children's relationships with adults, and thus distorted the formation of a benign superego and ego ideal. We are almost totally ignorant of how sado-masochistic sublimations and introjections were managed. Melanie Klein has observed that 'external and internal situations are always interdependent, since introjection and projection operate side by side from the beginning of life' (Klein, 1985, p. 21). We know very little about how these processes operate in children in our violent and disrupted society so that they do not inevitably introject and act out the violence that they have experienced, vicariously or immediately.

Pathogenic Aspects of Apartheid

The question 'Can a society be described as pathogenic?' soon leads to sterile debate. The classical psychoanalytic view is that there are inescapable tensions between individuals and their society and culture, because in being an individual in society 'each individual has surrendered some part of his assets - some part of the aggressive or vindictive inclinations in his personality' (Freud, 1985). Individuals live within collectivities which may lessen or inflate this surrender.

The group or society may encourage or discourage affiliative situations and relationships, or aggressive and hostile ones may be stressed or played down. Moreover, narcissism may be stimulated or lessened. Society too may facilitate or inhibit those situations and relationships which nourish one group's need to be distant from others who are rationalised as hostile or threatening, or ambivalently attractive and therefore threatening.

The never-completed developmental task of adults and children is, therefore, to reconcile two conflicting emotional demands: the need for a sense of autonomy and self and the need for emotional dependence. Adults and children both need a safe emotional base to retreat to and to move away from. They also have to reconcile, as far as is possible for the individual, their aggressive with their affiliative needs. The struggle to deal with these conflicting emotional needs leads to anxiety and individuals develop their own 'mechanisms of defence' to minimise the pain of anxieties that no human can evade.

According to Anna Freud the earlier developmental task is to deal with the primary instinctual demands which can often be experienced as overwhelming. Later this is complicated with having to deal with the demands of the super ego, which can be just as overwhelming as the instinctual urges. The mechanisms of defence defend the ego from anxieties that arise from the child's internal, internalised and external world. 'We can already speak with greater certainty about the parallels between the ego's defensive measure against external and against internal danger. [For example] repression gets rid of instinctual derivatives, just as external stimuli are abolished by denial' (A. Freud, 1966).

In *apartheid*, South Africa children were raised in *double-jeopardy* in defending themselves against those aggressive needs that must be sublimated (or otherwise disposed of). Black children, treated as Others by the dominant white culture, were members of a targeted scapegoat group and were exposed to legitimated and institutionalised aggression. Then they were at risk of receiving even worse aggression if they failed to repress (or otherwise deal with) a hostile response to institutionalised aggression. Yet, the natural aggressive needs that contribute to the formation of the ego and superego still required conditions in which they could develop normally. But there was no 'normality' in *apartheid* South Africa! There were no non-violent models, and no social sublimations necessary for a non-aggressive child rearing. There were even fewer influences to enable the growing child to acquire forms of self-control that were not slavishly over-controlling and over-conforming, or else, antisocial in nature. In other words, there was an absence of influences that might have enabled children to avoid developing such a punitive superego that could prevent uncontrollable emotions from being transformed into narcissistic destruction of people and property as symbolic representations of the all-powerful dominant and aggressive society.

'Identification with the aggressor' or a powerful other is a common method of dealing with anxiety-provoking people or situations (A. Freud, 1966). De Zulueta (1993) also reminds us of the tendency of abused children to blame themselves for what happens to them, because in becoming 'bad' the child makes her objects 'good'. The child's need for her abusive rejecting parent is thus salvaged, but the price is a terrible sense of guilt (p. 154). There were blacks who survived *apartheid* emotionally by rationalising that the whites meant well, and who half-believed that there was something 'bad' or 'primitive' about blackness, compared with being white. The whites, after all, had power, skills and wealth. An essential part of healing today is to generate a collective sentiment that being black is not bad.

A pathogenic society thus deprives individuals of the *emotional space* to develop those spontaneous affiliative, affectionate and libidinous relationships thatsupport the development of a strong ego and a benign superego upon which a sense of autonomy and competence depends.

Children who have been deprived of benign adult care because of war or social turmoil, may be driven to look to one another for emotional support, and may thus develop their own 'group superego' with its idiosyncratic psychopathology. Shortly after World War II, Anna Freud and Sophie Dann rescued six infants from *Theresienstadt* concentration camp. The infants were closely dependent on each other, rejected adult help and clearly had formed an intense love and concern for one another's survival, which probably saved their lives in the camp (Freud and Dann, 1951). Anna Freud observed that the children were hypersensitive, restless, aggressive, difficult to handle. 'But they were neither deficient, delinquent, nor psychotic. They had found an alternative placement for their libido and...had mastered some of their anxieties and developed social attitudes'. They had effectively developed their own group superego, values and norms. Many black, and some white, South African children have been forced by *apartheid's* depersonalising tumult to respond similarly (Straker et al., 1992).

Many black children responded to *apartheid's* denigration of their identity by responding assertively or as violently as *apartheid* itself. The aggressive values of peer-groups struggling to assert their authenticity was often internalised and the frustrated anti-apartheid, anti-adult anger was often deflected onto those fellow children who appeared to be less committed politically. This situation in which children are 'self-sealed' for adults, raises questions about the capacity of their collective superego to adapt to changing social conditions in which emotional contact with adult superego models must be made. Hostile impulses against the adult world must give way to identification with adults so that a new superego may develop; this may raise unsettling attempts of self-evaluation and further splitting of the already fragile ego.

It has been argued that the instability of child-adult relationships in South Africa has produced 'not a child with the wrong superego but, centrally, no superego at all' (Van Zyl, 1990). The controversial psychopathy of so many young black South Africans, and the attendant ability to commit violent acts without apparently suffering remorse, can be explained in just this way. Of course the same conclusion might be made of white police and officials! But this argument is inadequate. Children's violence was also modelled on adult violence, and on the legitimation of this violence in a macho culture. The aggression shown by youth was not motivated simply by a superego distorted by society, but was an introjection of the terrifying violence and depersonalisation that was both the reality and a phantasy of most of the population. It is still far from clear whether whites felt depersonalised in the same way by the constraints on their spontaneity and by their direct or indirect involvement in violent and psychological oppression of blacks. From a research perspective this must surely be given priority in a society apparently committed to reconciliation. For the dominant group, the collective superego was aggressive and punitive which motivated fanatical, puritanical and violent social, and political beliefs and actions.

Van Zyl (1990) also holds the view that non-violence was virtually prevented by the success and ubiquity of violence, and (as I see it) by the institutionalisation of official and unofficial violence in a very wide range of situations. The whites' almost total monopolisation of social control and effective leadership, made it almost impossible for non-violent leadership and methods of non-violent problem-solving to acquire emotional roots. Moreover, until very recently non-violent African leaders with whom young (and old) people could identify were models of impotence, not models of success.

Finally, South Africa is still strongly collectivised and made up of many self-sealed groups. This political and social feature is strengthened by a narcissistic sense of group identity, and has impelled individuals to deny the integrity of other groups and their members. Moreover, the gross inequalities of authority, power and access to the nation's economic wealth, has for long blocked the growth of the emotional rudiments of democracy. A nation of Others, strangers and aliens is unable to enjoy the collective learning of peaceful conflict-resolution. Gross inequalities seriously damage the growth of self-esteem and a sense of confidence in one's idiosyncratic skills and talents. However, the most gross of the collective narcissisms does seem to be abating.

Social Traumata and Depersonalisation

The reality, threat and phantasy of social violence in South Africa has created much individual trauma, either directly or vicariously. A major and disabling consequence of the traumata of apartheid is *learned-helplessness*. Learned-helplessness has been defined as a condition 'characterised by an expectation that bad events will occur and that there is nothing [in reality] one can do to prevent their occurrence. [It] results in passivity, cognitive deficits and other symptoms that resemble depression' (Rosenhan and Seligman, 1984). But it may be interrupted by episodes of counter-violence, or by active attempts to assert the reality of the self - by political activity, directed towards personal liberation. The expectation of bad events may arise from present or historical social experience, or it may be a fixation into infantile-helplessness - either realistic or induced by socially-imposed or personal phantasy. In either case, such experiences or phantasies 'lead to the establishment of a substructure in the budding psychic apparatus' (Heimann, 1989), and the child never quite overcomes infantile helplessness, even when a mature ego appears to be formed.

Symington (1993) discusses the relation between trauma and the narcissistic option. He writes that the essence of trauma is that a psychic stability based on steady expectation has been shattered, and so the traumatised adult or child responds either by living 'anaesthetised against whatever the painful thing may be', or by propelling himself into the pattern of the traumatising agent, e.g. by accepting the dependency of the infantile role imposed by oppressive authority (p. 73). Rappaport (1968) and Bettelheim (1960) describe what is perhaps the most long-lasting of trauma-producing situations: the destruction of the ego and of the sense of an autonomous self.

Apartheid forced millions of individuals to doubt their authenticity and identity as *individuals*, and by coercing them to collude with their oppressors and the oppressive social system often added to feelings of helplessness, shame, guilt and anger. Children (and adults treated as 'children') saw in the mirror of the significant powerful Others a distorted image of a powerless and immature self.

Franz Fanon (1971, 1986) was concerned as a black psychiatrist about the 'False Consciousness' that is imposed on black people in a racist-colonialist society. He elaborated the theme that black people have absorbed through their daily experience that to be fully human is to be white. But it was impossible to become white, so many people were forced to be white in phantasy. The result was a deep ambivalence about being an 'inferior' black: self-hatred, shame and distrust of being black, a diminished sense of competence and a low sense of self-esteem. Both the ego and the ego ideal have too little emotional space in which to develop adequately. Liberation is, therefore, both political and psychological, and becomes healing if the imposed white mask is torn off and a 'False Consciousness' replaced by a sense of pride in being black and by heightened self-esteem and self-confidence. Fanon saw de-colonization as the beginning of a process of recreating a culture in which blackness was no longer synonymous with an 'inferiority complex'.

In detail, the depersonalisation brought about by apartheid has five main features:

1. The grief, depression and suppressed anger brought about by learned-helplessness and imposed low self-esteem.

2. Economic, political and social arrangements severely discouraged individuals from working with others and from loving and relating to them spontaneously. Many relationships were severely and

narrowly stereotyped, and only the brave and committed evaded stereotyping.   Moreover, inter-group hostility, violence and paranoiac suspicions were legitimated and specific groups were targeted as victims.

3. *Apartheid* was based on an irrational, indeed bizarre, system of ideas which as they were obsessively elaborated, became more and more distant from the reality of how a fragmented and turbulent society could survive in the long run. There are analogies between the cognitive defences of many severely disturbed schizophrenics and the defensive, idea-systems of *apartheid*. The very concept of *apartheid* is arguably pathogenic. A nation was compelled to live a lie and to deny it. In a nominally deeply Christian nation, what amounted to an essentially anti-Christian ideology demanded an endless and exhausting intellectual and emotional effort of its supporters - active or passive - to rationalise it as a morally valid and socially realistic view of society. The 'victims' were thereby turned into the perpetrators, because *apartheid* generated a neurotic attempt to undo the guilt-producing problems that it had itself generated by ever more elaborate rationalisations. In this way severe depersonalisation also occurred in the adherents of *apartheid*.

4. *Apartheid* was collectively and individually unstable, because it deprived most of the people of any meaningful control over their own lives, and because it erratically uprooted whole communities for ideological reasons. Those with power needed more and more power and authority to reassure themselves that externally the control would last, and internally that they were justified morally. Those without power had to learn more and more elaborate ways to lessen their feelings of impotence and to maintain a bare level of self-esteem.

Apartheid was so agressively intrusive and emotionally draining for everyone that even the most simple wish-fulfilling dreams could only be a partial and an uncertain refuge from the daytime assaults on the individual's self-esteem. Moreover, there is no actual escape in dreams from poverty and gross insecurity. The victims of apartheid were exposed, visible and vulnerable. Their 'Otherness', their uncanny nature, was transformed magically into the politically dangerous. As Freud (1919) described, it was therefore easy and common for whites to 'ascribe evil motives to [them and also] to attribute to these intentions a capacity to achieve their aim in virtue of certain special powers' (p. 396).

5. *Apartheid* had considerable power to create victims. The obsessively detailed prescriptions of appropriate and inappropriate behaviour and feelings, allowed few assurances that one could behave correctly and gave no encouragement to a sense of authenticity and autonomy. It was, for example, dangerously easy for black people to be perceived as behaving in hostile or aggressive ways, or to be imagined as politically suspect. It was common to be perceived and treated as an inferior member of an inferior group. Or, one might be perceived as a danger because one was too dependent, too ingratiating - or too temptingly attractive. 'Uncle Tom' and 'Aunt Mavis' were no safer than any woman, man or child who found ways of resisting depersonalisation and who asserted his or her reality. The sadistic quality of the 'control' is well-documented and needs no elaboration here. What is too little acknowledged is the intensely guilt-provoking ambivalence of the feelings of the many controllers themselves.

Towards a Collective Psychotherapy

The healing process, individual or collective, has to replace infantile dependence, emotional fragmentation and the repressed anger arising from frustration and anxiety by a developing sense of autonomy and self-control, authenticity, competence and wholeness. For individual psychotherapy, Fenichel (1982) recommended that patient and therapist should be actively engaged in dissipating 'tendencies towards regression, toward the misinterpretation of reality, towards the longing of passivity and dependence, toward wish-fulfilling phantasies'. Collectively, through education and political and religious group activity, intellectual and emotional resources must be mobilised so that the depersonalising and traumatic conditions of reality can be countered. The therapeutic process must reverse the social and cultural forces that were depersonalising and ways must be found to stimulate the individual's repersonalising so that there is the freedom in which to construct one's own identity, and to explore and enjoy one's own feelings and skills.

In what follows, I refer directly to the problems of children, but similar, even identical, considerations apply to the adult 'children' of apartheid. Enforced infantilisation created emotionally impoverished adults, and emotionally impoverished adults do not build a creative society for creative individuals.

A beginning can be made from four promising, though psycho-dynamically disappointing, declarations:

1. The Declaration of the Rights of the Child (adopted by the UN in 1959).

2. The Children's Charter of South Africa (adopted in 1992).

3. The African Charter of Human and People's Rights (adopted in 1992).

4. The African Charter of Human and People's Rights (adopted in 1986).

None of these declarations, however, goes much further than legalistic statements of rights and duties, or goes beyond clichés about 'the right to happiness and education'. All lack a psychologically orientated preamble that might have obliged any person in a position of authority to: (1) use that authority moderately and only in ways that could enhance an individual's feelings of security and independence, and their acquiring better skills and a sense of competence; (2) to become aware of their emotions about authority, to constantly check these emotions and relationships, and to be alert to the tendency to value authority for its own sake; (3) to be sensitive enough to convey to those over whom authority is exercised, that they are valued as individuals and are not treated merely as subjects of authority; (4) to face and accept the challenge that authority has to earn and retain the trust of the individuals and groups subject to their authority.

The largely entrenched authoritarianism of *apartheid* remains damaging to South Africans. For example, child care legislation and practice is dated, woefully paternalistic and depersonalising. The Child Care Act of 1983 has no reference to children as *people* with a moral right to be consulted, listened to and respected about what happens in their lives. The ethos and practice is weighed heavily on 'control' and rehabilitation within institutions. The Act obsessively details the powers of authorities to separate children from their families and detain them, so that effective control of children (in some circumstances to the age of 21) was practiced by the same magistracy and penal system as the one empowered to have children whipped, detained or imprisoned. Goldstein et al. (1979, p. 65) recommended that 'the child in any contested placement should have full party status and the right to be represented by counsel' - rights that are almost unheard of in proceedings that have involved African children.

Changing the Emotional Ethos

Both the ethos of institutions and the wider national ethos are far from being emotionally democratic. Change is slowly but noticeably taking place, but it is not widely understood that institutional, social, political and legal changes are worthless unless they are inspired and motivated by emotional change.

In the new South Africa, while social and political freedoms are growing - in legal form at least - so, too, political attitudes that were once repressed are becoming conscious. The collective defence mechanisms and resistances that formerly served to contain tensions are becoming less suitable to the changing tensions. Moreover, it can now be possible politically to replace phantasy thinking by realistic thinking. The challenge from psychoanalysis to South African institutions is that there is in each of us 'a spontaneous well of subjectivity that simply does not contain in any immediate sense the categories of [social and political life]...yet plays a powerful determining role in social life' (Kovel, 1988). Therefore, institutions and the collective life of the society need to enrich and strengthen the ego and the True self, moderate the over-severe and punitive superego, and provide a wider range of spontaneous outlets for affiliative and libidinous relationships.

The most basic change is for children, women and men to be released from enforced dependency, and the most practical start might be within education. Both Sigmund and Anna Freud were concerned with the implications of psychoanalysis for education. Teachers at all levels are, to some extent, parental models and their attitudes towards, and feelings about, their quasi-children may be influential. Education should stimulate independence, self-confidence, a sense of self-esteem as well as basic skills. Teachers' training should set teachers free to encourage freedom. Education should be child-centred and ego-enhancing, recognising the role of the group and of phantasy in mental development, minimising rote learning and greatly increasing project work. Anna Freud was greatly interested in how play, music and the arts could help in the germination of both children's skills and their confidence in using them.

Some Broad Institutional Changes

The most appropriate and workable changes are probably in education and child welfare. Changes there would influence other institutions. First, all issues that concern the lives of children should be removed from the control of the police, courts and other personnel whose training and emotional allegiance is to the penal system rather than to children. This carries implications for the selection and training of those involved: 'control' should be replaced by cooperation and partnership, punishment by understanding and the chilly notion of paternalistic welfare replaced by the risky warmth of love. There is an urgent need to create conditions in which emotional growth is helped and not hampered by the staff and the ethos in control. The 'facilitating environment...must have certain qualities if the maturational processes in the individual child are to take effect and the child is to become a real person in the sense of feeling real in a real world' (Winnicott, 1987). Adults, too, need a facilitating environment in which they can develop 'the feeling of being free to choose and of being able to create anew' (ibid, p. 230).

The costs of the bureaucracy of law and social welfare, and the capital and running costs of staffing and maintaining reformatories, places of safety and prisons would be better spent in combatting the impoverished social and emotional worlds in which children and adults have been forced to live, and in forming and reforming a modern, psychodynamically and practical training for those who work with children and adults.

Moreover, supporting foster homes is often more 'facilitating' than the present institutions, which do little or nothing to encourage children or adults gradually to widen their social relationships and to find an emotional base from which to explore their world and return to freely if a need is felt for emotional security. In the U.K. since the early 1920s, there have developed institutions which avoided institutionalisation, with adults and children sharing responsibilities and a democratic psychology (see Bloom, 1956; Dockar-Drysdale, 1993; Durrant, 1993). There is a need in South Africa for smaller institutions where staff could - and should - strive consciously to avoid institutionalisation, and where the ethos should be on creating and maintaining the normal, emotional give-and-take of family and community life. The richness of variety of adults in the life of the quasi-family should be enhanced by welcoming volunteer carers from the community, and unhealthy institutional inwardness could also be lessened by access to telephones, uncensored letters (with help for the illiterate) and a policy of sharing and joining in local activities. Inmates' advocates should be empowered to monitor the institutions and to protect inmates from insensitive or over-zealous officials, and from unofficial harm or dangers. There is need for an effective Ombudsman and for independent emotional care for inmates of all institutions. The various children's protection units should become what the name implies: children too often need protection from the heavily over-controlling and punitive welfare and penal systems. It is reassuring that the present government is actively working to change the savage penal philosophy in South Africa.

Second, for many years, schools will need to be both shelters and places for formal education, and to have more productive relations with local communities, and between staff and students. The historical and present pressures on schools, and the heavily anti-educational ethos, conceal the basic defects of the present system, which functions erratically and without a climate of achievement in communities where survival has been more urgent than education. Teachers and administrators seem to ignore that the impact of schools on children is similar to that of the family. The family and the school 'don't have their effect through the specific skills they transmit, but through their values, climate, quality of relationships. Children [and adults] learn by internalising the attitudes, values and ways of meaningful others. And then, whatever content you expose children to, they learn it' (Schorr, 1988, p. 234). Teachers, like other adults, cannot evade responsibility for helping children to adopt those attitudes and skills that will enable them to attempt to create an emotionally tolerable environment.

Third, a political decision is implied in all practices which determine how people are to be treated. Far too many children, and adults treated as children, are lost within the welfare and penal institutions with far too little concern about the institutions' emotional and social influence. A healthy political system is one where adults and children are enabled to avoid colluding with the powerful educational, social and cultural encouragement of learned-helplessness. In South Africa, children and adults need to be incited to take their lives into their own hands. A beginning is being made, but the weight of authoritarian attitudes and practices still hinders individual and group efforts to try for independence.

Conclusion

South Africa has barely begun to capitalise on 'the emancipatory potential of psychoanalysis that is embedded in its rich account of intra-psychic forces and interpersonal dynamics' (Meyers, 1994). Further, psychoanalysts were the pioneers of listening to and taking seriously the voices of those who had been excluded because they were different: the emotionally disturbed, both adults and children. Psychoanalysis is unique in sensitivity to the paradox that humankind shares the essentially identical psycho-biological nature, yet people often have their amazing but 'normal' idiosyncrasies.

In South Africa we still have to accept at a deep emotional level that blacks and whites are essentially equal, yet individual blacks and whites have developed their personal defences against the stresses of *apartheid*. From his youth Freud was concerned about the relationships of individuals to their society and in his early paper 'The claims of psychoanalysis to scientific interest' he observed that 'the neuroses themselves have turned out to be attempts to find individual solutions for the problems of compensating for unsatisfied wishes, while the institutions seek to provide social solutions for these same problems' (Freud, 1986, p. 52).

Psychoanalytic psychotherapy in South Africa should, for example, be more explicitly concerned with how individual blacks and whites developed their personal defence mechanisms. We should also be concerned with the dynamics of how differing social conditions encourage different patterns of splitting by blacks compared with whites. Therefore, 'one interesting implication...is that political organisations should pay more attention to the psychological development of their members, for reasons of effectiveness as much as for humanitarian reasons' (Samuels, 1993). Furthermore, government itself should consider the effects on psychological development of laws and political practices.

What Anna Freud (1964) wrote about children's welfare can be adapted to the main features of adult psychotherapy. 'The best interests of the child are served...by all measures which promote his smooth progression toward normal maturity. The latter, in its turn, depends above all on the coincidence of three factors: on the free interchange of affection between child and adult; on ample external stimulation of the child's inborn, internal potentialities; and on unbroken continuity of care' (p. 228). Adults, too, need freedom to interchange affection, a stimulating and supportive environment, opportunities and encouragement to develop their potentialities and a government that is free from preoccupation with power, control and punishment.

References

Andreas-Salomé, L.(1987), *The Freud Journal*, London: Quartet Books.
Bettelheim, B.(1960), *The Informed Heart*, New York: Free Press.
Bloom, L.(1956), 'Psychological aspects of self-government in the residential treatment of the delinquent child', *Mental Health*, vol. 16, pp. 6-16.
Bloom, L.(1994), 'Ethnic identity: a psychoanalytic critique', *Psychology in Society*, vol. 19, pp. 18-30.
Dawes, A. (1994), 'The emotional impact of political violence', in A. Dawes and D. Donald, (eds), *Childhood and Adversity: Psychological Perspectives from South African Research*, Cape Town: David Philip.
de Zulueta, F.(1993), *From Pain to Violence: The Traumatic Roots of Destructiveness*, London: Whurr Publishers.
Docker-Drysdale, B.(1993), *Therapy and Consultation in Child Care*, London: Free Association Books.
Durrant, M.(1993), *Residential Treatment: A Cooperative, Competency-based Approach to Therapy and Programme Design*, New York: Norton.
Fanon, F.(1971), *The Wretched of the Earth*, Harmondsworth: Penguin Books.
Fanon, F.(1986), *Black Skin, White Masks*, London: Plenum Press.
Fenichel, O.(1982), *The Psychoanalytic Theory of Neurosis*, London: Routledge.
Freud, A.(1964), 'Psychoanalytic knowledge and its application to children's services', in *The Writings of Anna Freud, vol. V*, New York: International Universities Press.
Freud, A.(1966), *The Ego and the Mechanisms of Defence*, New York: International Universities Press.
Freud, A. and Dann, S.(1951), 'An experiment in group upbringing', in *The Writings of Anna Freud, vol. IV*, New York: International Universities Press.
Freud, S.(1908), 'Civilised sexual morality and modern nervous illness', Harmondsworth: Penguin Freud Library, vol. 12.
Freud, S.(1913), 'The claims of psychoanalysis to scientific interest', The Penguin Freud Library, vol. 15, Harmondsworth: Penguin Books.
Freud, S.(1919/1985), 'The uncanny', Harmondsworth: Penguin Freud Library, vol. 14.
Fromm, E.(1945), *The Fear of Freedom*, London: Kegan Paul.
Goldstein, J., Freud, A. and Solnit, A.J.(1979), *Before the Best Interests of the Child*, New York: The Free Press.
Heimann, P.(1989), *About Children and Children-No-Longer*, London: Tavistock/Routledge.
Kennedy, R.(1993), *Freedom to Relate: Psychoanalytic Explorations*, London: Free Association Books.
Klauber, J.(1989), 'The Role of Illusion in the Psychoanalytic Cure', in J. Sandler (ed), *Dimensions of Psychoanalysis*, London: Karnac Books.

Klein, M.(1985), 'The psychoanalytic play technique: its history and significance', in M. Klein, P. Heimann and R.E. Money-Kyrle (eds), *New Directions in Psychoanalysis,* London: Maresfield Library.

Kovel, J.(1988), *The Radical Spirit,* London: Free Association Books.

Levenson, M.(1991), *Modernism and the Fate of Individuality,* Cambridge: Cambridge University Press.

Menzies Lyth, I.(1988), *Containing Anxiety in Institutions,* London: Free Association Books.

Meyers, D.T.(1994), *Subjection And Subjectivity: Psychoanalytic Feminism and Moral Philosophy,* New York: Routledge.

Per, L.(1992), 'Themes of aggression and violence in the therapy of a young adult activist', *Psycho-analytic Psychotherapy in South Africa,* vol. 1, pp. 7-17.

Rappaport, E.A.(1968), 'Beyond traumatic neurosis: A psychoanalytic study of late reactions to the concentration camp trauma', *Int. J. of Psycho-analysis,* vol. 49(4), pp. 719-731.

Rosenhan, D.L. and Seligman, M.E.P.(1984), *Abnormal Psychology,* New York: Norton.

Rustin, M.(1991), 'Psychoanalysis and Social Justice', in M. Rustin, *The Good Society and the Inner World: Psychoanalysis, Politics and Culture,* London: Verso Books.

Samuels, A.(1993), *The Political Psyche,* London: Routledge.

Schorr, L.B. and Schorr, D.(1988), *Within Our Reach: Breaking the cycle of disadvantage,* New York: Anchor Books.

Stein, H.F.(1990), 'Adapting to doom: The group psychology of an organisation threatened with cultural extinction', *Political Psychology,* vol. 11(1), pp. 113-145.

Straker, G., Moosa, F., Becker, R. and Nkwale, M.(1992), *Faces in the Revolution,* Cape Town: David Philip.

Swart, J.(1990), *The Street Children of Hillbrow,* Johannesburg: Witwatersrand University Press.

Symington, N.(1993), *Narcissism: A New Theory,* London: Karnac Books.

Symington, N.(1994), *Emotion and Spirit: Questioning the Claims of Psychoanalysis and Religion,* London: Cassell.

Van Zyl, S.(1990), 'Freud and a Political Role of Psychology', *Psychology in Society,* vol. 14, pp. 4-16.

Winnicott, D.W.(1987), 'Freedom', in *Home Is Where We Start From,* Harmondsworth: Penguin Books.

Wolfenstein, E.V.(1993), *Psychoanalysis and Marxism: Groundwork,* London: Free Association Books.

7 Apartheid's Children: The Emotional Costs

Introduction

In examining the effects of the trauma of apartheid upon children, 'perhaps the most central thought that emerges is the value of the notion of *reliance,* i.e. why and under what circumstances some children and not others are able to resist apparently similar adverse circumstances' (Donald and Dawes, 1994, p. 270). I am no more sure of an adequate answer than other social psychologists, but it seems highly probable that the answer is related to the flair that some children have to coax at least one adult to form meaningful relationships with them, and for a child to create a sense of ego identity within a meaningful and emotionally supportive group. Some part of the answer was given to me by Thabo, then aged about 12, who, when I asked him how he has survived, responded with obvious pride, 'I'm quick, Len!' Thabo's quickness consisted largely in his ability to be taken up as a mascot and protected by white university students. Thabo and other children showed me that the overall portrait of black South African children as casualties of extreme deprivation, apartheid and poverty may be unjustifiably pessimistic and may indeed fail to do justice to these children's resilience, courage and enduring capacity 'for universal achievement' (Liddell et al., 1993, p. 14).

From the outset I faced an insoluble problem: how can the direct consequences of apartheid be distinguished from phenomena that accompanied it but would probably have happened even without apartheid? As a social policy, apartheid obstructed the full and free development of the individual and collective identities of African children. In Fanon's chilling word, it imposed a 'mask' of imposed identity behind which growing children were forced to find their own ways to create their individuality. But apartheid directly and indirectly exaggerated the effects of such colonial and post-colonial disruptions as the creation of a landless urban African proletariat, the breakdown of communities and families, poverty and the gross inequalities of educational and occupational opportunities. Apartheid politics were typical of the stubborn, often violent, resistance of authoritarian governments to sharing power and authority democratically.

I do not claim to solve the insoluble problem. This chapter is a modest attempt to share and interpret some of the experiences of some African children and young people who have had to support and nurture themselves in a society that made it difficult or impossible for adults consistently to nurture, support and protect them. It will be apparent that I find inadequate those analyses of apartheid that study it on 'the assumption of a rational human being acting in accordance with his interests ...[My] understanding works in the opposite direction - not to reveal the hidden rationality of the bizarre...but the irrationality of social reality itself' (Ward, 1988, p. xv).

Procedure

This chapter emerged spontaneously out of my daily life. I did not think this odd because my professional interests have long ago led me to welcome that although 'some roles are planned by the researcher...others are invented on the spot, constituting creative responses to unanticipated situational events' (Hunt, 1989, p. 11).

Early in 1993 I found myself in Grahamstown, South Africa, in an 'unanticipated' situation where unforeseeable events and relationships moved me to ask research questions. The unanticipated situation was that I found myself chatting with two Xhosa youngsters, then aged about 13 and 15, who responded with interest when I asked them if they would tell me the stories of their lives and who allowed me to make notes while we chatted. From this beginning other Xhosa boys drifted to my house, some of whom were able to chat freely. Some were street-wise enough to use the situation as a novel addition to their techniques of begging, but almost all the youngsters seemed both flattered and relieved that an adult would take an interest in their lives. I rejected the stories of a few boys which seemed melodramatically false. It was often impossible in the circumstances to check the details of the stories. At the same time I began asking the African friends, at Rhodes University, of my African adopted son (who was a postgraduate student) if they would share their life stories with me.

Altogether between April and July 1993 I collected the life stories of about 30 young people, aged between about 13 and 23, of which I studied 26. I gave no direction to the boys about the stories. I simply stated that I was interested in the youngster's 'very own' story of his life and that he could start with anything that was important. I also stated that adults know little about children's lives and it might be helpful in the new South Africa to understand what children thought about their lives. I asked if I might make notes while we chatted, and I stressed that it was important that I would not give away his or his family's identity. On the other side, I stressed that I was interested in the youngster's own lifestory - a private and personal possession. Our conversations were private and individual. The younger children preferred to sit on the stoep of my house, which is sufficiently sheltered to prevent eavesdropping, yet is near enough to the road to permit an easy exit. The youngsters spoke in English of widely varying quality, but it was always comprehensible and sometimes unexpectedly vivid.

I made no attempt to select a specific sample. In the circumstances this would have been impracticable. But if the estimate of social workers was accurate that there were about 50 'homeless' youngsters in Rini, then my sample was more than 50 per cent. I was visited freely by the youngsters, and was usually informed that a friend had said that I was collecting lifestories. I refused to pay for the stories, but I offered food and drink which was accepted. It seems probable that I was not exploited as a naïve dispenser of sandwiches and coffee: twice during 1993 when there were potentially violent political situations, many boys came to shelter in my garden, which they felt was far from the danger in the town, in a quiet area near the university.

Unlike most researchers with children and young people, I had no official or quasi-official position to legitimate my questioning. It was known that I was attached to Rhodes, but I was emphatic that I had no official position that related to my interests and that I was in no way connected with the police, or with welfare agencies, the schools or churches. I had no institutional links like Wilgespruit, with whose staff I could consult and compare mv experiences (see Straker, 1992, pp 144-45). The generalisations that I have drawn from the material are therefore largely my own and no doubt partly reflect my earlier professional interest in the problems of young people in changing sociopolitical situations in Zambia, Nigeria and South Africa (see Bloom, 1960, 1972, 1978 and 1982). I had very little professional support in organising and analysing my material, but I was able to discuss the probability of my generalisations with my African son and with a psychoanalytically-oriented senior PhD student.

I did not ask the boys, or the five undergraduates, if they had had stable and emotionally satisfying families, but it soon became clear from their stories and the manner in which they told them. Of the undergraduates, only two seemed to have had a stable and emotionally satisfying childhood. All the youngsters had had a childhood that was broken or emotionally unsatisfactory. It was, however, often impossible to distinguish the immediate personal problems that caused the instability from the indirect, impersonal effects of apartheid. Three of the youngest children seemed to be 'of' the street, i.e.'they abandoned (or have been abandoned by) their families, school and immediate communities, before they were 16 years of age, and [have] drifted into a nomadic street life' (Richter, 1988, quoted in Swart-Kruger and Donald, 1994, p. 108). One of the boys was of Xhosa and white Afrikaaner parentage and had been rejected by both his white and his African families. His closest friend had repeatedly run away from his grandmother and was taken back to her by the police. He gave many indications of psychological disturbance. A third boy, of Xhosa and white parentage, was depressed and had had no contact with his white and African families for at least six years, according to a social worker.

It is always difficult to test the reliability and validity of field-work, however, my generalisations are not inconsistent with other studies of children and young people in contemporary South and southern Africa. At the very least my generalisations may add to the accounts of diversity and range of experiences which childhood offers: 'Generalisations about any culture of childhood will rest in small enclaves of children sharing substantive commonality of experience and opportunity' (Liddell, 1994, pp. 21-22). Generalisations about children depend partly upon our adult understanding of the children's culture, but perhaps even more, our generalisations depend upon our sensitivity to how the children understand their culture, value or reject it, and have feelings about it.

The Context of Childhood and Youth

We often tend to forget that children do not passively react to their culture and society, but that they actively attempt to manipulate their relationships so that their culture and society go some way to satisfying children's needs rather than those of the significant adults in their lives. Now 'children have emerged from the shadows to invade the arena and the history books usually reserved for adults ... Any examination of current political developments and influences ... must include children as an active and visible force, quite apart from their less visible but more deep-rooted effects' (Burman, 1986, p. 4) as a distinct and numerous section of the total population. Burman distinguishes three critical features of South Africa that influence children, to which must be added the strikingly youthful distribution of the population: (1) 'social engineering and socialisation', (2) 'definitions and divisions' and (3)'the rapidity of social change'.

Social Engineering

Burmann argues that 'since 1948 the South African government has placed more faith than is usual in most countries in the use of direct legal intervention to organise the most personal details of people's lives ... a host of regulations and laws bolster these divisive controls' (Burman, 1986, p. 5). She finds five major interacting results: (1) children from different communities have been isolated from each other and spontaneous relationships have often been very rare or even impossible; (2) there has been an increase in bilingualism, perhaps paradoxically; (3) there is conflict between the government's aims for socialisation and the results of their policies, for example, even the impoverished 'Bantu education' encouraged critical ability and the emphasis upon 'ethnic and cultural differences' has encouraged the growth of black pride and black consciousness; (4) the authoritarian ethos of South Africa has (I believe) taught children to evolve their own techniques to resist authority, and leads Burman to suggest that (5) 'to understand control in S.A. we must examine power in the basic units of society' (Burman, 1986, p. 7). It seems likely that just as children are oppressed bv adults so they will learn to oppress others and to evade or manipulate adult authority.

Definitions and Divisions

Burmann refers to the 'chaos' created by the varied and sometimes contradictory definitions in 'racial' and cultural terms. A question that is not yet fully researched is therefore: how do children in different groups and at different ages classify or define themselves? When, and in what circumstances, do children classify themselves as adolescents, as adults, as mature and ready for independence? I had little information about these questions.

Children and Change

Burman reminds us that South Africa is a country with rapid and fundamental economic social and political changes. But it has (I consider) been unique in the interactions of urbanisation, mass migrations, 'detribalisation', and such apartheid social engineering as influx control and enforced population removals. Burman suggests that in South Africa there are striking 'discontinuities of experience between children and their parents and grandparents [so that] children in many situations in   South Africa are having to work out their own destiny, values and lifestyle to an extent far greater than is usual in more settled societies' (Burman, 1986, p. 11). Moreover, I believe that they often have to protect themselves from the oppressive adult world (and from hostile or exploitative children) to a degree inconceivable in more settled and less conflictual societies.

Liddell et al. (1991) review studies of childhood in South Africa historically. They are critical of the clinical and psychometric biases of South African developmental psychology, which they assert support negative views of African abilities and mental health, and that pathologise African children by ignoring or minimising sociocultural influences on their development. Liddell et al. recognise five enduring features of African childhood and socialisation that have been influenced by 'apartheid': (1) sex differences in child rearing, (2) authority and social control, (3) female-headed households and maternal affection, (4) the valuation of children and (5) the emphasis upon social responsibility and adaptability. Overall, Liddell et al. stress that even under apartheid children were not defenceless and that there has been both change and stability in the influences of apartheid on childhood socialisation and relationships. I would add that the emotional needs of childhood are enduring and relatively immune to social and cultural attempts to define and control them. The findings of Liddell et al. are confirmed by the historical sociology of Walker (1990). Walker observes *inter alia* that there has been 'the emergence of new family forms in the urban area, centred on women and their children, in which men were largely transitory figures' (Walker, 1990, p. 20). Moreover, 'both the indigenous ruling class and the colonisers agreed, though for very different reasons, on the need to restrict the mobility and autonomy of African women' (Walker, 1990, p. 18). Social domination was reinforced by the political domination of apartheid and even now children are controlled to a degree no longer acceptable in more settled democratic urban-industrial societies.

Liddell et al. note that there have always been marked sex differences in, for example, the social and economic demands made of boys and girls and in the interactions of parents and children. Apartheid 'has done much to entrench' these differences (Liddell et al., 1991, p. 7). By contrast, respect for elders and authorities has weakened, because of the breakdown of the extended family and community, and (I believe) because of the rejection of the adult world that has failed to protect the children from apartheid and insecurity. Children and young people have been forced by the pressures of apartheid to become politicised, to form peer groups for their protection and for protest, and this has distanced them from adults and authority. Liddell et al. doubt whether the female-headed household in Africa has the same 'social significance or the same deleterious effects on children as ... in the First World' (Liddell et al., 1991, p. 9). However, apartheid politicised and exacerbated the emotional consequences of such families. Migrant labour policies and poverty forced fathers to leave their households and forced mothers and children to fend for themselves, often in desperate circumstances. But Liddell et al. find 'striking' the persistent depth of maternal affection and the valuing of young children. Social responsibility and responsiveness are still valued and taught by mothering-ones, and for this the society must thank the many grandmothers and great-grandmothers, often themselves poor, who care for children left with them by mothers unable or unwilling to care for them. There is, even now, a vestigial communal caring for children that has protected many children from the hurts of abandonment and adult neglect.

'It is exceptionally difficult to tease out the effects of the ordinary context of violence [physical, social and psychological] which is common to South African children's lives ... In many ways, being violent to children is legitimised' (Dawes, 1994, p. 188). It is still too soon after the 1994 changes in political power to distinguish short-term from long-term effects of violence and the more resilient from the less resilient children. lt may well be that the children and young men with whom I spoke in Grahamstown had (to some extent) developed their own resilience and avoided severe emotional damage.

Children and Adults

South Africa is strikingly youthful and fragmented. This demographic feature influences attitudes towards children. Adults, African and white, are overwhelmed by the armies of children who are often stigmatised as anarchic, unruly and too numerous to be controlled without adult heavy-handedness. African children suffer more than white, because African children are doubly controlled: by both African and white authoritarian adults. The persistence of practices that legitimate deference towards adult authority indicate adult unconscious fears about young people. In this society of young people, most adults are young enough to fear the vitality and close competition of the rising generation. Adult phantasies have forced children to live within an unstable and narcissistic adult political psychology. As in Northern Ireland, the former USSR and Yugoslavia, our children have been forced to share adult wars, violence and rivalries and have learned that power is based upon force. The aggressive collective narcissism of adults is communicated to children, who direct it back towards the adult world that they perceive as exploiting children and failing to respect them.

The symbiotic relationship between children and adults contains both dependence and rivalry especially during adolescence, when covert or overt sexual and social rivalries are developing. For example, a so-called street child, *C.*, aged about 13, told me about his life: he advised me about the best rubbish bins in which to find clean food to cook, and how to evade police raids. He was forced to be both child and adult. He had no long term contact with adults, yet had to use the world of adults although it had rejected him. And he had cynically and intelligently learned to manipulate it. Many children have been forced into a defensive narcissism that is analogous to the collective narcissism of adults. 'The core of narcissism is a hatred of the relational - a hatred of something that is inherent in our being' (Symington, 1993, p. 18). Moreover, the defence of narcissism denies that individuals can only survive by relating to others. *C.* was on the edge of a narcissistic retreat from the world: he felt that he needed others for his survival but he was utterly cynical about his relationship to adults and the adult world, which was there to be used but not trusted.

The Development of Emotional Security

I once asked *S.* (aged 20) what sort of person he would like to become if he could be any sort of person. He replied: 'A white person!' His sardonic and emphatic tone insinuated: 'Of course! Wouldn't you if you'd had my life?' Like many, maybe most (we do not know), young Africans, he identifies himself as a Black African, and his Rastafarian beliefs reinforce his sense of identity, but like many Africans he is ambivalent about this strongly asserted identity. He contrasts his experiences and life-chances with whites of his own age, but he is unsure whom to blame for his impoverished life. His sense of self is such a tangled tissue of negative and positive fragments that it is a struggle to harmonise them as well as circumstances and his innate strengths and sensitivities permit. But he hopes that a new South Africa will set children as well as adults free.

And what do circumstances permit ? Too few African children have enjoyed Winnicott's 'average expectable environment'. For too many children the expectable environment has been alienating, violent and both lonely and grossly overcrowded. But it may be optimistically (though cautiously) noted that 'violence is always context-bound ... Children interpret the content of violence in terms of socialised expectations and cultural context ... Children living in areas where there is some hope of liberation are less affected by living with conflict. Perhaps in South Africa young people may cope better over the next few years, as hope increases for a negotiated and just settlement' (Liddell et al., 1993, pp. 21-25). Frightened and angry children have lived in a world in which adult caring and protection have been gravely eroded by apartheid. 'My grannie can't help me', a 15-year-old boy told me, 'she's too old'. But there was no other adult. His family was one of the thousands that had rarely had an adult male for protection. I suspect that beneath the bravado there is fear, anxiety, stress and turbulent feelings of depersonalisation and of revenge against the adult world that has abandoned and neglected the children that it ought to have protected - but was unable to. The punitive and authoritarian ethos of child care and education fosters feelings of guilt: these terrible things have happened to us, because we children have been wicked and deserve the punishments that we get from adults. For too many children there are no 'good enough mothers' (as Bowlby and Winnicott describe them) because of the obstacles of poverty and social disruption. Many children unconsciously feel that the lack of good mothers (and fathers) is because the children are bad. Children find that the world that adults present them with is dangerous, yet the world of childhood is no safer as a refuge. Adult carers came and went with bewildering unpredictability as poverty and apartheid laws forced adults to adopt a nomadic way of living; and the harsh treatment of children (and adults) demonstrates the institutionalisation of 'the taboo on tenderness' (Suttie, 1988). Symington is concerned about the emotional consequences of growing up nomadically without a stable 'life-giver', the deepest

emotional contact with another. If there is not a life-giver then the child
may turn inward and become locked in an intense narcissism, but this self-
love is rarely, if ever, a true love, but is permeated with self-hate: 'no-one
loved me, so I'm unlovable. I hate myself for being unlovable'. Children
may reject the life-givers that they unconsciously long for because they fear
that the life-giver has rejected them. 'When an infant is born physically, it
does not necessarily mean that it has been born psychologically or
emotionally. The emotional birth rests upon a choice' (Symmington, 1993,
p. 34). But there can be no true choice if reality prevents the child from
choosing; the turbulence of apartheid made the conditions of choosing
immensely difficult.

Healthy adults are emotionally interdependent upon each other, in
contrast to 'the largely skewed dependence of infancy' (Greenberg and
Mitchell, 1983, p. 161), but interdependence can only develop where it is
emotionally and physically safe and where the child senses that it is both
encouraged and safe. It must be safe for the developing child to share
emotions and experience with others, to project feelings and introject them,
to accept that our relationships are rarely unambivalent but are often an
effervescent interaction of love and hate, affiliation and distancing. There
can be no healthy development if the child had no freedom nor security to
choose a life-giver. Moreover, a child who is a passive recipient of an
imposed life-giver has not the emotional freedom for the essential emotional
adventuring of finding a meaningful life-giver. South African children,
particularly those deemed to be in need of care, still have too little
emotional freedom within the authoritarian practices and attitudes of 'care'
to develop a spontaneous capacity to become 'a differentiated individual for
co-operative relationships with differentiated objects' (Fairbairn, 1946, p.
145).

The Development of Identity

Apartheid imposed group identities and permitted little room for children to
search for the relationships, situations and values that suited them. The
enforced group identity is an impoverished identity: it forces many
individuals to adopt False, a compliant, self and their idiosyncratic, private
and personal sense of self is blocked from developing. A Manichean view
of the world permeates relationships. The world is dichotomised into
sharply split good and evil groups - adults and children, and strangers

(ethnic or national, social class, male and female) are readily interpreted as potentially or actually threatening because of their *difference*. Africans and whites became each other's shadows. A new psychology for a new South Africa needs to be bolder and more open in discussing and healing these divisions.

Paradoxically, apartheid damaged children by both its long life and its erratic instability. Family and community life was destroyed, and many children were emotionally damaged by the arbitrary upheavals of their relationships with adults. Moreover, children only develop a healthy sense of self where society encourages individuality. Apartheid was deeply hostile to individuality. The dominant ideology was a complex system of hierarchies of worth and worthlessness and in the obligation to conform to social norms uncritically. And the ideology and the practices lasted during several generations.

Consider, for example, *C.*, aged about 13, whose father is probably white and whose mother is Xhosa. *C.* is a so-called 'Coloured' child, who in Europe would probably pass for a fair-skinned Arab. By his seventh year he had been rejected by his father and his father's family, was also rejected by his mother and her family and became a nomadic homeless child. He found himself a substitute family with other so called 'street-children', and acquired another identity, one that was acceptable by a pariah group and regarded with hostility by most adults. In 1992 he was taken into care by the family and child welfare organisation, by whom he was assessed as a 'redeemable child', and once again he found himself with an imposed identity. Once in care he was sent, against his wishes, to a Place of Safety, where he will lose his autonomy and authenticity. His contacts with the world outside the institution will be severely restricted, his freedom to chose friendships with adults and children limited, and he may become yet another victim of neat but unimaginative institutionalisation. *C.* has two ways open to maintain a viable continuity of self. The unhealthy way is to surrender to the imposed definition of 'redeemable child'. The other way is to appear to surrender, and to resist the stigmatising process in whatever ways his ingenuity allows. The individual experience of *C.* is magnified by the collective definition of people perceived as units in groups.

The True and False selves are responses to children's needs to feel protected against their internal and external threats and dangers. Children need to feel that they are real, autonomous selves in control of their loving and aggressive emotions, and both valued by others and valuable in their own self-esteem. Children also live in a world which must provide them with adults who spontaneously love, protect and support them. If the adults in a child's world lack spontaneity and love, then the child will have to struggle to feel spontaneous love for others. Too many children have had to make do with adults whose own hardships and insecurity have diminished their ability to give strength to their children. The rigid and constraining racism and class structure of apartheid have created many lives that are characterised by 'a sense of futility born of compliance' (Winnicott, 1988, p.127). The True self depends upon emotional freedom, and 'freedom arises out of the emotional intercourse between one person and another. More accurately, there can be no freedom unless there has been such an experience established into the structure of the personality' (Symington, 1990, p. 102). The obsessive structures of apartheid effectively diminished and restricted the freedom for children to explore the wide experience of emotional intercourse in which spontaneity, responsibility and social sensitivity can alone develop.

Solidarity depends upon trust and trust depends upon spontaneous and democratic relationships between adults and children. Too many children feel like *S.*, aged 20, who said: 'I stay alone. My mother stays alone ... I think I'll suffer forever ... they never buy me a shirt ... Nothing good when I was little. All was painful. All was struggle. I was always crying with hunger. No place to sleep ... I've never even been told my birth date'. Not surprisingly, *S.* is an active organiser of a small, intimate quasi-family of youngsters, giving the love that he has never had but often imagined. The group has developed a solidarity, regarded with suspicion by child welfare workers, who cannot accept that the youngsters are creating a meaningful solidarity that society has never provided nor allowed them to form. For many children the safest response to adults is a quick, superficial submission, to 'learn to effect a balance between a life-saving apathy in regard to the environment and an ever-ready alertness' (Rappaport, 1968, p. 721). But it is not only the homeless and the institutionalised children who develop their own adult-rejecting norms, but all those children who have learned how dangerous are adults in a society that is hostile to children.

It is a commonplace of developmental psychology that children are influenced by their peer groups. The stigmatising of so-called 'street children' or the homeless reinforces the children's ambivalence about adults, who may be idealised unrealistically as magic-helpers (Fromm, 1945), or more realistically rejected because of their power to reject, beat or refuse to love the children. Adult aggression and rejection is an additional force to press children to live emotionally within the only family or support group that they feel they belong to. There can be little doubt that children who are so effectively banished from democratic and spontaneous relationships with supportive adults will experience obstacles to developing a sense of self-worth and identity. They may, moreover, experience problems of greater or lesser severity in adulthood in making spontaneous relationships, attachments and normal sexuality. If 'violence [is] a by-product of psychological trauma ... processed into rage' (de Zulueta, 1993, pp. xi) adults should be amazed and thankful that so few children are violent in a world that traumatises them, and compels them to adapt to adult violent norms.

Identity Confusion

Identity confusion is encouraged by a world in which adults are distant and dangerous. Children cannot easily form benign relationships if adults have a fairytale capacity to vanish and reappear and have unchallengeable powers to do damage or harm to children. For many children development is 'a struggle for power and destruction and the fear of retaliation' (Greenberg and Mitchell, 1983, p. 123). African children have had particular problems in establishing permanent, supportive relationships with adults and in exploring their identity in a world in which there is no benign stability. Children are often almost obsessed with their fragmentary relationships with adults and the transition from child to youth to adult is unnecessarily painful.

   T., aged 20, was not alone in pleading for adults to change their attitudes towards young people. Adults ought 'to say the truth ... and try to encourage youth to help themselves in all their talents and moods that young people know what they are ... And give good schools and respect us. And then we'll respect them. But the township adults are very cruel. They are against us'. *L.*, aged 13, was as cogent, as we walked past the police station: 'If the government built more schools, they wouldn't need jails'. Winnicott wisely observed that 'it may be hard for people who have had fortunate environmental experiences to understand [that] ... if we deprive a child of transitional objects and disturb the established transitional phenomena, then the child has only one way out, which is a split in the personality with one half related to a subjective world and the other reacting on a compliance basis to the world which impinges' (Winnicott, 1992, pp. 187-88). A major and delicate task for a new South Africa will be to evolve some form of collective psychotherapy, integrated with economic and social reconstruction, to allow children to grow up without traumatic disturbances so that they may develop a spontaneous True self that no longer has to fear the psychic destruction caused by social practices that make splitting commonplace.

Towards Putting Young People Back Together Again

The cynicism of many children about adults is well-merited, and often well concealed behind a superficial compliance. I asked *B*. (aged 14) if he went to church and what he believed. He replied: 'I believe in the food and clothes the church gives us!' Cynicism is a sublimation of anger, and repressed anger is an integral attitude of many children who have been abused *as individual people* by the world of adults. In South Africa the never-faced problem of establishing an emotionally satisfying authentic democracy is that in our adult relationships with children conformity is preferred to independence, obedience to enterprise, aggression to love and distance to affiliation and comradeship. Children are people too! Their status and dignity as individuals must be assured so that they can be enabled and empowered to manage their lives, while yet being sensitive to the lives of their fellows. The arbitrary interventions by adults reduce children to the status of parcels to be delivered, stored or otherwise disposed of. For example, within the obsessively detailed definitions and provisions of child care legislation and practice from 1960, children have no effective rights in decisions, about their lives and only the most meagre opportunities to express their feelings, opinions and wishes. The bureaucratic framework is so tightly controlling that it shows no appreciation of children's needs for emotional space in which to develop emotionally and socially. Children need to live in a society that does not denigrate or demean them because of their sex, age, wealth or poverty, ethnic, national, religious, or other arbitrarily defined category. All children need to feel wanted, valued and respected even, or especially, those who are in some ways, unlovable and difficult.

The immediate need is for psychologists, psychiatrists, social workers (and other professionals), to be assertive in advocating human rights based upon the human needs for independence, emotional space for the growth of identity, and of one's unique talents and intelligence. And above all, for freedom from the constraints of adult-imposed impotence and poverty.

References

Bloom, L.(1960), 'Self concepts and social status in South Africa', *Journal of Social Psychology,* vol. 51, pp. 1-10.

Bloom, L.(1972), 'Values and attitudes of Zambian youth, studied through spontaneous autobiographies', *African Social Research,* vol. 14, pp. 288-300.

Bloom, L.(1978), 'Values and attitudes of young Nigerians: responses to social change', *West African Journal of Sociology and Political Science,* vol. 2, pp. 99-115.

Bloom, L. 1982), 'Lying and culture: a West African case-study', *Journal of Psychoanalytic Anthropology,* vol.3(2), pp. 175-84.

Burman, S.(1986), 'The contexts of childhood in South Africa: an introduction', in S. Burman and P. Reynolds (eds), *Growing up in a Divided Society,* Johannesburg: Raven Press.

Dawes, A.(1994), 'The emotional impact of political violence', in A. Dawes and D. Donald(eds), *Childhood and adversity,* Cape Town: David Philip.

de Zulueta, F.(1993), *From pain to violence: the traumatic roots of destructiveness,* London: Whurr.

Donald, D. and Dawes, A.(1994), 'The way forward: developmental research and intervention in contexts of adversity', in A. Dawes and D. Donald (eds), *Childhood and adversity,* Cape Town: David Philip.

Fairbairn, W.R.D.(1946), 'Object-relationships and dynamic structure', in W.R.D. Fairbairn (1952), *An Object-relations theory of personality,* New York: Basic Books.

Fromm, E.(1945), *The fear of freedom,* London: Kegan Paul.

Greenberg, J.R. and Mitchell, S.A.(1983), *Object relations in psychoanalytic theory,* Cambridge, MA: Harvard University Press.

Hunt, J.C.(1989), *Psychoanalytic aspects of field work,* London: Sage.

Liddell, C.(1994), 'Diversities of childhood in developing countries', in L. Eisenberg and R. Desfarlais (eds), Culture and medicine: international perspectives on mental health, Cambridge, MA: Harvard University Press.

Liddell, C., Rapodile, J. and Masilele, P.(1991), 'Historical perspectives on South African children', *International Journal of Behavioural Development,* vol. 14(1), pp. 1-19.

Liddell, C., Kvalsig, J., Strydom, N. and Qotyama, P.(1993), 'The young lions! South African children and youth in political struggle', in L. Leavitt and N. Fox et al. *International perspectives on political violence,* Hove: Lawrence Erlbaum.

Rappaport, E.A.(1968), 'Beyond traumatic neurosis', *International Journal of Psycho - analysis,* vol. 49, pp. 719-31.

Richter, L.(1988), 'Street children: the nature and scope of the problem in southern Africa', *The Child Care Worker,* vol. 6(7), pp. 11-14.

Straker, G., with Moosa, F., Becker, R. and Nkwale, M.(1992), *Faces in the revolution: the psychological effects of violence on township youth in South Africa,* Cape Town: David Philip.

Suttie, I.D.(1988), *The origins of love and hate,* London: Free Association Books.

Swart-Kruger, J. and Donald, D.(eds) (1994), 'Children in the South African streets', in D.Donald and A. Dawes (eds) *Childhood and adversity,* Cape Town: David Philip.

Symington, N.(1990), 'The possibility of human freedom and its transmission (with particular reference to the thought of Bion)', *International Journal of Psycho-analysis*, vol. 71(1), pp. 95-106.

Symington, N.(1993), *Narcissism: a new theory*, London: Karnac Books.

Walker, C.(1990), 'Women and gender in southern Africa to 1945: an overview', in C. Walker (ed) *Women and gender in southern Africa in 1945*, Cape Town: David Philip.

Ward, I.(1988) Introduction, in J. Kovel *White racism: a psychohistory*, London: Free Association Books.

Winnicott, D.W.(1988), 'Clinical varieties of experience', in D.W. Winnicott *Through paediatrics to psychoanalysis*, London: Hogarth Press.

Winnicott, D.W.(1992), *Deprivation and delinquency*. London: Routledge.

8 Quasi-family, Quasi-psychotherapy: Six Years of Living Together, Black and White, in South Africa

'This mournful truth is everywhere confessed,
SLOW RISES WORTH, BY POVERTY DEPRESSED'.
(Dr Johnson: London: Poem written in imitation of Juvenal's Third
Satire, lines 176, 177)

Introduction

In an ideal world home is where we start from, and that home is integrated into a stable and supportive community. For nearly a century in South Africa, most African children have been prevented, by poverty and by the legal and social turmoil of apartheid, from growing up in stable homes - emotionally, socially and physically tolerable. Children have had to defy and survive psychic and material impoverishment and create for themselves such makeshift homes as they could. Like Anna Freud's and Sophie Dann's children from the Theresienstadt concentration camp, 'a combination of fateful outside circumstances' uprooted hundreds of thousands of African children and chance sent three of them to my house.

Coming together

In April 1992, it was barely two years since apartheid's laws were abolished. The laws had gone, but many practices and attitudes lingered on. I was teaching psychology at a university and lived in a white, middle-class neighbourhood in a conservative cathedral town. No Africans lived in the area, which was effectively out of bounds to them except for hawkers, job-seekers, a few students and many begging boys. An African postgraduate student shared my house, and we grew used to youngsters begging at our

157

front gate. We fed the children and felt helpless to do more for them. Most of our neighbours were indifferent, but two households were openly hostile and only one neighbour openly supported us.

In 1992 an African child was foolhardy to be in the white man's town, and knocking on his door was bravery indeed and could be dangerous. Late one night in April there was an unusually persistent knocking: at the door (protected, of course, by burglar bars), stood a small boy, seemingly about 12 years old, shivering in tattered cast-off clothes, apprehensive but jaunty. He begged courteously for food and coffee and as he ate he chatted about his life as a 'street-child' in fluent but wildly street-made English. He left, and we were surprised when he reappeared the next night. He taught us his Xhosa name (Ayanda) and asked if he could bath and wash some clothes. He told us more about the poverty of his great grandmother, who raised him as an infant and movingly described how (like other children) he had had to leave his great grandmother to find shelter with other poor, homeless children. He had had to hide from the violent police (black as ferocious as white), learned to beg for food, clothes and shelter from university students and survived until 'I found your home in 1992 and got settled'.

The third night that he returned he announced: 'You've got a big house. Can I move in and you can look after me...I'm very clean and quiet'. We agreed but insisted that his granny must agree, he must attend school and keep out of trouble. He moved in, stopped truanting and soon scored 80% in school tests. A few days later he introduced his friend, Bongani, who was older, frail and deeply depressed. He pleaded for the silent Bongani, and reluctantly we let him move in. The two grannies came to discuss the future of the boys and to check our *bona fides*. We passed. We were trusted and one night Ayanda warned me for the first time: 'never forget, Len. We're *your* kids now!' I tried to persuade the boys to accept that we could not know how permanent or temporary our relationship would be and gradually we evolved the *modus vivendi* that transformed a house into a home that housed a quasi-family.

A week or two passed and one evening the boys invited Danilé to dinner. He was older, wore unconventional dreadlocks (which later caused him to be rejected from school), barely spoke, ate little and seemed deeply depressed, defeated and wary of rejection. Only after several visits did he begin to talk freely and eat. So he, too, moved in and slowly matured into a warm and caring elder-brother and an intuitive (if sometimes irresponsible) son. He had lost four years schooling and is still sharply aware of his lack of education and wasted skills and talents.

By late May 1992 I was sheltering three teenagers. During the first night that Ayanda slept in the house, he wet his bed and came to me apologetically in the morning with the sheet. It was then clear that I was providing more than a shelter: I was now going to be living three inseparable roles: mother, father and psychotherapist, and that from situation to situation my role would change unpredictably.

We still live together, but the boys have neither neglected their grandmothers nor lost their township friends, some of whom visit us freely. The boys have chosen to live in - not between - two interacting worlds, and each has formed his individual style to reconcile, minimise and avoid conflicts between them. I, too, live in their two worlds, and I am aware that it is far easier for me than for the boys to keep those worlds far enough apart to feel comfortable.

Recurring Themes

Four broad themes recur in this chapter as in life:

1. The question 'What is a quasi-family?' poses both ethical and substantive issues. What, for example, are the responsibilities that the members owe each other? Are they the same for a 'real' family as for a 'quasi-family'? How do individual histories and cultures influence the relations between family members? How do relationships between family members change?

2. How do love-hate relationships develop in the family, and how are they influenced by individuality and cultures? Have adults the right to influence the spontaneous flow of feelings - if, indeed, they are able? Is love in the quasi-family 'real', some sort of analogue of 'love' in psychotherapy? Is love in the quasi-family more than, indeed different from, an unending succession of transferences and counter-transferences that must be resolved, ignored or lived through?

3. In South Africa, black-white relationships are still tainted by racism. In our quasi-family, the formation of their adolescent identities was complicated because they are African and I am white.

Whom did they think they were and were becoming? Whom do they feel that I think they are? Does 'their' culture and that of 'whites' mean anything to them?

4. The boys come from a euphemistically 'disadvantaged' background. This suggests that they have had to overcome obstacles to developing self-esteem, competence and independence. Has our quasi-family been able to provide a safe enough emotional base in which 'Real' selves can be developed to offset the 'False' self imposed on them by society and culture? Indeed the following questions could be asked: what do they see as their culture? What do they feel about it?'

Dawes and Donald succinctly set out the difficulties facing those who wish to explore the conflicting influences shaping the developing young adult:

'Childhood' is defined by a society, and if that society consists of dramatically conflicting values - as does South Africa - then 'childhood' will be defined in several, contradictory ways. White 'children' are still seen as different from African 'children'. I doubt the use of searching for 'the universal normative child' with whom to compare an individual child. What *is* useful is to try to appreciate the individual child's efforts to deal with the survival tasks which confront them ... the notion of adaptive power ... is as much an assertion of the active, agentic child as a force in its own development, as it is an assertion of the social forces that interact with, and thus are shaped by, that very capacity for adaptation. (Dawes and Donald, 1994, p. 23)

Some Methodological Cautions

Anna Freud has remarked that 'the analyst comes on the scene as a disturber of the peace ... He destroys compromise formations ... bringing the unconscious into consciousness ... hence ... the ego institutions respond to the analyst's purpose as a menace' (Freud, 1993, p. 29). I, too, was a disturber of the peace when Ayanda, Bongani and Danilé moved into my home. Like any analysand they *chose* to expose themselves to the menace of an intimate relationship. Like any analyst I have had to try to be sensitive to the stresses of transference and counter-transference and to the unpredictable shifts of how we interpret reality and our moment-to-moment feelings about each other. And 'what is meant by "reality"? It would seem to be something very erratic, very undependable ... what remains over when the skin of the day has been cast into the hedge ...' (Woolf, 1988, p. 104).

Danilé once told me: 'When I talk about the past it hurts me. I can see in my eyes exactly what was happening: my home, the surroundings, the people. And when I go out I feel I'm going to meet it all again'. In psychoanalysis, founded upon personal statements, it is a problem to separate reality from the accumulated repressions and elaborations of the past. This is no less a problem in everyday life - and one of its delights and dilemmas. Life is a construction: '"world making" is the principal function of mind, whether in the sciences or the arts ... [And biographies] and autobiographies are a continuing interpretation and reinterpretation of our experience ...' (Bruner, 1987, pp. 12, 13). That Danilé is hurt by his past - the reality as he feels it - and that this is ever-present to him, tells much about his perception of his world. The next step in understanding Danilé is to share with him what in his childhood situations and relationships might account for his pessimism. Bruner asks the interesting question 'What are the "possible" lives that are a part of one's culture?' (Bruner, 1987, p. 15), and asserts that 'there is no such thing psychologically as "life itself" ' (Bruner, 1987, p. 13) because individuals always live *their own lives,* even when they are unacceptable, rejected parts of a culture. Ayanda, Bongani and Danilé were labelled as 'poor', 'homeless', pariah 'street-children', and have resisted these labels imposed upon them. How have they resisted? Do these demeaning labels still demean them? Shortly before I wrote these lines, Ayanda was reminiscing about his past (as he often did cathartically), and in answer to my question: 'How did you survive when you were a little someone?', replied: 'I was cute and students were kind. *And* I was quick and didn't want to go under ... But sometimes I wouldn't give a damn even if I didn't wake up next morning. I'm sure other kids felt like that...' But he continued to wake up, even when life was as uncertain and stressful as ever, and although his imposed definition as a beggar showed little sign that it might change.

'Ethnicity' and Culture

In their introductions to *Black Hamlet* (Sachs, 1937/1996), Dubow and Rose elaborate the methodological problems of psychoanalytic research across cultures. I am not convinced that the problems are necessarily as grave as they imply, but they are relevant to this paper and must be met. Briefly, I doubt that psychoanalytic enquiry applies only within western cultures, and I am convinced that none of the obstacles to understanding oneself, others and relationships within a culture differs fundamentally from striving for understanding between cultures. Understanding, intuition, empathy between individuals in one culture, evoke the same problems of emotional and cognitive communication as relationships between human beings anywhere (see, for example, Bloom, 1993).

Dubow and Rose ask the key questions: whose voice are we hearing in the narrative? Whose story is this? Who is transformed and by whom? Whose desire or fantasy are we dealing with here? What does Wulf Sachs [the analyst, story-teller] want of John Chayafambira [the subject of the story]?' (Sachs, 1996, pp. 32, 39). Sachs wrote in the late 1930s and late 1940s, when 'race relations' were highly volatile in South Africa, rapid and mass proletarianisation was uprooting millions of Africans, racist laws were proliferating and black-white contacts were almost entirely confined to master-servant relationships. Sachs' purposes in his book were: 'to show that the structure of the "native mind" is identical with that of whites'; and 'to demonstrate this in terms of the universal applicability of Freudian analysis' (Sachs, 1996, p. 11). Sachs' politically radical opinions tended to push him into 'a strong element of judgemental paternalism' (Sachs, 1996, p. 23) so that he made decisions to 'awaken' John and improve his life - as Sachs saw it. Rose asks if it was possible to cross the barriers of 'language and distrust ... Or rather, we should notice how hostility across the racial barrier ... is inseparable from the fully psychoanalytic question of what speech, in terms of its internal and external boundaries is capable of' (Sachs, 1996, p. 46).

Perhaps in the 1990s it is less acceptable to overstate culture-as-strangeness and to be diverted from individual dynamics. Even though language and communication constitute social behaviour, individuals communicate and behave in terms of their own emotions and cognition. Words gain life when they are understood as belonging to the individual as well as to society. '[One] may hear the words but be deaf to the background noise and information of the [speaker's] world by which the words are given life ... If we are sensitive we can learn our personal communication insensitivities' (Bloom, 1993, p. 204). When, for example, Ayanda first introduced himself as a beggar I did not 'hear' if he was proud or ashamed. Nor did I know how he got the label, nor what was its significance in his local, Xhosa culture - nor to him. But I could ask or infer and he soon let me 'hear' the word's emotional meaning for him. He said that 'When the township kids knew that I was a beggar, they teased me. 'Beggar! Beggar! He's a beggar!' I was worried. I'd thought they knew the situation I was in. And they grown up enough to understand! But what could I do? I was angry!' He later made close friends among other children who had to beg and felt proud that he - like his friends-survived poverty and the hostile police and adults.

In our early conversations I consciously attempted to avoid being patronising by freely admitting my ignorance and sometimes pretending to be ignorant and in need of the boys' explanations and interpretations. I was always open about my own values and political beliefs, and we soon learned that we could criticise each other's beliefs and opinions without arousing hostility. I, for example, never concealed my scepticism about religion and my disapproval of the commercialism of some aspects of Xhosa spirituality. We avoided the linguistic problem of what to call me by tacitly adopting the culturally-appropriate title, *Madala* (old man). I was soon able to tease Ayanda by calling him jocularly, 'young man', and then my name became used without any overtone of saucy familiarity. I am now 'Len' even when we are in the township and this is accepted even by older people.

Unlike a practising psychotherapist I have not had the support, advice and cautioning of a colleague with whom to discuss anomalous moods and counter-transferences. Unlike a more conventional fathering one I have had few close and understanding friends of the family. Most of my white friends and acquaintances have said or implied when I needed to share my problems and my feelings: 'I told you so!' It seems to be assumed that problems arise because the boys (it is assumed) are unwilling or unable to shed their past. The myths persist that 'you cannot expect them to leave their largely unwestern culture', so it is naive to try to bridge black-white (or African-non-African) cultural gaps. Moreover, 'As you are white, you are assumed to be rich and can therefore expect to be exploited, even if the exploitation is not malicious'. Even among 'liberal' whites I sense an uneasiness and a reluctance to accept us as a family. On the contrary, my African friends and acquaintances (who were not just South African, let alone Xhosa), are unanimously supportive. Africans seem untroubled that the boys are black and I am white, and they respond to our family problems matter-of-factly with a brisk but sympathetic: 'What do you expect in a family of four, all living together?'

As sometimes happens in psychoanalytic therapy, the boys directly probe my motives and relationships, and all of them (especially Ayanda) challenge me if they feel that I am too quick to make a judgement before fully understanding the implications of a situation: 'You must *overstand!',* he insists. Recently, for example, I was angry when Danilé appeared after midnight, drunk and with an unknown girl. Was my indignation a father's prudence or envy? My bourgeois resistance to finding a stranger trespassing on my property? A trace of a puritan objection to loose sexual behaviour? Danilé was too drunk to talk and I bundled him off to his room. In the morning he explained his uneasiness at sleeping alone without his girlfriend and baby and spoke feelingly about his cultural and personal shyness that made him try to hide the situation from me. Whatever my motives and my lack of understanding, his direct and reasonable explanation diverted me towards his world and its ethos and away from my own possible misinterpretation. His spontaneous response, confirmed by the other boys' similar behaviour, is an informal check on what in psychotherapy would be counter-transference frictions. In any family a critical, counter-transference friction may arise from 'the expectation of the [adults] which may be a reflection of "If youth but knew..."' (Speigel, 1965, p. 390). It is tempting to hope and expect too much from children, and too easy to underestimate the emotional and cultural obstacles that they have to overcome. Parents too often say or imply: 'I fought poverty and won through to my profession - so you can!' or 'I never won enough from life -so you must win in my place!'

    The boys' Xhosa friends and family (and my own friends) often play unwittingly the role of 'supervisor', so that I have become sensitive (I hope sufficiently sensitive) to avoid the mistake that 'the culture of research becomes equated with the individual's family... Anthropologists frequently talk about being 'adopted' by members of the culture of study... [so] wishes generated in a family context can impose themselves on the ongoing cultural encounter' (Hunt, 1989, p. 37). One of the more effective ways to avoid being 'adopted' is to enjoy non-research relationships in a wide, normal range, but even non-research relationships and the informal curiosity of friends about our family life are an inadequate substitute for analytic supervision and discussion. My informal relationships are, however, a constant reminder of the dangers of unconsciously confusing the roles of parent, teacher and psychotherapist (and more besides), and are an encouragement to self-scrutiny. But no amount of unsupported self-scrutiny can immediately warn if one is unconsciously acting one role while consciously verbalising another.

    Whenever there is emotional contact or commitment individuals cannot avoid psychic change arising from their mutual influence - negative or positive. Call this 'transference' and 'counter-transference' or what you will, whether the contact is within one's own culture or in 'an encounter with another culture [there] is an alternation of excitement, discovery, frustration, embarrassment, liberation, depression, elation, puzzlement and only occasionally the kind of abrupt and disconcerting surprises implied in the term "shock"' (Kracke, 1987, p. 60). Love and hate, attraction, repulsion and indifference could be added. Kracke speaks of 'transference ... in the intercultural experience [as] an intense experience which is likely to stir up phantasies and memories ...' (Kracke, 1987, p. 65). Experiences and feelings *now* are saturated by emotions from *then* and *there*. Two examples illustrate how our family situation was coloured by my lingering anxiety:

1. Kracke notes that in another culture one person becomes important as a friend who becomes an informant, guide and reassurer, much as a good parent or sibling. He or she often becomes the lightning-conductor for the anxieties and turbulence aroused by unfamiliar or threatening situations and relationships. Ayanda and Danilé are my lightning-conductors, who have often made me sensitive to relationships and problems that have aroused my emotionality.

2. Kracke describes how he 'had difficulty dealing with ... the recurrent demand for gifts and the lack of expression of gratitude when receiving one' (Kracke, 1987, p.75). Like many quasi (and real!) fathers I often feel tense when I have to share my money, clothes and desirable odds-and-ends with my teenagers. But I have learned that giving and sharing here are powerful emotional bonds between people, and are particularly salient for boys who have only experienced poverty. Gifts are not simply gifts in the western sense; giving and receiving demonstrate and strengthen the caring feelings of parents and children for each other. Often the boys (at home and when in a restaurant) spontaneously give me a portion of their food and would be hurt if I refused it. We even have a family joke: 'Have a little symbolic something'. Even Danilé's baby tries to feed us. Food has magical and real qualities: it can nourish or poison, physically or emotionally; it can be accepted or rejected, and how it is offered, accepted or refused indicates deep, primitive attitudes and relationships. Like food, money is both real and symbolic. My anxieties about spending and running-out are only partly realistic

and are more symbolically associated with unconscious fear that our family could come to an enforced end if we no longer have enough money (love) to share. (Bloom, 1984, 1991, *passim*)

Dubow and Rose discuss the problems of 'culture shock'- culture incompatibility might be more descriptive. One sign of incompatibility is 'judgemental paternalism': 'Do it my way, please!' easily slides into 'Do it my way. I know best!' Such judgements are essentially rooted in the assumption of inequality, even when they are expressed courteously. From the start of our close relationship I nearly always felt 'culture-comfortable', but even now I welcome the open and direct challenge of the boys to alert me if I am slipping into a paternalistic, judgmental stance. 'You don't understand!' one of the boys will begin and then he would go on to explain why we were not at one. Usually we do come to an understanding, or at least I am aware that my ways and the boys' differ. Sometimes it seems that I am unconsciously refusing to understand, so I have had to learn to be sensitive to the areas where mutual emotional misunderstandings are possible.

Living as a family has also alerted me to Ferenczi's dilemma: psychotherapy is either too hot or too cold. So is parenting! Neutrality is hard to maintain, and Freud consistently and realistically warned against contaminating therapy with unresolved counter-transference and transference emotions and identifications. It is a truism that family relationships swing between extremes of cold distance and over-intense warm emotionality, but just as patients (or clients) can be therapists, too, so can children be therapists to a parent.

It is too easy to repress our emotionality by denying that 'we are human. If we know we are reacting, if we are fully conscious of the reasons why one or another type of reaction ... causes us discomfort, then we are saved from any kind of actual response by this very awareness' (Sharpe, 1978, p. 58). Alas, we are rarely 'fully conscious' of our reasons, and we do often fly into an 'actual response'. Therapists are helped to avoid a *post hoc* reaction by their patient's response and if they have effective supervision or collaboration. A parent is similarly helped, as I have often been, by the boys' intuitively adopting a psychotherapeutic role. Their response: 'Why are you so angry now ... ?' does not always dispel or divert my anger or misunderstanding, but it often does. Bongani usually responds by his forensic, argumentative skills that encourage my own liking for debate. Danilé plays a helpless role and arouses my protective feelings. Ayanda stands his ground, tells me why I am angry and offers me tea and sympathy. Their friend and frequent visitor, Xolani, can often make me see the humour or ridiculousness of the disagreement. Because of the distance between the generations in most South African cultures, and because of the persisting authoritarian relationships of African fathers to their children, the boys are unusual in their growing sensitivity to my moods and their skill in diluting my authority in my role as an elder, a father.

Family: Reality and Dream

'The mystified invisible loyalties that so characterise a culture or historic group not surprisingly operate at the social level of the family ... The term 'family myths' explains just such a process of 'homeostatic' mechanisms in family life' (Stein, 1994, p. 190). In family myths, as in other relationships, what we feel or think that we are doing and what is unconsciously happening, do not always coincide. The family myth is 'the way the family appears to the members, that is, a part of *the inner image* of the group ... [But it] 'explains' the behaviour of individuals in the family while it hides its motives' (Ferreira, 1963, p. 56). One family's myth that they are steady may be regarded as volatility by another! A family's myth of their loyalty to each other may conceal deeper disloyalties. Every family has its competing internal and external allegiances and has its myths to conceal them from itself and from the outside world. In our family the main division is between what I imagine are middle-class English norms, and what the boys imagine are Xhosa. I believe that it is a reality and not a myth that we succeed in preventing our norms from clashing in most circumstances where a clash might be expected.

The boys have created for themselves a refuge, from what Ayanda witheringly describes as 'the ghetto', where they are shielded from the poverty, overcrowding, few incentives to achieve and the social and emotional problems of their childhood; but they retain and enjoy the affection and liveliness of their families, friends and township social life. Their memories of deprivation and social turmoil have not been deeply repressed, but are still recalled, sometimes dispassionately, sometimes with bitterness, often with pride that they have survived when other children have gone under. All care for their grandmothers and visit them daily; all have taken me to visit their grandmothers and friends and have had me accompany them - as their father not as a friend - to social and ceremonial events where I was expected to join in as befits my role and status. Danilé has many times sadly taken me to the site of his shack (now burned down) which he shared, as a family of brothers, with four childhood friends with whom he is still close.

The boys were already closely bonded when they settled in my house, because they had survived together for several years when they lived in the storm drains or 'under the bridge'. As a family we, too, have developed a strong sentiment of mutual dependence, and we feel increasingly free to express negative feelings about, and to each other, without fearing that we are rejecting or distancing each other. I seem to satisfy the boys' needs for dependence and for their freedom to express a younger child's spontaneous affection - and from time to time I have to tolerate an adolescent's prickly *noli me tangere* - 'hands off!' I have inevitably become both a good and a bad father: protecting, nurturing, controlling and frustrating; offering opportunities to develop skills and helping them to feel more secure emotionally; but also, because of being a good father, inevitably lessening their rejection and suspicion of adults. They are simultaneously more dependent, because they are more openly loving, and more independent, because they are more skilled and self-confident. I am obviously 'white', yet foreign and untypical of the conventional South African white man or woman: 'You're not afraid of Africans, like most of them!', Bongani commented. The boys were impressed that I am ready and willing to share an affection that they have had seldom and from few adults. I am ready to receive affection, even when it is ambivalent or cupboard love. I arouse ambivalence both because I am an individual good-bad adult, and because I cannot avoid symbolising the boys' relationships with adults beyond the family, which (with good reason) they sense as hostile to children and young adults.

Parent and children roles develop: 'characterological change does not take place through interpretation, but through experience, "micro-internalisations" of the [parents'] functions as a self-object' (Greenberg and Mitchell, 1983, p. 357). Children gradually become aware of themselves as self-objects, if they find significant adults with whom to identify and if those adults reward the children emotionally for their developing self-awareness.

The boys' self-awareness, although in some indeterminate sense influenced by society and culture, seems more idiosyncratic than Social Identity Theory suggests. In a conference paper Campbell (1996, p. 49) shows how South African township youths construct their identities: they switch on (and off?) to meet the social situation. In South Africa's complex and volatile society identity must therefore be very changeable. What holds together the bits of identity? What might be the constant relationships in early childhood that help the child to resist the capriciously imposed definitions of self? (See, for example, Bloom, 1994.) The boys are probably typical in their close relationships with the grandmothers who raised them; but political, religious and social affiliations are also strong. Recently, I asked Danilé: 'What held you together in those tough times?' After much thought he replied:

> I was scared to die. But the way that we were living - our dream was to enjoy life - we felt there *was* no life for us. The doors were closed. You know that feeling: we could see we'd already died while still alive. There was this feeling: if we'd been born again it would be better. I'd ask myself, 'Why was I born into this world?' My Rastafarian beliefs helped a lot. I just changed to be a Rasta because of the suffering. Rastas helped me to forgive and taught me a lot about that if I'm into being poor, I shouldn't worry so much. Every day I'm around, every day I'm around, I'm living. We Rastas gathered together, we lived natural, made our own shelter, plants to eat, clothes. It gave us a way of living ... It's very protective that thing. Even now I still feel that I could be a Rasta ...

In a quasi-family the tensions of letting go of, and holding on to the family, are increased by its impermanence. However much the adults and children (or one of them) long for a perpetual family, the longing is going to be disappointed and the longing depressed or denied. The adults, often phantasised as guarantors of the fairy-tale that the family will live happily ever after, may arouse hostility or resentment because they are unable to provide a firm guarantee. I, too, have found it disturbing that our family is essentially impermanent: 'You're not 68, you're 28!' protested Bongani when I teasingly announced that I could not go on for ever. The boys often talk about the future, as if to make sure that it is within our control and everlasting, but Danilé is particularly uneasy about his future and cannot be reassured.

The end of the family, like the end of the analysis, provokes both liberating and unsettling emotions. The latter must be worked through as a sort of mourning. In everyday life these emotions may be obscure. For example, one evening Luvuyo (who often visited us) curled up tightly on the floor and said quietly: 'Luvuyo dead, dead now'. He had been told by social workers that he was going to be 'taken into care', regardless of his fears and wishes and with bureaucratic insensitivity. He *was* dead! We never had so dramatic a parting, but whenever I travel the boys are disturbed, steal symbolic bits of me and hide them. A few days ago, once again Ayanda pleaded with me 'Don't desert us!' and was only reassured when I reminded him that I have always returned. But there may always be that one time when I cannot return. It is impossible to reassure adequately even the normally secure child, and I may have been insensitive to reassure the boys by praising them for having survived so bravely before they found me. But recalling the past possibly 'reactivates the depressive position ... as it relives all the traumatic partings of childhood' (Berry, 1987, p. 109). Moreover, individuals must tolerate two sensitive 'positions: that of an object suffering a loss, and that of a subject imposing an absence' (Berry, 198, p. 109). The narcissistic question 'What is going to happen to me if you go?' is made more painful by the guilt-producing 'And what is going to happen to you? What have we done to make you leave us like this? What have we done to deserve this?' These emotions may be projected onto the departing adult: 'You have done a bad thing to us. You are a bad person to leave us'. There is no way to determine if we have, collectively, the emotional strength to accept the opportunities and uncertainties of our future, nor if we will be able to avoid searching regressively for another comfortable womb. In every intimate group the members test how far it is safe to assert their individual autonomy before the group relationships break beyond repair.

Parents and children get angry with each other, but beyond anger there is 'another phase ... of the attack against the parents. It's a pure withdrawal. But ... the withdrawal is not enough. There follows the hostility and hate which he uses to try to cut the bond with the parents. So that eventually withdrawal won't be necessary anymore because the parents are no good anyway' (Sandler and Freud, 1985, pp. 509-510). But these feelings, too, are ambivalent: Bongani's angry withdrawals often barely conceal repressed anger, against me and he loudly threatens that he is leaving and does not care where he goes or what will happen to him. And it is all my fault! But this anger is always transformed into an appeal for understanding and acceptance, mediated for him by one of the other boys.

Adults likewise are ambivalent about their children. Children can be overtly idealised and unconsciously rejected; unconsciously felt as an irksome bond and consciously treated as attractive; they can arouse an adult's repressed sexuality, and because of guilt that attraction evokes, they can stimulate aggression, hostility and punitiveness. Adults may fear unconsciously that they are tempted yet threatened by their children's exuberance and the acting out of childhood omnipotence. An adult's guilt if he or she rejects a child may be too painful to contain and like a compelling counter-transference may be over-compensated for by a compelling idealisation of the child.

If a quasi-family does break up, then the children may be thrust into adulthood too hastily, before they are prepared for it, or they stay fixated in childhood attitudes although their physiology and their world may force them to act grown-up. Recently, Danilé (himself a father) pleaded and screamed for me to pay for him to ride on the merry-go-round, begging for 'only one ride!' and alternating cries of 'you *must* do this for me!' with 'I'll do *anything* for you!' He was both pleading for a kid's ride, and trying to hold the family together by regressing to being the infant for whom the family would have to stay together to satisfy and protect.

Can a quasi-family develop a normal family romance, even if there is not a mother-surrogate at hand? The boys still ask directly about my female friends: 'Will she be a mother to us?', and seem indifferent if she is African or white. A 'mother' has been invented, firstly by the youngest and later by the others. The oldest boy has been most persistent in addressing one white visitor as 'mother' despite her robust irritation in rejecting the title. The boys are not bothered because 'She's a South African white who doesn't overstand us!' Some part of the boys' persistence may be a ploy, a semi-serious attempt to obtain cash, food or a cigarette, but it seems unlikely that their perseverance is only a cynical manipulation of white guilt. The boys know that they will be rejected, yet the compulsion to beg jokily for symbolic nurturing is strong. It is suggestive that they all have very close physical relationships with their girlfriends, and they are so affectionate with Danilé's baby that it seems that their girlfriends are both friends and mother-surrogates, and that they identify themselves with the happily mothered baby.

Looking Back

We now feel that we have largely succeeded in reconciling our individual needs with social and cultural norms and constraints. We have, moreover, come to understand and tolerate each others' individual style and moods. Our African friends and relations take this unusual family in their stride, accepting that we are living in two overlapping and interacting cultures. The family has become a safe container in which to act-out infantile (and adolescent) frustrations, anxieties and stress. But the question must be asked - even if it cannot yet be answered - who among the boys will be emotionally secure enough 'to discover ways of distancing himself and of accepting the unknown?' (Berry, 1987, p. 114) when he is too old to live as a child in a family? Will their early lack of a secure, stable and loving family discourage them from being the containers of their own lives? The love that the boys show for each other, for their girlfriends and for Danilé's baby gives grounds for optimism.

Some Sources of Tension

The main sources of tension between us have been about food and about the boys' sexual relationships. Our time together, although long enough to be a significant proportion of the boys' lives, is not yet long enough to give enough information about 'the ontogenesis of the self-representation of the defences' (LeVine, 1992, p. 42). A few psychodynamic snap-shots may be illuminating.

Food

For the first three months that we lived together, the boys alternated between refusing food or eating very sparingly and eating voraciously, compulsively, as if tomorrow there might be nothing to eat, or that they might not be alive to do the eating. I would find foodstuffs hidden in clothes and furniture, food intended for the next day would vanish from the fridge and when we shopped excessive quantities of food or tempting items would be 'smuggled' into the trolley. Danilé would, for example, slip 'Tinkies'- a biscuit aimed at the very young - into the shopping. Gradually the compulsion to consume has lessened as our relationships have grown more stable, but even now when my mood alarms the boys they insist that we prepare an unusually ample and elaborate meal that we must share. And even now, if Bongani or Ayanda are annoyed or disappointed they pointedly refuse to eat what I have cooked.

Anna Freud has analysed feeding disturbances, and two of the conditions that she describes are that the pleasure of eating may change, or feeding may become associated with sex or aggression (Freud, 1968, *passim)*. She points out that feeding is the child's first experience of the immediate gratification of an instinct and - we may add - that the instinctual gratification is complicated, amplified, diminished or distorted by the relationship between the feeder and the being-fed. The boys now accept that a delay in wish-fulfilment is not unbearable. Anticipation may even be pleasurable and tension is not always relieved by immediate gratification. But even now there is sometimes aggression associated with their feeding. I am absorbed by means of the food that I provide, or rejected by way of the food that is spurned. Food must be devoured so that it (I) can be safely stored away and not lost. However, not only is the 'good me' absorbed but the 'bad me' is digested, destroyed and expelled. One of the boys first let me know that he trusted me when he shared with me his secret that he knew where to find the rubbish bins with the best, clean food to cook. He was also telling me that he did not have to fear that I might withhold my nurturance. Danilé's feeding still veers between abstemiousness and near gluttony, and seems to relate to his psychosexual anxieties. Refusing food is refusing the feminine in his personality, because food symbolises life and life, in the form of a baby, is created by a woman: 'Don't want to carry a baby. I don't want the female who is inside me'. According to Anna Freud, food disorders are complicated with 'guilt feelings arising from sexual competition with the parents' (Freud, 1968, p. 58), among which are the dangers that accrue as the child grows into a potential rival - and knows that he so growing. The child who refuses to feed is presenting the parents with the message: 'I don't want to grow up. I won't eat.and then I can't grow up. Don't feed me and force me to grow up'. More disquieting is the unconscious: 'I'm scared to grow up because if I do grow up I could hurt you because you stood in my way'.

Sex and Culture

It is a truism that 'projection and displacement of aggression [and sex] are responsible for much of the strain, suspiciousness and intolerance in the relationships between individuals' (Freud, 1968, p. 72). The LeVines have studied three major causes of strain and conflict between the generations among the Gusii of Kenya. (Are they a representative East African culture?) It was found that the most disturbing tensions were in three areas: incest and avoidance; greed and jealousy; and 'other people's eyes'.

Incest and avoidance The Gusii 'practise an elaborate form of intergenerational avoidance ... between all kin who address each other with child and parent terms' (Le Vine, 1992, p.43). Their world is peopled by those who must be avoided and those who need not be, and there is a powerful preoccupation with the temptations of sexual contact, embarrassment [and arousal?] if the cultural protocol is violated.

The Xhosa avoidance protocol is that I, as a parent, should not know about nor meet the boys' girlfriends. For several months girls were smuggled into the house at night after I was thought to be asleep or occupied, and I pretended to be unaware. The boys, however, discreetly disrupted the household routine to let me know that they had had a secret visitor. Gradually the girls were allowed by their boys to become visible and eventually they became extensions of the family. And I found myself with Danilé's baby as a quasi-grandchild! The boys had made me play the father's role of pretending to see nothing, and the boys played their part of avoiding embarrassment. But I was also having to accept their sexual and social maturation and unconsciously, therefore, their rivalry. Nearly always I have been able to reconcile my Londoner's insouciance about sex with the boys' Xhosa anxiety, but my concern has broken through when health problems have arisen. At first the boys felt ill at ease with the tension between their asserting independence and my care about their health and safety, which led me to control their adventuring. They have felt increasingly confident that they can assert their independence without behaving foolishly, and we have frequently discussed the dangers of AIDS, the pros and cons of the pill, what it means to be gay or lesbian, and my help has been solicited when traditional medicine has failed to cure a genito-urinary infection.

Emotional discord may be caused by cultural or by personal disagreements, or more often by a combination of both. The protest: 'You don't understand me!' often means 'You don't understand how I'm having to cope with me and my culture!' Danilé, for example, soon felt free to introduce his two steady girlfriends and to hint about his sexual adventuring. He discusses frankly his sexual needs and is sensitive to my age, tactfully letting me know that he appreciates that I cannot be expected to share all his feeling. But as his deeper unease became manifest, I had to recognise his *cultural* need to act the part of a macho (but gentle) Don Juan, and we had jointly to accept his *individual* need to conceal from his peers his repressed homo-erotic needs by his Don Juan activities. Interwoven is his anxiety to create a mini-family of his own in which he can express his affection openly and his love unaggressively. At another extreme, Bongani is as secretive about his sexual relationships as about his social, and experiences great difficulty in sharing his feelings. Ayanda and Danilé solicit my reassurance, yet they still sometimes assert their cultural need to keep their sexual and social activities hidden from elders. Both still probe my knowledge and attitudes about 'modern' or 'western' sexual norms, and indirectly test whether I am embarrassed, disturbed or scared by their sexuality and social maturity.

Each boy, in his own way and with his own needs, tests my attitudes towards his sexual attitudes: collectively they both distance me and draw me close. Few Xhosa teenagers, however urban, would be so bold and sophisticated as to make these approaches. The boys have comfortably distanced themselves from some of the constraints of their culture, and have often discussed and approved of the contrast between the conservatism of the elders and my modern (as they see them) attitudes.

Greed and jealousy Le Vine asks 'Why is everyone expected to be jealous of any improvement in anyone else's life?' (1993, p. 45). He suggests that the Gusii find it difficult to share. The boys differ in their ability to share: Ayanda shares readily, with one eye on what is expected in our house. Bongani finds sharing very difficult. Danilé enjoys sharing, so the boys, although equally deprived when they were infants, respond individually to the cultural norm of sharing. They seem unusually ready to identify with those less fortunate, and show little envy of those much more fortunate. I seem not to be regarded as another rich white man: the boys have long been concerned to shop economically and to advise me how to avoid being charged what we call 'white man's prices'. The boys are affluent compared with most of their peers in the township, but this never seems to have aroused much envy. Many of their friends are glad that the boys no longer live in poverty, and they are careful not to arouse jealousy because boasting would be unwise, unkind and unacceptable. But they cannot help but announce their affluence by wearing nice clothes, and have developed their own rituals to deflect jealousy by letting it be known that they earn with their practical, marketable skills.

'Other people's eyes' Gusii children learn that being looked at can bring danger, so that 'visual interaction is largely excluded by the code of avoidance and respect' (Le Vine, 1992, p. 46). Humans 'see' with their feelings even more than with their eyes. It is not surprising that the ritual masking of the face or hiding other attractive, and therefore vulnerable, bits

of the self is re-enforced by a false self, a persona created as an idiosyncratic defence. Ayanda's cheerful extrovert charm is immediately responded to, and is acceptable to his Xhosa and non-Xhosa friends; but behind the mask is a shrewd and wary young man. In such an intensely crowded community as the township, physical avoidance and interaction is almost impossible, and the boys often discuss their 'visibility'. Wearing a false self can be an essential and effective physical-cum-emotional avoidance. Even though I have no social or magical powers, like the Xhosa elders I have eyes, and it took the boys more than a year before I was permitted a glimpse through their cultural and personal masks. Now we all rarely wear our masks at home.

'Other people's eyes' can both praise and censure: this was obvious when Bongani and Danilé announced in December 1995 that they must follow the rituals of circumcision by going into 'the jungle' as *abakhwetha* (initiates) and emerge as fully men. Their close relatives simultaneously praised the boys for being mature enough to make this decision, and criticised them for leaving it so long. They were content - not surprisingly - that I, a non-Xhosa but quasi-father, would foot the considerable bill. Like the boys, I was both praised for acting appropriately and criticised for the delay. I was disturbed by the boys' insistence: other *abakhwetha* had recently (and since) been severely mutilated or had died because of clumsy and insanitary circumcision, and I doubted that the ritual had any cultural or educational use for modern, urban youth. Unconsciously, no doubt, I feared that my quasi-children would be replaced by quasi-adults of whose relationship to me I was uncertain. We debated lengthily my mingled praise, encouragement and censure; the boys anxiously assured me that they would be the same Bongani and Danilé when they became men.

It has been shown that violence is an essential element of initiation, so that 'in agreeing to let their children be initiated and in participating in the proceedings the adults are willingly submitting to an attack on their children and by extension on themselves' (Bloch, 1992, p. 9). In addition, adults may get a vicarious sadistic satisfaction, because the boys are being punished for growing up to be the rivals of the adults. In being sexually mutilated the boys' manhood is desecrated, yet they are pronounced adult men, capable of fertilising. 'The community is promised permanence if it is willing to allow its young to 'die' at the hands of the 'ancestors', who actually expel the initiates from the place of life ... [but allow] the young to return ... under the leadership of the elders' (Bloch, 1992, p. 19).

Our quasi-family was accepted as a family, and I did not feel special simply because I am white, and participated fully in the rites and celebrations. Before and during their month in 'the jungle' the boys expressed strongly their conflicts about the rites. They argued that they must be initiated like their peers or they would be mocked and called 'boys!', but they considered that the rites, advice and exhortations are irrelevant. In 'the jungle' they prudently and secretly used antibiotics and organised a courier service to send me letters daily and to bring them food secretly.

The circumcision dramatised the force of other people's eyes: we all felt noticed and judged, approved but yet a source of mystery to the community. We were made to feel how close and how far apart we are, emotionally and culturally. Every family symbolises a division of loyalties between a narrower and a wider world, and our living together has made us all consciously try to integrate our values. The boys, their friends and many of their relatives knew that I had reservations about the circumcision, and the boys appreciated my reluctance and willingness to be involved. During this period I never felt that I was treated differently from any understanding Xhosa father.

Basic and Partly-resolved Issues

A family, like humanist psychotherapy, should be a Winnicottian 'facilitating environment' that sets individuals free to be themselves without the destruction of themselves or others. Ayanda, Bongani and Danilé have been emotionally robust enough to *create their family* in which they have developed their distinctive emotional styles and techniques for survival. Since 1992 they have also created a family in which they - and I - have largely succeeded in balancing what our cultures demand of us and what we need as individuals. We have found that we are free to express our feelings to each other and the boys are developing a positive sense of self, in which their confidence, self-esteem, independence and ability to give and take love, give them a realistic expectation that they will survive their futures. No child is insensitive to living with poverty, and family and social turmoil, and every child's strategies for survival are his or her own. Like Anna Freud's Theresienstadt children, Ayanda, Bongani and Danilé are 'neither deficient, delinquent, nor psychotic', because even despite their adverse childhoods they have to a considerable extent 'found an alternative placement for libido and, on the strength of this ... mastered some of their anxieties and developed social attitudes' (Freud, 1951, p. 154). They were fortunate that they were able to develop close, and sometimes lasting, relationships with students who were as caring as elder siblings, nonjudgemental and (because they were white) unconsciously dramatised their love and concern for the boys. Later, the boys found that they were able to relate to me as we developed a mutual feeling of care and support for each other.

Most of the local 'street-children' are now institutionalised, but Ayanda, Bongani and Danilé rejected the temptation to exchange their painful yet independent lives for the material security and loss of independence in an institution. This seems a strong indication of their emotional stability. Moreover, although like most people, they sometimes experience depression and self-doubts, their mutual support, political and social awareness, and their enduring relationships with their caring grannies have helped them to grow into hopeful young men.

Nunn (1996) describes six 'good reasons why hope should be considered to a greater degree than it has been in the past ... [among which are] notions such as learned-helplessness, which have been influential in the development of new forms of therapy [and] are being increasingly reformulated to include the perceived future' (Nunn, 1996, pp. 227-228). He further observes that 'individual hopes may wax and wane but perceptions of one's global future are very stable' (Nunn, 1996, p. 231). Although Bongani and Danilé sometimes feel depressed about their ability to compete in the emerging competitive South Africa, their feelings are less intense as their capacity to understand and deal with reality grows, and as they interpret challenge as increasing opportunities for Africans. 'Hope provides the anticipation of relief, is enhanced through verbalisation, sustained by a credible leader, and controls mood to enable survival behaviour .... [There is a] close relationship between coping responses and the perceived future' (Nunn, 1996, p. 238). The boys are aware of their educational weaknesses, but they know that their other skills and talents can give them strength for an independent adulthood. Moreover, they have learned effective techniques for dealing with those in power or authority, both Africans and whites. Their fluent oral English, their blend of confidence and humour, the poise that they have acquired while living in the white man's town, have taken them far from the (unhappily still common), unfocussed aggression or submissiveness of many young people towards authority.

Four unresolved issues remain: first, although the emotional relationships within the quasi- and the real family are essentially similar, the responsibilities of the members to each other differ. We do not have strong formal kinship ties, but caring and supportive attitudes are strong and persistent. For example, when Ayanda was robbed and badly assaulted, Danilé traced the assailant and beat him severely. When Ayanda came across a drunken Bongani wandering dangerously in the township, at some risk to himself he escorted Bongani home. What, then, are the limits to such acts of caring? When does responsibility for other family members end? What right has a member to disrupt the family relationships by leaving it or distancing himself.

There are no objective limits to caring or responsibility: each individual sets his own limits according to the strength of identification with other members and to the collective ego. It may be, too, that a close sense of group loyalty depends partly upon the threat to the group by the wider society. The boys feel that they belong to each other, because their culture and most adults, have made them feel that they survived by their forming themselves into a family of brothers.

Second, in the family, as in the more structured psychotherapy, members both love and hate each other spontaneously. In a family it may be far more difficult to resolve love-hate relationships that can develop unpredictably, erratically and apparently from nowhere. Psychoanalysts are professionally aware of the frictions caused by transferences and counter-transferences, but in a family there are no professional techniques to control these frictions. The boys and I often hug each other, but I feel no need to refer to Ferenczi for approval of my mothering or fathering. But there are analogies between relationships in the family and in psychotherapy. If 'the sign of countertransference lies in what the analyst habitually accepts from the patient and what he habitually ignores ... [the analyst] refuses to recognise the individuality of the patient because we project archaic images onto him ... We continually resume our dispute with our own archaic internal objects' (Klauber, 1987, p. 37). In a family, too, some relationships are accepted and some emotions readily shared, and others rejected. Emotional tensions and satisfactions emerge and vanish, but their origins may be too well hidden for them to be diffused. Parents and children *should* feel free to hug each other, although it has been argued that 'however highly the [adult] may prize love he must prize even more the opportunity for helping his [children] over a decisive stage in ... life. [They have] to learn from him to overcome the pleasure principle, to give up a satisfaction which lies to hand ... in favour of a more distant one, which is perhaps altogether more uncertain, but which is both psychologically and socially unimpeachable' (Freud, 1924, p. 170).

In both psychotherapy and in a family 'love consists of new editions of old traits and it repeats infantile reactions. But this is the essential characteristic of being in love' (Freud, 1924, p. 168). There is always the danger that relationships are being exploited to satisfy the adults' unconscious needs, to respond negatively, angrily or vengefully to infantile frustrations, or to echo pleasurable relationships of the past. Children, too, unconsciously recreate the past to enrich or to redress the present. Therefore, in a family the spontaneous situations and relationships are often seen to be spontaneous, and they are neither easily understood, nor controlled nor focused on the here-and-now. This volatility cannot be avoided, because the very richness of family life is based upon the irrepressible feelings, phantasies and relationships of childhood. In a quasi-family, adults must be especially sensitive to their emotional vulnerabilities as well as to those of children who have had a homeless or otherwise traumatic childhood, and who may reject adults while unconsciously craving and soliciting their attention and love.

However, we *are* a family and not in group therapy! We feel like a family: we do not feel like a therapist and clients who have not chosen to be clients. My professional and my paternal egos do sometimes conflict, but they are often far apart because parental concern comes first, and such concern must respect the children's privacy, eccentricities and awkwardnesses, and must take for granted their integrity. Psychoanalysis is a mutual engagement of quite another kind, with its own goals, relationships and commitments. A parent, like an analyst, if he is to be worth anything, should be free emotionally to enjoy 'the rich variety of every type of human experience that has become part of [him], which would never have been [his] either to experience or to understand in a single mental life, but for [being a parent]' (Sharpe, 1978, p. 122).

Third, a major part of growing up is our success or failure to understand our psychic life and our social relationships so that we have a 'feeling of coherence and identity' (Widlöcher, 1987, p. 137). It is not enough to be socially acceptable and to play competently the social roles that are expected of us. We must also feel integrated, comfortable that our idiosyncracies and inconsistencies, our differences from others (no less than our similarities), are respected and valued by the significant-others in our lives. We need to feel that we are needed for our own self, even despite the pricklier bits of our self, and we need to feel that we have emotional space in which to feel real and a person.

Apartheid forced millions of children to doubt their identity and their sense of self by arbitrarily and oppressively imposing on them an inferior and demeaning 'False Self'. The institutionalised aggression of apartheid made it difficult for many children to develop a healthy 'self-representation system ... that is, an internal representation for the child of a loved self, a secure self, and a personalised self' (Widlöcher, 1987, p. 143; also see Bloom, 1996a,b). Yet many African children have grown into mature and stable adults. Why do some children resist the depersonalisation caused by a violent, segmented and dehumanising society, while others are more resilient? Children may themselves survive by being protective mothers or fathers to other children. Luvuyo's caring for his deeply disturbed friend Xolani, and Ayanda's protecting the older but vulnerable Bongani, almost certainly saved all four boys from emotional disintegration.

The less vulnerable children have many qualities - we should never forget their courage - of which perhaps the most salient are that they have social skills, warmth and openness, and are 'well regarded not only by their peers but also, and perhaps more important, by themselves' (Segal and Yahraes, 1979, p. 285). In addition, the less vulnerable have been able to identify 'with at least one figure among the adults who touch their lives [and have] a well-developed sense of personal identity' (Segal and Yahraes, 1979, p. 286). A narcissistic self-regard is therefore not necessarily emotionally unhealthy but may be an emotional strength. It is only partly true that 'stress and adversity' serve as a 'training ground': not only do some children fail to transform adversity into opportunity because of their weak ego and ego-ideal, but the significant adults in their early lives may be models of defeat who were unable to encourage the child's skills and emotional strengths. Children's vulnerability may, therefore, be caused by an interaction of internal and external influences. Bongani was raised in circumstances as unfavourable as Ayanda's, yet Bongani is as pessimistic and hurt by disappointments as Ayanda is optimistic and able to wrench some advantage from unpromising circumstances. Ayanda was valued and needed in relationships that were emotionally meaningful to him; Bongani was not.

In South Africa being 'black' or 'white' raises its own problems of identity and vulnerability: group identifications were enforced and valued. Ayanda, Bongani and Danilé are probably anomalous in their success in developing multiple commitments and identifications, some of which conflict while others do not, some are interrelated, and others are segmented or encapsulated. They have lived in several worlds as several Ayandas,

Bonganis and Danilés, yet they are three strikingly different individuals, each with his distinctive style of dealing with his drives, needs, wants and relationships. Our family as a retreat has probably made this individualising easier. My peculiar status as an outsider, a psychologist and writer, and my own un-South African independent nonconformity has provided them with a rare and somewhat exotic model.

During most of their crucial adolescence the boys have lived freer of personal and cultural judgements than their peers: their choice of commitments and the depth of their conformity has been *theirs* and have been supported by me and a handful of my African and white friends. The family has been a cultural and personal refuge, as once were the Rastas, and from both the boys have developed attitudes towards the future that are supportable and personal to them, even where they do not conform to 'traditional' Xhosa culture or relationships.

Mitchell and Black (1995) suggest that Erikson's and Kohut's ego psychologies are complementary: 'Erikson explored the phenomenology of selfhood. Taken together, they (along with Winnicott) opened up the problem of personal subjectivity and meaning for psychoanalytic exploration' (Mitchell and Black, 1995, p. 141). None of them has nullified the classical Freudian psychobiology of unconscious drives and psychic processes - nor could they. All three boys grew up in a culture of anti-law, maybe anti-white, poverty-induced thieving. To survive physically and emotionally children have had to steal, get away with it and develop a super-ego that allowed them to forgive themselves. Ayanda seems to have hated himself for stealing and hated the society that forced him to. Bongani seems to have neutralised his super-ego by withdrawing from social pressures and relationships. Danilé seems to hate himself for having had to steal to survive, and like Ayanda he has an astonishing capacity to forgive the unforgivable society and the individuals who drove him.

Fourth, crucial to whether children 'learn' learned-helplessness is whether they are stigmatised as disadvantaged and then prevented from fighting free of the label. In South Africa there has been a sharp division between the advantaged and the (euphemistically labelled) disadvantaged. Disadvantage provides models that suggest that low self-esteem and incompetence are elements of identity and as difficult to defy as poverty. The experience of Ayanda, Bongani and Danilé shows that one should be wary of assuming that a culture of poverty is inescapable. All three boys joined groups and activities in which they had a measure of success, even if it were only to construct a wind and rain proof shelter, to learn to prepare food, to beg for food and clothes and a place to wash. All have now discovered that they have skills that could earn them independence; none has retreated into the phantasy world of becoming an entertainer or sportsman. All have kept a guardedly optimistic world-view from their time as Rastas, and they have fashioned their own styles of assertiveness.

Conclusions

Our family experiences show that cultural and social differences between individuals are not insurmountable obstacles to empathy and understanding. We learned to talk and empathise with each other, even when personal or cultural misunderstandings have made it difficult to reach each other. So it is in psychotherapy, and as in psychotherapy everyday relationships are often transference relationships, so we have had to appreciate our unconscious and irrational needs for each other. Sandler *et al.* (1989, p. 284) showed that 'to a degree that would not be possible in normal life, infantile impulses, phantasies, object relationships, conflicts, and solutions become alive in the present...' In an emotionally close and long-lasting quasi-family whose members have come together because they need each other, intense transferences are not only possible, but inevitable. Some of our problems of living together have been the acting-out of that 'irrational relatedness to another person' that is the very stuff of human existence. In the family, as in psychotherapy, 'what we are dealing with is the need of a person to have another person to fulfil this need' (Fromm, 1994, p. 120).

Ayanda, Bongani and Danilé have been wantonly hurt emotionally by a callous society's indifferent or hostile adults: inevitably the quasi-family became a quasi-therapeutic group despite my wishes. The boys and I act out our conflicts and relationships. Together we try to understand the negative emotional and social messages of the adults in their world, by bringing them into consciousness. The authoritarian adult world tried to impress upon them that they were worthless because they were poor and without families or communities to support and encourage them. The boys have had to fight for themselves to feel worthwhile individuals - authentic, independent and proud that they have survived *as individuals* and not failed as victims. The fight continues!

References

Berry, N.(1987), 'The end of the analysis' in J. Klauber, J. Symington, R. Kennedy, P. Casement, N. Berry, D. Widlöcher and H. Thomä (eds), *Illusion and spontaneity in psychoanalysis*, London: Free Association Books, pp. 99-130.

Bloch, M.(1992), *Prey into hunter: the politics of religious experience*, Cambridge: Cambridge University Press.

Bloom, L.(1984), 'Psychological aspects of wealth in poorer societies', *The Journal of Psychoanalytic Anthropology*, vol. 7, pp. 189-208.

Bloom, L.(1993), 'Psychotherapy and culture: a critical view', *The Psychoanalytic Study of Society*, Vol. 17. New York: International Universities Press, pp. 181-211.

Bloom, L.(1994), 'Ethnic identity: a psychoanalytic critique', *Psychology in Society*, vol. 19, pp. 18-30.

Bloom, L.(1996a), 'The emotional damage of apartheid: a psychoanalytic view', *Psychoanalytic Psychotherapy in South Africa*, vol. 4, pp. 55-70.

Bloom, L.(1996b), 'Apartheid's children: the emotional costs', *Changes* , vol. 14, pp. 148-158.

Bruner, J.(1987), 'Life as narrative', *Social Research*, vol. 54, pp. 11-32.

Campbell, C.(1996), 'Identity salience in context: the social identity of South African youth', Abstract in Social Psychology Section, *Proceedings of the British Psychology Society*, vol. 4, pp. 49.

Dawes, A. and Donald, D.(1994), 'Understanding the psychological consequences of adversity', in A. Dawes and D. Donald (eds), *Childhood and adversity: psychological perspectives from South African research*, Cape Town: David Philip, pp. 1-27.

Ferreira, A.J.(1963), 'Family myth and homeostasis', *Archives of General Psychiatry*, vol. 9, pp. 55-61.

Freud, A.(1937/1993), *The ego and the mechanisms of defence*, London: Karnac Books.

Freud, A.(1946/1968), 'The psychoanalytic study of infantile feeding disturbances', in A. Freud, *Indications for child analysis and other papers: the writings of Anna Freud*, vol.IV, New York: International Universities Press, pp. 39-59.

Freud, A.(1946/1968), 'Notes on aggression', in A. Freud, *Indications for child analysis and other papers: the writings of Anna Freud*, vol. IV, New York: International Universities Press, pp. 69-72.

Freud, A.(1951/1968), 'An experiment in group upbringing', in A. Freud, *Indications for child analysis and other papers: the writings of Anna Freud*, vol. IV, New York: International Universities Press, pp. 163-229.

Freud, S.(1924/1991), 'Observations on transference-love (further recommendations on the technique of psychoanalysis III)', in S. Freud, *Psychopathology*, London: Penguin Freud Library, vol. 10, pp. 159-171.

Fromm, E.(1994), *The art of listening*, London: Constable.

Greenberg, J.R. and Mitchell, S.A.(1983), *Object relations in psychoanalytic theory*, Cambridge, MA: Harvard University Press.

Hunt, J.C.(1989), 'Psychoanalytic aspects of fieldwork', *Sage university paper series on qualitative research methods*, vol. 18, Beverly Hills, CA: Sage.

Klauber, J.(1987), 'Implied and denied concepts in the theory of psychoanalytic therapy', in J. Klauber, J. Symington, R. Kennedy, P. Casement, N. Berry, D. Widlöcher and H. Thomä (eds), *Illusion and Spontaneity in Psychoanalysis*. London: Free Association Books, pp. 35-45.

Kracke, W.(1987), 'Encounter with other cultures: psychological and epistemological aspects', *Ethos*, vol. 15, pp. 58-82.

Le Vine, R.A.(1992), 'The self in an African culture', in D.H. Spain (ed), *Psychoanalytic anthropology after Freud*, New York: Psyche Press, pp. 37-48.

Mitchell, S.A. and Black, M.J.(1995), *Freud and beyond: a history of modern psychoanalytic thought*, New York: Basic Books.

Nunn, K.P.(1996), 'Personal hopefulness: a conceptual review of the relevance of the perceived future to psychiatry', *British Journal of Medical Psychology*, vol. 69, pp. 227-246.

Sachs, W.(1996), *Black Hamlet*, Baltimore: Johns Hopkins University Press.

Sandler, J., Holder, A., Kawenoka-Berger, M., Kennedy, H. and Neurath, L.(1989), 'Theoretical and clinical aspects of transference', in J. Sandler (ed), *From safety to superego*, London: Karnac Books, pp. 264-284.

Sandler, J. with Freud, A.(1985), *The analysis of defence: the ego and the mechanisms of defence revisited*, New York: International Universities Press.

Segal, J. and Yahraes, H.(1979), *A child's journey: forces that shape the lives of our young*, New York: McGraw Hill.

Sharpe, E.F.(1978), *Collected papers on psychoanalysis*, New York: Brunner/Mazel.

Speigel, L.A.(1965), 'A review of contributions to a psychoanalytic theory of adolescence: individual aspects', in *The psychoanalytic study of the child*, New York: International Universities Press, pp. 375-394.

Stein, H.F.(1994), *The dream of culture: essays on culture's elusiveness*, New York Psyche Press.

Widlöcher, D.(1987), 'The self as illusion', in J. Klauber, J. Symington, R. Kennedy, P. Casement, N. Berry, D. Widlöcher and H.Thomä (eds), *Illusion and Spontaneity in Psychoanalysis*, London: Free Association Books, pp. 130-148.

Woolf, V.(1988), *A room of one's own*, London: Grafton Books.

9 After the War is Over: Truth and Reconciliation? Reflections from South Africa

Introduction

In 1945, barely seven months after the collapse of Nazi Germany, the Nuremberg trials of former Nazi leaders and officials opened. In 1993, one of the first Acts of South Africa's transitional government set up a Truth and Reconciliation Commission (TRC). It was charged 'to provide for the investigation and establishment of as complete a picture as possible of all gross violations of human rights committed...during the period 1 March 1960 to 5 December 1993, and emanating from the conflicts of the past...' The fundamental purpose of the TRC and the Nuremberg tribunal was to present 'a well-documented history of...a grand, concerted pattern to incite and coerce the aggressions and barbarities which have shocked the world'. (Taylor, 1992, p. 54). Both the tribunal and the TRC were concerned with crimes against humanity. Both confronted the problems of bringing sanity to insane societies.

In this chapter, I compare and contrast the TRC and the Nuremberg tribunal, and I suggest some social, political and psychological implications and shortcomings of their work. I examine some analogies between the workings of the TRC and the processes of psychoanalytic psychotherapy, in particular the end of the work and consider some emotional and social issues that may stay unresolved when the TRC's mandate has ended in 1998.

The International Military Tribunal

On August 8 1945, the International Military Tribunal (IMT) was set up by a Charter 'for the trial and punishment of the major war criminals', and in Article 6 (c) it included and defined 'CRIMES AGAINST HUMANITY...persecutions on political, racial or religious grounds...whether or not in violation of the domestic law...' (Taylor, 1992, p. 648). Other 'general principles' in Articles 6, 7 and 8 dealt with responsibility and culpability and stated that 'the fact that the Defendant acted pursuant to order of his Government or of a superior shall not free him from responsibility' and 'the official position of defendants...shall not be considered as freeing them from responsibility'.

The trials began with a statement by Justice Jackson, who on behalf of the prosecuting nations, emphatically made 'clear that we have no purpose to incriminate the whole German people...the German, no less than the non-German world, has accounts to settle with these defendants' (ibid., 168). On October 1 1946, the Tribunal announced its judgements, penalties and executions.

The Truth and Reconciliation Commission (TRC)

The aims of the TRC are both cathartic and educational. The preamble to its functions declares that 'it is deemed necessary to establish the truth in relation to past events as well as the motives of and circumstances in which gross violations of human rights have occurred and to make the findings known in order to prevent a repetition of such acts' (p. 2). The Commission was charged, *inter alia*, with 'the restoring of the human and civil dignity and the rehabilitation of victims of gross violations of human rights'. To encourage confessions of violations, the Commission is empowered to appoint a committee to hear applications for amnesty and about 8,000 applications had been received by the deadline in May 1997, some of them from very senior politicians, administrators, police and military personnel. It is 'the most original feature of the South African process [that] there is only individual amnesty, granted only to those who personally apply for it, only for those past misdeeds of which they make full disclosure and only where they can demonstrate a "political objective"' (Ash, 1997, p. 34). Thus the granting of an amnesty was intended to depend on the committee's judgement of the claimant's *bona fides*, that he has made a full disclosure and shown signs of contrition.

The TRC has held frequent, open and accessible hearings throughout South Africa, which have been fully reported and freely discussed. The ruling party in the government has itself been accused of violations during the struggle for freedom - in effect, a civil war - and has made available its records, and admitted and regretted its violations where it has been found to be at fault. No such frankness has been shown by the former government, nor collectively by any official (or unofficial) group or organisation.

Unlike the Nuremberg tribunal, the TRC does not sit as a court of law and its procedures uneasily blend formality and informality. There is no formal presentation of indictments against specific individuals, nor any formal presentation and challenge of evidence. There is not, therefore, any formal examination and cross-examination, no plea taken of 'Guilty' or of 'Not Guilty', nor a formal verdict from which an appeal can be made. Indeed there seems nothing but the fairness of committee members and the vigilance of the media to protect individuals from exaggerated or false accusations. The least informal procedure is the reading of confessions, which seem to have been drafted by cautious lawyers.

After Nazi Germany: After Apartheid South Africa

At its simplest, both the Tribunal and the TRC were concerned to reveal and document that 'this is the evil that was done, this is who did it; here is why they did it and how they felt' (Joffe, 1996, p. 21). The Nuremberg trials concluded: and this is how they shall be punished. The conclusions of the TRC are less dramatic: an historical report and, it is hoped, recommendations for political, social and educational programmes that might modify racist beliefs and prevent racist practices.

Both the Tribunal and the TRC have indirectly and unintentionally initiated a changing political psychology, 'a decision to face pain rather than evade it' (Symington and Symington, 1996, p. 6). Of the many sources of emotional pain, perhaps the most overwhelming are shame and guilt, and one of the sources of healing is self-awareness. Collectively, self-awareness in South Africa has barely begun, unlike the remarkable efforts in post-Nazi Germany.

Fischer, in his discussion of the Nuremberg trials, compares two opposing myths that rationalise a 'kind of collective amnesia' by many Germans about Nazi Germany. Similar myths prevail in South Africa. One German perception 'had hardened [by the 1980s] into a mythology of absolute evil, residing outside historical space and time'. The contrasting view was that Nazi persecution was not 'a unique act but was to be expected from a political religion that presupposed extermination as a necessary element of its world-view' (Fischer, 1995, p. 575). Both perceptions eliminate individual responsibility for the atrocities that were carried out by specific individuals who followed or made specific decisions.

Apartheid South Africa and Nazi Germany share many collective attitudes, a self-justifying ideology and similar racist policies and practices. The 1935 racist Nuremberg laws and the legal framework of apartheid have much in common. For example, both deprived groups of basic civil and human rights and effectively excluded them from citizenship, reducing them to mere subjects; both prohibited friendships, marriage or sexual relationships between groups; both reserved education and training, jobs and professions to specific groups; and both determined where groups could live and restricted their rights to meet or worship together. And just as the Nazis were obsessed with the problem of who was a Jew, so were apartheid officials obsessed with the multiple problems of which 'group' individuals of uncertain 'racial' identity should belong to. Not surprisingly from the early 1930s (and even in the late 1990s) many 'white' political, social and religious leaders were actively pro-Nazi.

Apartheid and Nazi ideologies were animated by a hatred of human equality and by quasi-magical fears of contact with peoples labelled as 'inferior' or 'primitive'. Apart from the Nazi attempts to annihilate groups, there is little to distinguish the two racist practices and ideologies. Although on a small scale compared with Nazi atrocities, apartheid governments maintained power by sanctioning or directly organising the torture, murder, imprisonment or segregation of individuals and groups who opposed them or were feared as a threat.

In South Africa and post-Nazi Germany, there are men and women from the past who are still active and whose racist beliefs are intact. A collective emotional problem is that those who once enjoyed or exploited the status and power conferred by their 'race' have lost that prop to their narcissism. Myths still persist to support racist and ethnic illusions and a question that may be asked about the TRC is: has its work weakened or dispelled these myths?

The TRC has tried to encourage genuine confessions and to expose the feigned. If it is moderately successful in dispelling myths, then it baffles those who would try to deny their guilt or complicity by diverting their responsibility onto 'the system'. One result may be to discourage the furthering of the myths by those whose narcissism benefits by them. G. M. Gilbert (the psychologist at the Nuremberg trials) considered that six of the senior Nazis in custody at the opening of the trials showed signs of remorse, and reported that Albert Speer alone 'frankly admitted the guilt of the Nazi régime [and wrote on his copy of the indictment] "the trial is necessary. There is common responsibility for such horrible crimes even in an authoritarian system"' (Gilbert, 1995, p. 5). No such frank admission has been made to the TRC, therefore the myth that apartheid was not evil but was a legitimate and ethical means to protect the beleaguered *volk,* has hardly begun to dissipate.

South African victims, their families and friends were robbed of their voices. Now these voices are heard again at the TRC. The very theatricality of the TRC may begin to destroy myths of group 'difference', where the passionate playing of the roles of victim and victimiser compels public attention. The refusal to play the role of a victimiser is compelling. Even those who accept the myths of racism cannot easily evade the reality that they are the same human beings as the victims who now face them. The myth begins to be destroyed by its glaring unreality.

Myth and Guilt

Hitler's Germany had 'willing executioners' (Goldhagen, 1997). Apartheid's advocates and supporters also lived comfortably within a myth that legitimated and motivated policies, deferred collective guilt and supported anti-guilt defences.

For apartheid to have thrived for nearly half a century, three conditions were needed to animate the myth of racism:

1. Leadership had to be so obsessively preoccupied with definable though phantastic dangers - 'communism', the *swart gevaar,* anti-Christ - that they believed that even torture and murder were justified to protect their endangered people.

2. Leadership had to be so persuasive and followers so gullible, cynical or indifferent that the 'dangers' were not seen as illusions.

3. Political, ideological and ethical opposition had to be stigmatised as dangerous, irresponsible and unrealistic because of its support of 'the dangerous myth of equality'.

The TRC, whether its members are aware of it or not, is involved in the demystifying of South Africa's past. Willingly and deliberately or not, the TRC is committed to a sort of collective psychotherapy that scrutinizes and interprets the mythical defences of those who have violated human rights. Moreover, the TRC, like psychotherapy, is often a theatre for the acting-out of the horrors of the past.

What, then, are myths? Individually and collectively, present life is invaded by unwelcome elements of the past. Myths are a major defence against the past, insulating us, not always adequately, from (i) internal tensions, anxieties and guilts and, from (ii) the real, symbolic and phantasy threats that arise from our perceptions and misperceptions of our external world. Individually and collectively we live by our myths, by our emotionally meaningful fictions, dreams and imaginative creations. Myths can only be dispelled if their history and psychodynamics are understood and confronted. Collectively, they can only be neutralised if social and political education based on their psychodynamics is designed to challenge rationalisations about the past.

Myth, then, is 'firstly and primarily, *mythos*, story, plot...a narrative that suggests two inconsistent responses: first, "this is what is said to have happened", and second, "this is almost certainly not what happened..."' (Frye, 1990, pp. 3, 4). Myth is 'a phantastic romance': even though it was said that Oedipus unlawfully, but in ignorance, married his mother Jocasta - and based upon this story psychological and social consequences followed - it is now doubted that these events did take place. However, it is still believed, even feared, that this 'phantastic romance' expresses or symbolises psychological, social and political truths. A myth is a pseudo-history, a truth that is also an untruth, but one that individually and collectively *needs to be believed* to neutralise an imagined or factual 'reality', too scary, threatening, disappointing, anxiety or guilt-provoking to be endured.

Ethel S. Person's study of 'the force of phantasy' goes beyond the early 'pychoanalytical formulations [that] viewed phantasy as primarily providing substitute gratification, a retreat from the external world' (Person, 1996, p. 1). Myth, too, is a retreat into an internal, dreamlike world. Person discusses how aggressive phantasies 'may be particularly persuasive when the inner needs and conflicts of the individual converge with the shared phantasies and myths of the group to which he or she belongs' (ibid., p. 190). The leaders' needs both motivate his (or her) politics and incite him (or her) to create and strengthen a convergent social and cultural myth that gives 'a sense of protection to those who participated in it...The reward for the actual (or phantasy) destruction of one's evil enemies is not only enhanced power but a fictive world of mythic grandeur, composed of hero warriors and pure women...[where individuals share] an illusory sense of strength, of participation in the Godhead, since they assume the power of life and death' (ibid., pp. 190-191). Person also shows how collective myths express the individual phantasy of the family romance: we *are* all one 'ethnic', 'race', national...group, whatever others may say we are! Implicit is the unsaid, repressed suspicion that we are *not* in reality one happy family with no jealousies, insecurities, conflicting interests or unacceptable libidinous wishes. She observes that 'the typical family romance phantasy acts as a balm to any current sense of narcissistic injury and it also provides an imaginative step into a future' (ibid., p. 99) where everyone lives safely and happily ever after. Hitler's Reich was going to last for a thousand years. Apartheid was for ever!

But *real* reality has a corrosive effect! In South Africa the apartheid myth was destroyed by the reality that South Africa was becoming ungovernable, and the costs of apartheid were bringing the economy into crisis. Moreover, the unstoppable processes of urbanisation, industrialisation and the demographic projection that by the year 2005 only 10% of the population would be 'white', exacerbated the self-destructive tendencies of apartheid ideology.

The characters in a myth are perceived as men, women and children who once-upon-a-time lived in that real-fanciful world. Myths, therefore, reveal the fears and hopes of those whose lives are dominated by them. The inhabitants of our myths share our thoughts and our feelings. We may enjoy those thoughts and feelings vicariously, or we may get rid of them by projecting them out of our lives. And 'if we can think of [those inhabitants] as characters in a drama...it can bring fresh light to a stuck situation by bringing a naïve viewpoint instead of the more abstract theoretical [i.e. depersonalised] point of view' (Symington and Symington, 1996, p. 48).

Dispelling the Myth: Lessons from Psychotherapy

The essence of psychotherapy is to reconnect the patient with relationships and self-awareness that exist 'in a space in which self and world can exist' (Woolf, 1985, p. 71). The TRC, like psychotherapy, is involved in a process of reconnection: victims and victimisers. The TRC confronts complex problems of discovery about the past and meets powerful emotional resistances to uncovering and interpreting matters that many people may wish were left hidden because they arouse guilt, shame, anger and anxiety.

Freud, in many papers, distinguished 'historical' from 'material' truth. *Historical* truth is a *constructed* part of a mythical world that is emotionally necessary as an escape from the 'material', the real world. Individually and collectively we live with our reminiscences of the unendurable bits of our history, which we rationalise, sublimate or repress and shape into a more bearable illusion about the past. The emotional work of the TRC implicitly and of psychotherapy explicitly, consists of 'liberating the fragment of historical truth from its distortions and...leading it back to the point to which it belongs' (Freud, 1938, p. 268). Other collective constructions cannot be ignored. Why did leaders and groups imagine and feel so passionately that it was safer to live within the myth's protection than to try to solve realistic problems rationally? To what symbolic dangers and anxieties were those who believed the myth's truth-untruth vulnerable? What injuries to the collective narcissism were feared if the mythical shelter ceased to be sheltering? The strains of reality *may* destroy the myth, but the process is strengthened when a re-orienting of values is a collective psychotherapy that exposes the emotional, untruthful, dysfunctional nature of the myth. Collectively, those who need the myth may consciously and unconsciously resist those who try to uncover the emotions, relationships and beliefs that inspire it. The members of the TRC have to be as wary as any sensitive analyst who explores the unconscious origins of transferences and resistances.

Transference and Resistance

The TRC is a quasi-judicial forum of men and women, whose official rôles do not define and limit their feelings about what they are doing. The emotional states and relationships that are evoked by the hearings could influence its proceedings and its findings, yet this problem has never (as far as I am aware) been recognised and faced. Freud (1910) saw that the analyst's unconscious feelings, ideas and understanding of the analytic situation are influenced by the patient and that such feelings could, indeed would, arouse positive or negative misinterpretations that make it difficult or even impossible to perceive clearly the reality of the patient's problems.

Since 1910, and especially since Heimann (1950), analysts have been educated to be sensitive to the normality of these distortions of reality, and to continually examine them so that the 'reality' with which the analyst and the patient is dealing is made conscious to both of them. One sign that the joint 'reality' is limited or distorted is what 'the analyst habitually accepts from the patient and what he habitually ignores' (Klauber, 1987, p. 37). The analyst and the patient thus unconsciously collude, so that by each satisfying the other's needs and relationships, an unwelcome piece of reality is concealed from them and thus fails to be confronted. On the other hand, an aspect of 'reality' is welcomed, encouraged and overemphasised. Symington (1983) imaginatively describes how one may be 'lassoed into the patient's self-perception' and discusses the advantages and problems in therapy of appreciating and escaping from it. Indeed, 'whenever two people meet there is an instant fusing so that a new being emerges...part of the psychic entity becomes fused with that of the other person' (Symington, 1986, p. 30). This fusion occurs even if they meet in circumscribed rôles, if there is any space for them to meet *as people*, even though the fusion may turn out to be fleeting and superficial.

The following emotional entanglements and distortions might credibly be expected of the TRC, participants and others interested and concerned: first, and perhaps most likely to cause distorted judgements, moods may be generated at a hearing so affecting that the TRC could be 'lassoed' so tightly into identifying with victims that it becomes difficult or impossible objectively to discover and assess the 'facts'. Conversely, victimisers seeking amnesty might be so deeply rejected as blameworthy, immoral or repulsive that their possibly genuine remorse might be disbelieved.

Second, it may be difficult to appreciate that a confessor is affected by a genuine depression caused by his guilt, shame or fear. He may therefore not be obdurate or insensitive, resisting making a full and fair confession, but is emotionally blocked from confessing. In making a confession, the confessor is exposing his ego and ego-ideal to the trauma of a reality that he has up-to-then rejected and denied. But alternatively, one defence against guilt and shame is flight into a quasi-manic excitement. Deeper, true feelings of shame may be hidden by a flood of wild, over-emotional speech. Writing about post-Nazi Germany, Money-Kyrle (1951) considered that very many Germans were deeply depressed after Germany's defeat and that there were two ways that depression might collectively be lessened. Either there might be a [manic?] effort to make reparations, or if this failed, there might be a 'renewed paranoidal attack on the objects they had injured' (Money-Kyrle, 1978, p. 244), blaming *them* for causing the problems that caused the guilt that caused the depression and the failure to relieve the depression. A similar fusion of moods is possible in South Africa.

Third, members of the TRC and the public have their own sensitivities and are sensitive to situations and relationships that by arousing fears, angers, hostility and excitement may blind them to an impartial enquiry into the causes of events. Emotional appeals, open or implicit, genuine or spurious, divert judgements away from analysing how 'historical' and 'material' truth have interacted in the life of an individual. If truth is to be reached 'what matters is how each individual and each group manages to become aware of its own specific self-deceptions and thereby learns to overcome them' (Mitscherlich, 1975, p. 17). The myths and phantasies that nourished the deceptions must become accepted as unreal, and their unconscious motivations revealed and diffused.

Fourth, the past must be mourned or its political ghosts will never rest. It is surprising that it is not collectively appreciated that the TRC (like other such tribunals) is the nation's principal mourner and that therefore it carries an emotional burden: the disquiet of those groups and individuals who are unable or unwilling to mourn because they cannot confront their individual or collective pasts.

Mourning is emotionally exhausting. It is both an ending and a beginning, it asks unanswerable questions and thrusts upon the mourner a final answer, and Mischerlich sees it as a form of restitution, where we work through our ambivalences or conflicts about the loss. Did I cause the loss? Could I have prevented it? *Should* I have prevented it? Am I secretly relieved that the loss is over and done with? *Should* I be relieved, or should I feel guilty or ashamed about what happened? Am I secretly proud that I had power to cause the loss, yet frightened by the power that I possessed? Am I scared of the power of revenge of those who have gone? Mourning, as Freud (1925) observed, is a gradual process that is easy for some people and painful for others. Some individuals and groups can accept that the loss means that our reality has changed irrevocably, but others seek to deny the change by retreating into hallucination. There *was* no loss; I did not cause a loss; the loss occurred despite my wishes.

Mitscerlich maintains that the inability to mourn has many motivations: rationalisations about the past may persist and guilt and shame may be denied by projecting it onto victims: 'they brought it on themselves', or onto the once-powerful leaders and apologists, 'they made us do it'. Another form of denial is the refusal to accept that loss occurred. It may also be asserted that the losses are exaggerated.

In post-Nazi Germany and post-apartheid South Africa denials have been declared by individuals and collectively. There can be no mourning if it is denied that there is anything or anyone to mourn! But denial is both cognitive and emotional: in order to feel guilt and remorse, individuals must work through the losses, accepting that what happened was no myth but was carried out by the individual and his fellows, and that it gives rise to feelings that must be accepted and worked through. Individuals must therefore meet head-on that they have lost chunks of their past by repressing unwelcome memories and events. Their repressed but integral thoughts, feelings, hopes, memories have to be made conscious, restored and accepted, neutralised and lived with. Delusional myths may retain their powerful cathexis, e.g. 'it's still the fault of the Jews' or 'the blacks still want to take our culture and our identity'. So scape-goating can be a substitute for mourning when it is too painful or difficult to strive to free oneself from the past in order to rebuild one's self, one's ego or relationships.

Members of the TRC are not free of their pasts, and like other men and women may find mourning too deeply disturbing to allow themselves, but failing to mourn may be no less unsettling. Like psychotherapists, members of the TRC have had to reconcile two conflicting situations, of which they are probably largely unaware: the past must be recalled, and acting-out of feelings about the past must be permitted yet contained. As the South African society finds both difficult or even impossible, the TRC is, inevitably, vicariously mourning for the wider society. It seems unlikely that the TRC members are aware of how dangerously easy it is to over-estimate how completely emotions and phantasies are controlled or sublimated, collectively even more than individually. Collectively feelings about the past should be monitored so that ghosts and their messages should be confronted and mourning achieved.

Forgiving, Repairing, Ending?

Melanie Klein attached great importance to the *need* for reparations - a fundamental, quasi-instinctive need. If the individual fails to make reparations that he feels emotionally satisfying, he may suffer guilt and depression. A normal ego cannot deal with a reality in which 'objects' have been wished away in phantasy, or have been damaged or destroyed in reality. Individuals who damage or destroy other individuals, whether in phantasy or reality, are admitting to themselves that they, too, are vulnerable. The inability to make reparations is a regressive refusal to accept blame and an unconscious attempt to revive the comforting illusions of childhood omnipotence. Adults, like children, neutralise self-blame by blaming others: the TRC has had to listen to politicians and police each blaming the other for atrocities, and both blaming the opponents of apartheid.

Nertus (1997) is sceptical of the psychological adequacy of war crimes tribunals, such as those in Rwanda and the former Yugoslavia. She admits that they have limited legal and political worth, but that they have done almost nothing to heal the social and emotional damage suffered by survivors and their communities. The failure of such tribunals is their inability and unwillingness (because of their political and legal constraints), to meet the urgency of symbolic and compensatory reparations.

'Breaking the cycle of violence' (Lumsden, 1997) and 'Boundary-making and reconciliation' (Stein, 1994) are very similar to the TRC's latent mission of breaking the grip of the ethnicity-obsessed past, in which all the ethnic groups feared that other ethnic groups would damage their collective identity. These fears boosted narcissistic defensiveness and aggression. The hearings of the TRC have been ominously silent about the ethnicity-consciousness that is far from dissipated in South Africa - this is unlike the Nuremberg trials.

Writing about the post-war Germany of 1946, Money-Kyrle (1978) predicted that a people depressed after being defeated may move out of depression in either of two directions: (1) if attempts at reconciliation by offering reparations are accompanied by real and symbolic remorse, then the oppressors' guilt and the victims' anger and feelings of revenge may be lessened. The society is then freed to become more stable, without the despairing and angry splitting into narcissistically hostile groups of persecuted and persecutors. But (2) if reparations are emotionally false, then guilt may be intensified as attempts to dispel it fail. The danger now is that persecutors, the narcissistically threatened, renew their paranoid suspicions of, and hostility towards, their former victims. New and old scapegoat groups will be targets of split-off guilt, anger and unconscious self-destruction. In South Africa (as in post-Nazi Germany), attempts at reconciliation and resistance to them, are already being manifested in an oscillation between guilt and self-justifying bravado; the mourning of death and pride at having caused it; anger and restitution; vengeance and forgiving.

Lumsden's analysis of 'breaking the cycle of violence' includes, (of particular relevance to a psychodynamic approach) education and communal rites: first, the ethos and relationships of the educational system have a direct (although limited) influence on the balance between attitudes of cooperation and conflict, of social exclusiveness or indifference to social distinctions. Teachers' relationships to learners are partially responsible for whether children have an ego able to deal effectively with reality, a benign or punitive superego and an ego-ideal that advances individual self-esteem or depresses it. Education cannot by itself modify individuals' attitudes, which are jointly created by the individuals' inner needs and perceptions interacting with social norms. But the relationships young people experience in education, and how they respond, to them contribute to whether they become as adults authoritarian or democratic, punitive or tolerant, open or narrow in their ethnic preferences. Or, will they become defensively narcissistic, separatist and ethnically hypersensitive?

Much of our life is passed in uncertainty about who we are. We often seek an answer by contrasting ourselves with those whom we are not. In this Alice-in-Wonderland forest where we look for ourselves, we are frequently depersonalised, alienated and estranged. 'Ethnic' identity is one common way to un-depersonalise individuals and groups. Education, if it is designed to restore teachers' and learners' self-esteem, self-awareness by empowering them with skills, unhostile relationships and a sense of identity, may partially compensate for poverty and ethnic narcissism and restore freedom.

Second, Lumsden's 'communal rites' are both symbolic and realistic, and are concerned fundamentally with the problem of 'containing anxiety in institutions' (Menzies-Lyth, 1988) and 'aggression and reconciliation' (Stein, 1994). Lumsden rites include 'the reintegration of warriors, purging of "death pollution", opportunity for participation, for experiencing sense of belonging' (ibid., p. 381). If 'effective social change is likely to require analysis of the common anxieties and unconscious collusions underlying the social defences determining phantasy social relationships' (Jaques, 1955), then an emotionally 'new' South Africa is both urgent and difficult to imagine. The lively ambivalence about the violence of the past has barely been noted, much less countered by an unequivocal condemnation of violence. For example, Mrs. Madikizela-Mandela has been both praised as 'the mother of the nation' and has defended herself defiantly against accusations that she was a planner and accomplice of assaults and murders. A former security policeman expressed his own ambivalence - characteristic of many of apartheid's killers who appeared before the TRC: '...he had a task, which was to kill apartheid's opponents. He did it, he did it with conviction and isn't sorry...The only thing he regrets is that he had lost the war, was exposed and had to confess'. Yet, he also claimed that 'we drank a lot, maybe because subconsciously we felt guilty...maybe there isn't forgiveness for people like me...' (Pauw, 1997, p. 29). The anxious defiance of Mrs. Madikizela-Mandela and a 'security' policeman's doubts about the morality of his job, barely conceal their reluctance to abandon their (politically approved) need to be warriors. The TRC has often been reluctant to test whether a warrior is a warrior no longer, or how many ex-warriors are still warriors psychologically. The 'purge of death pollution' has been meagre and spasmodic, and with no significant attempts to combine it with a mass, collective mourning. However, despite the persistence of ethnic separation - and what could one expect in the short time since 1991? - participation in symbolic and actual activities of belonging is fairly common, though emotionally shallow.

Winnicott's description of individual 'manic defence' seems to apply collectively to South Africa in the late 1990s. It is 'intended to cover a person's capacity to deny the depressive anxiety that is inherent in emotional development, anxiety that belongs to the capacity of the individual to feel guilt...and for the aggression in the phantasy that goes with instinctual experience' (Winnicott, 1958, pp. 143-44). Collectively and individually we fly from the guilt that we cannot tolerate or appease into a search of enemies - phantasy or 'real' - who we can imagine are responsible for our unwelcome guilty feelings. In South Africa, victimisers and victims still live unconsciously as enemies inhabiting the myths of the past. 'We-ness', empathy and toleration of difference have not yet substantially begun to replace 'they-ness' and dehumanisation. The ritual taboos on emotional, social and physical contact are only slowly being eroded. However, the collective need for enemies and aggression is still nurtured by the mass media, and by the punitive ethos of an authoritarian society in both its urban and its rural sectors.

'Manic defence' can only be moderated as guilt is diminished, and guilt is only diminished as the need for aggression is replaced by a self-confident True Self. Stein's discussion of peace research suggests we may collectively lessen the strength of aggressive impulses and behaviour. He argues persuasively that the dynamics of small and large groups are similar, so that reconciliation, avoiding the making and phantasising of enemies and offsetting feelings of vulnerability, powerlessness and low self-esteem are similar in small and large groups. The most demanding problem in group dynamics is, probably, how to ease talking and working through unconscious phantasies, conflicts and fears instead of allowing them to be acted-out violently (Stein, 1994, pp. 381-396). Phantasies give rise to 'an ideology which evolves out of [and re-enforces] group memory'.

Stein shows how a 'group memory' develops that becomes a sort of 'group-trance', with phantasies of 'we-ness' that are re-enforced by phantasies of a feared 'other-ness'. Segments of reality are thus distorted and 'Others' are perceived as, and felt to be, dangerous, uncanny, needing to be obsessively scrutinised. The more intense the scrutiny, the more is hostility or danger attributed to the Uncanny Others. A 'cycle of hostility and projected hostility' and 'witchcraft anxiety' (ibid., p. 389) is started, and once started, paranoid fears and anxiety feed upon themselves.

How then, is it possible to break the cycle, to reconcile the *soi-disant* witch-hunting persecutors with the persecuted witches? Can the Uncanny be transformed into the benign and familiar? Collectively, as individually, the therapy is in the recognition that one is dealing with a phantom, ghost or witch, who is no realistic danger to anyone. **They,** Others are only dangerous when they symbolise split-off 'bad' bits of ourselves. Stein suggests that collective therapy, like individual therapy is to be aware of all the defences that consign Others into an emotionally distant world, e.g. displacement, projective identification, projection and denial, and, above all, to be sensitive to constructing a Manichean world split into 'good' Us and 'bad' Them. He also stresses the importance of talking together, and finding every opportunity for co-operative, mutually beneficial action between groups: groups appreciated as made up of individuals who have precisely the same humanity as us.

Perhaps the enduring evil of apartheid's ethnicity is that enforced collectivity has triumphed and individuals have not yet been rediscovered. The TRC, despite its mandate and its good intentions, has discreetly avoided confronting South Africa's persistent ethnicity.

References

Ash, T.G.(1997), 'True Confessions', *New York Review of Books*, vol.XLIV(12), pp. 33-38.
Fischer, K.P.(1995), *Nazi Germany: A New History*, New York: Continuum.
Freud, S.(1925/1991), 'Mourning and Melancholia', in S. Freud, *On Metapsychology*, Penguin Freud Library, vol. 11, Penguin Books, Harmondsworth.
Freud, S.(1938/1973), 'Constructions in Analysis', in S. Freud, *Standard Edition*, vol.XXIII, pp. 255-270, London: Hogarth Press.

Frye, N.(1990), 'The Koine of Myth: Myth as a Universally Intelligible Language', in N. Frye, *Myth and Metaphor*, Charlottesville: University Press of Virginia, pp. 3-17.
Gilbert, G.M.(1995), *Nuremberg Diary*, New York: Da Capo Press.
Goldhagen, D.J.(1997), *Hitler's Willing Executioners*, London: Abacus Books.
Heimann, P.(1950), 'On Counter-transference', in P. Heimann, *About Children and Children No-longer*, (1989), London: Routledge.
Jaques, E.(1955), 'Social Systems as a Defence against Persecutory and Depressive Anxiety', in M. Klein, P. Heimann, and R.E. Money-Kyrle (eds), *New Directions in Psychoanalysis*, (1985), London: Maresfield Library.
Joffe, J.(1996), 'Goldhagen in Germany', *New York Review of Books*, vol.XLIII(19), pp. 18-22.
Klauber, J.(1987), 'Implied and Denied Concepts in the Theory of Psychoanalytic Therapy', in J. Klauber et al., *Illusion and Spontaneity in Psychoanalysis*, London: Free Association Books.
Lumsden, M.(1997), 'Breaking the Cycle of Violence, Peace and Conflict'. *Journal of Peace Psychology*, vol.34(4), pp. 377-383.
Lyth, I.M.(1988), *Containing Anxiety in Institutions*, London: Free Association Books.
Mertus, J.(1997), 'The War Crimes Tribunal: Triumph of the "International Community", Pain of the Survivors', *Mind and Human Interaction*, vol.8(1), pp. 47-57.
Mitscherlich, A. and M.(1975), *The Inability to Mourn*, Grove Press, New York.
Money-Kyrle, R.(1978), 'Social Conflict and the Challenge to Psychology', in *The Collected Papers of Roger Money-Kyrle*, Clunie Press, Strath Tay, pp. 198-219.
Pauw, J.(1997), 'The Electrician: Looking into the Face of Evil', *Mail and Guardian*, vol.13(47), Inside section pp. 28-29.
Person, E.S.(1996), *The Force of Phantasy: Its Power to Transform our Lives*, London: Harper Collins.
Stein, H.F.(1994), 'Peace Research: Aggression, Boundary-making and Reconciliation in Balint Groups', in H.F. Stein, *The Dream of Culture*, New York: Psyche Press, chapter 16.
Symington, N.(1983), 'The Analyst's Act of Freedom as Agent of Therapeutic Change', *International Review of Psychoanalysis*, vol.10, pp. 783-792.
Symington, N.(1986), *The Analytic Experience*, London: Free Association Books.
Symington, J. and N.(1996), *The Clinical Thinking of Wilfrid Bion*, London: Routledge.
Taylor, T.(1992), *The Anatomy of the Nuremberg Trials*, Boston: Little Brown-Back Bay Books.
Winnicott, D.(1958), 'The Manic Defence', in D. Winnicott, *Collected Papers: Through Paediatrics to Psychoanalysis*, London: Tavistock, pp. 129-144.
Woolf, V.(1985), *Moments of Being: Unpublished Autobiographic Writings*, New York: Harcourt, Brace Jovanovich.

DATE DUE

JUL 0 3 2002			
NOV 2 1 2003			
JUN 1 8 2007			
APR 0 5 2004